Festive Quilling: 20 Beautiful Christmas Ornaments

First published in 2024

For permission requests, write to the author at the following email: [anushanagappan@gmail.com]

Author, Designer, Editor, and Photographer:
Anusha Rajendran

ISBN : 978-93-6163-295-2

Disclaimer: The author and publisher have made every effort to ensure that the information in this book was correct at press time. The author and publisher do not assume and hereby disclaim any liability to any party for any loss, damage, or disruption caused by errors or omissions, whether such errors or omissions result from negligence, accident, or any other cause.

CONTENTS

INTRODUCTION

Welcome to "Festive Quilling: 20 Beautiful Christmas Ornaments"!

The holiday season is a time of joy, celebration, and creativity. There's something magical about decorating your home with ornaments that not only look beautiful but also carry the warmth and love of handmade craftsmanship. This book is designed to guide you through the enchanting world of paper quilling, offering step-by-step instructions to create 20 stunning Christmas ornaments that will add a unique, personal touch to your festive decorations.

Why Paper Quilling?

Paper quilling, also known as paper filigree, is an art form that involves rolling, shaping, and gluing strips of paper to create intricate designs. This craft is perfect for all ages and skill levels, providing a wonderful way to express creativity and make personalized decorations. The delicate and detailed nature of quilling makes it ideal for creating Christmas ornaments that are both elegant and festive.

What You'll Find in This Book

In "Festive Quilling: 20 Beautiful Christmas Ornaments," you'll discover a diverse collection of designs ranging from classic holiday motifs to modern interpretations. Each project includes:

- **Detailed Instructions**: Step-by-step guidance to help you through each stage of the quilling process.
- **Materials List**: Everything you need to gather before you start crafting.
- **Tips and Techniques**: Expert advice to make your quilling experience enjoyable and successful.

Each ornament is designed to be achievable yet striking, providing a sense of accomplishment and joy once completed.

Getting Started

Before diving into the projects, the introductory chapters cover essential quilling techniques, tools, and materials. Whether you're new to quilling or looking to refine your skills, these sections will equip you with the knowledge and confidence to start crafting your own beautiful ornaments.

A Festive Journey

As you work through these projects, you'll find yourself immersed in the festive spirit. Creating these ornaments is not just about crafting but also about making memories and traditions. Hang them on your tree, give them as heartfelt gifts, or use them to adorn your home – each piece you create will bring a touch of handmade charm to your holiday celebrations.

Thank you for choosing this book as your guide to paper quilling Christmas ornaments. Let's embark on this creative journey together and make this holiday season truly special with the art of quilling.

Happy quilling and Merry Christmas!
Anusha

TOOLS AND MATERIALS

To ensure you have everything you need to create beautiful paper quilled Christmas ornaments, here is a comprehensive list of tools and materials required for the projects in this book

1. **Circle Template Ruler**: For making precise and consistent shapes.
2. **Quilling Board**: A board with various sized circles to help make uniform coils and shapes.
3. **Brush**: For applying varnish over the finished decor
4. **Scissors**: For cutting quilling paper strips to the desired length.
5. **Tweezers**: For handling small pieces and placing them precisely.
6. **Slotted Quilling Tool**: Essential for rolling paper strips into coils.
7. **Fine-Tip Glue Applicator& Glue**: For applying glue precisely to small areas. Can fill in the applicator with any Clear-drying glue for securing the quilled shapes.
8. **Ribbon or Thread**: For creating loops to hang the ornaments.
9. **Clear Varnish or Sealant**: To protect and preserve your finished ornaments.
10. **Quilling Paper Strips:** Various colours and widths (10 mm wide and 3mm wide) to create different parts of the ornaments.

By equipping yourself with these recommended quilling supplies, you can enhance your paper quilling experience and achieve professional-looking results. Each tool and material play a crucial role in creating beautiful and intricate quilled art, ensuring that your projects are both enjoyable and successful. Each project in the book will guide you through using these supplies to create stunning decorations that will bring holiday cheer to your home. Happy quilling!

1
2
3
4
5
6
7
8
9
10

TIPS AND TECHNIQUES

Creating stunning paper quilled Christmas ornaments requires both creativity and skill. Here are some essential tips and techniques to help you achieve beautiful results with your quilling projects:

1. **Selecting the Right Materials**
   - Use high-quality paper quilling strips to ensure clean cuts and consistent shapes. Thicker paper may be used for more durable ornaments. For beginners, pre-cut strips are ideal as they come in a variety of colours and sizes.
   - Different projects require different widths of paper strips. Narrow strips (3mm) are suitable for detailed work, while wider strips (5mm, 7mm and 10mm) are better for larger, bolder designs.
   - Use the glue that dries clear and be strong enough to hold the paper without causing it to warp.

2. **Rolling and Shaping Techniques**
   - Maintain even tension while rolling paper strips to create uniform coils. Uneven tension can result in coils that are too loose or too tight, affecting the overall appearance.
   - ·Use a quilling tool with a slotted tip for rolling paper strips. This tool helps achieve consistent coil sizes and shapes.
   - Learn to manipulate your rolled paper into various shapes like teardrops, marquises, and tight coils. Practice making these shapes consistently to build a strong foundation for more complex designs.

3. **Precision in Gluing and Assembly**
   - Apply glue sparingly to avoid excess that can seep out and affect the paper's appearance. A fine-tip applicator or needle can help you control the amount of glue applied.
   - Allow each layer of your quilling design to dry thoroughly before adding additional elements. This prevents pieces from shifting or misaligning during assembly.
   - Use tweezers to position quilled pieces accurately. This ensures clean lines and cohesive design elements.

4. **Enhancing Your Design**
   - Experiment with colour theory to create visually appealing designs. Complementary and analogous colour schemes can enhance the aesthetic of your quilled pieces.
   - Incorporate patterns and textures by varying the width of the paper strips or combining different quilling shapes. Adding contrasting textures can create depth and interest.

5. **Troubleshooting Common Issues**
   - If your paper strips are wrinkled, flatten them under a heavy book before use. For minor wrinkles that occur during rolling, gently smooth them out with a bone folder or your fingers.
   - If glue seeps out or leaves residue, clean up any excess before it dries with a cotton swab. Ensure you are using the appropriate amount of glue for each step.
   - If pieces shift or misalign, carefully lift and reposition them while the glue is still wet. Use a gentle hand to avoid damaging the paper.

7. **Storage and Maintenance**
   - Store your quilling strips flat and in a cool, dry place to prevent them from curling or becoming damaged. Use a dedicated quilling kit or organizer to keep tools and materials in good condition.
   - Keep your tools clean and free from glue residue. Regular maintenance of your tools ensures they function effectively and last longer.

Mastering quilling requires patience, practice, and a keen eye for detail. By following these tips and techniques, you can overcome common challenges and enhance your quilling projects with confidence. Embrace the process of learning and experimenting, and let your creativity shine through every quilled creation.

BASIC QUILLING SHAPES

In the art of paper quilling, mastering basic shapes is essential for building more intricate designs. These foundational shapes form the core of many quilled artworks, enabling you to create everything from simple patterns to elaborate compositions. This section will guide you through the process of creating the essential quilling shapes, providing you with the skills needed to embark on your quilling journey.

TIGHT COIL

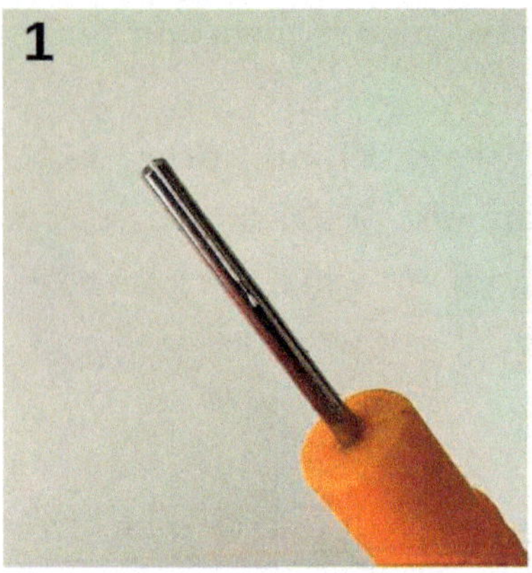

Notice the slot at the top of the slotted quilling tool

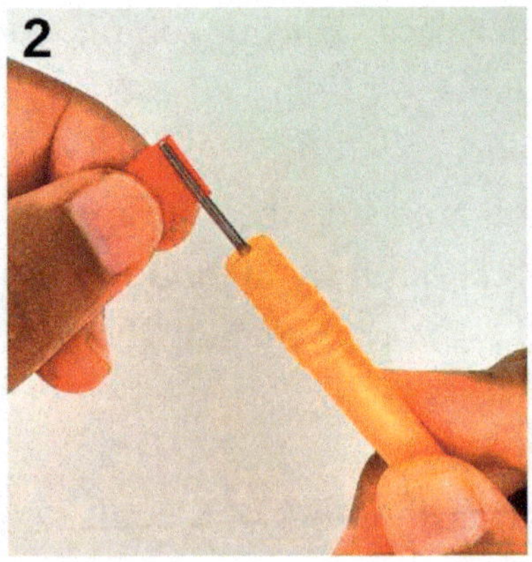

Start with a quilling strip of your desired colour and length. Insert one end of the strip into the slotted quilling tool.

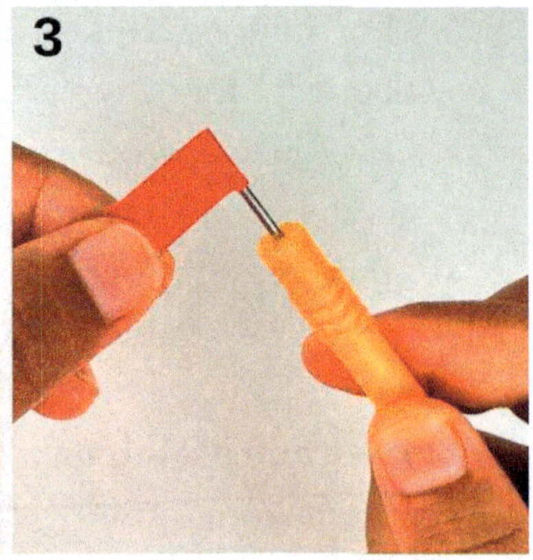

Begin rolling the strip tightly around the tool.

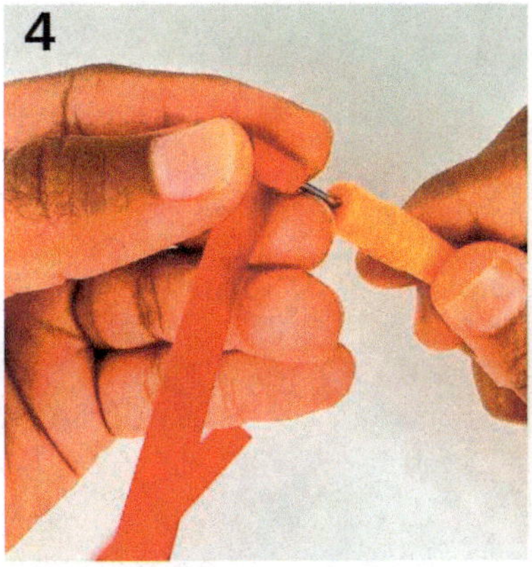

Maintain even pressure to keep the coil uniform

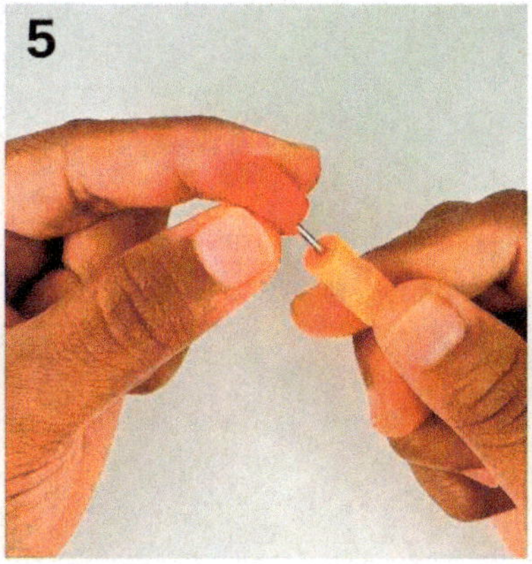

Continue to roll till the other end of the quilling strip

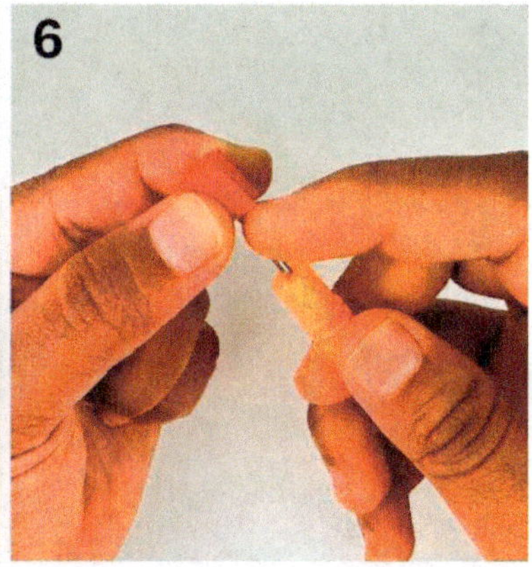

Once the strip is fully rolled, gently remove it from the tool

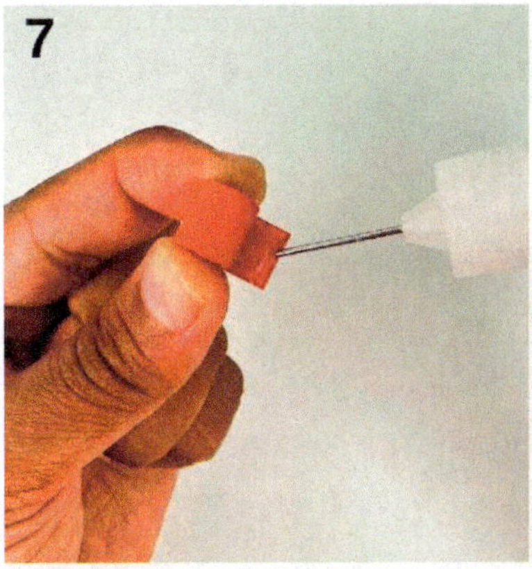

Apply a small amount of glue to the end of the strip

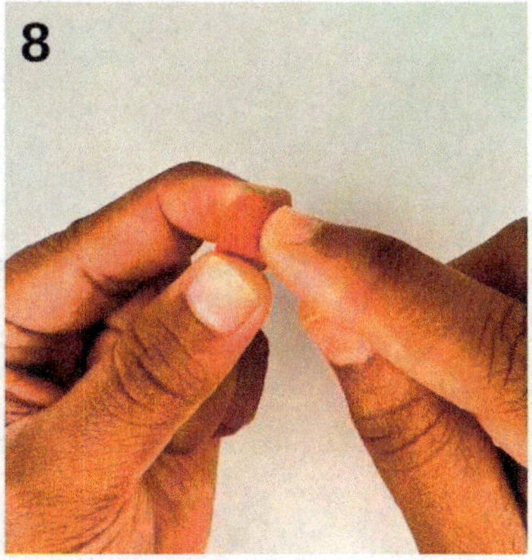

Press and hold for few seconds to secure it in place

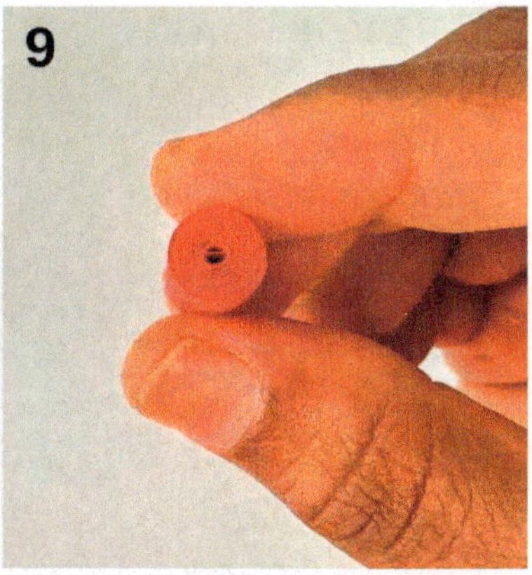

Tight coil is done

LOOSE COIL

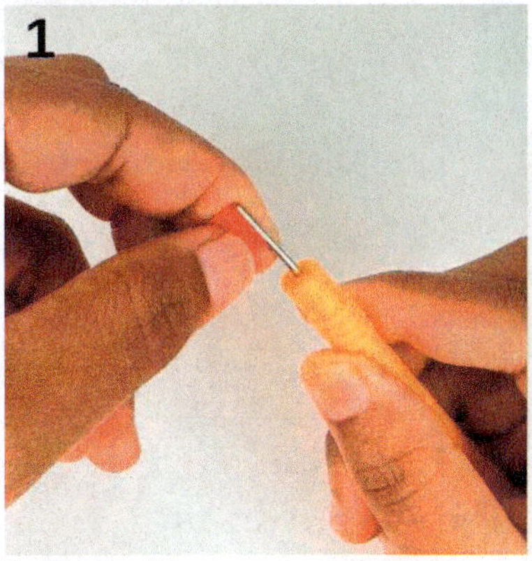

Follow the same steps as for the tight coil

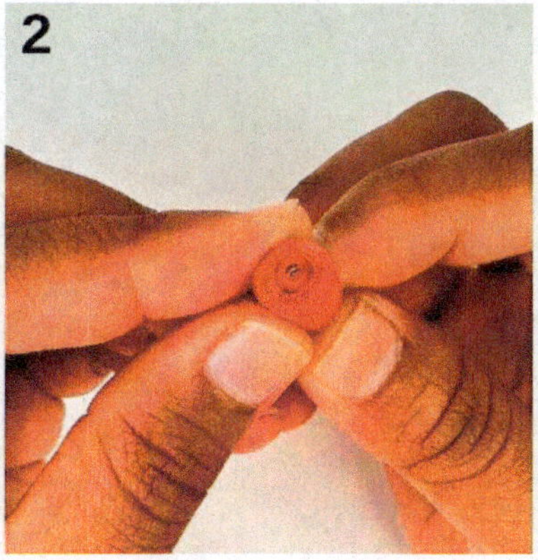

Hold the tight coil between the fingers after removing it from the tool

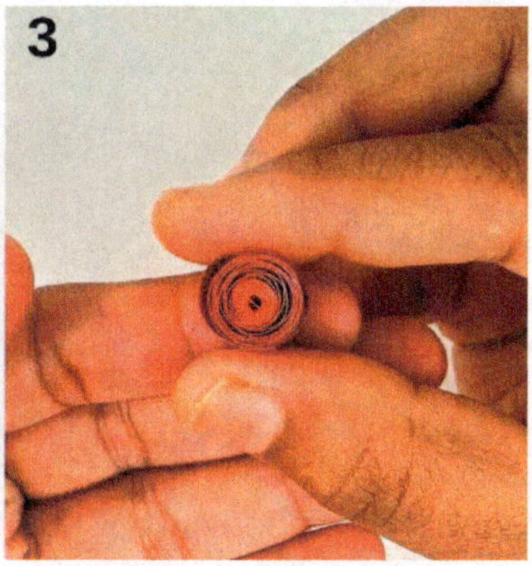

Allow the coil to loosen slightly

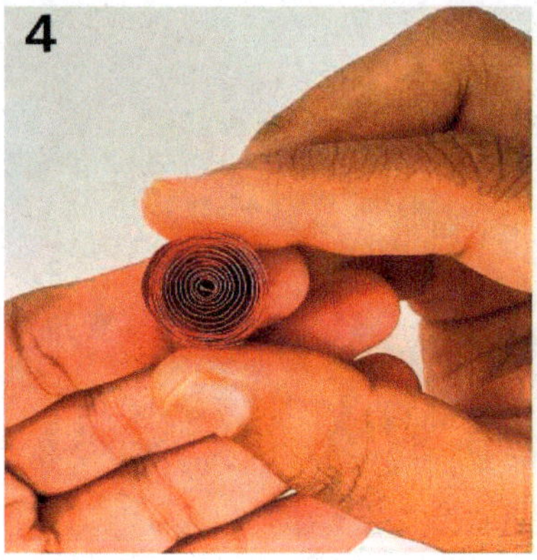

Adjust the looseness according to your required size

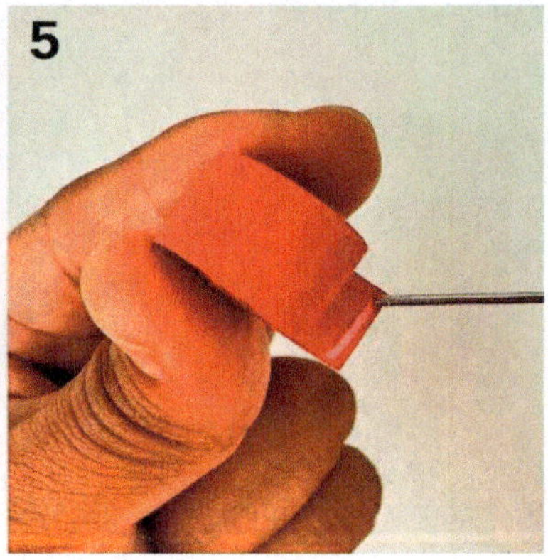

Apply glue to the end of the strip to hold the coil in place

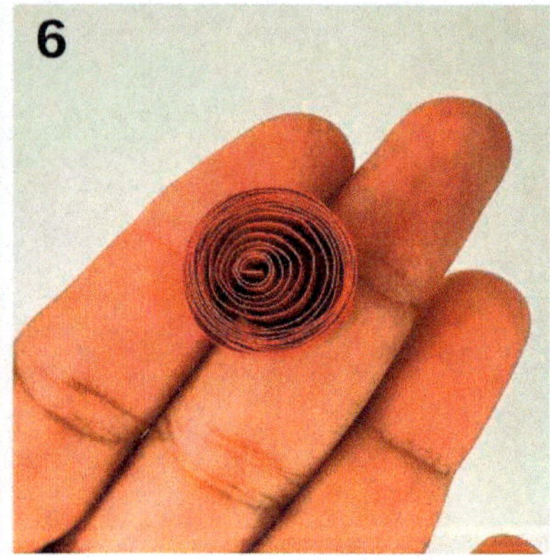

Loose coil is ready. This will be the base for making different quilled shapes

TEARDROP SHAPE

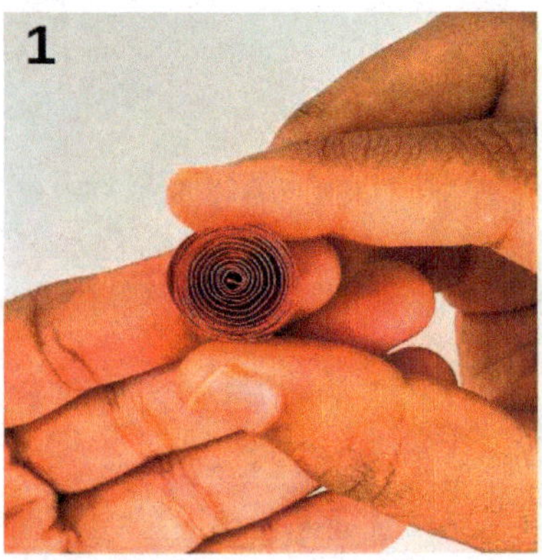

Begin with a loose coil, as described above

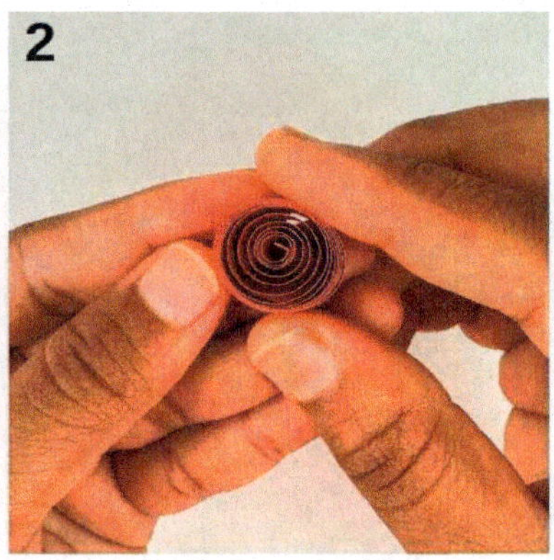

Place the loose coil between the fingers as shown

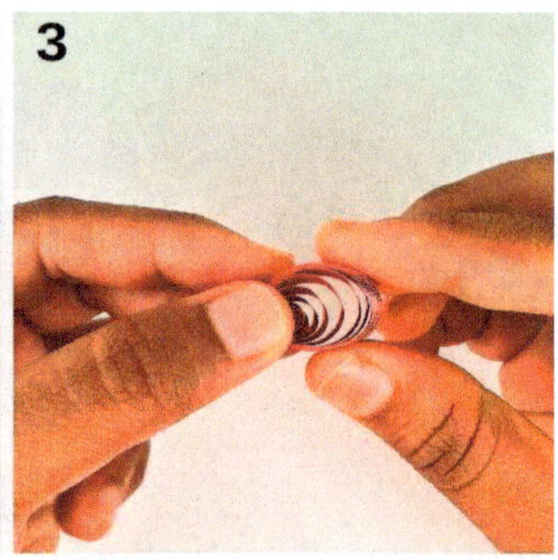

Hold the centre of the loose coil

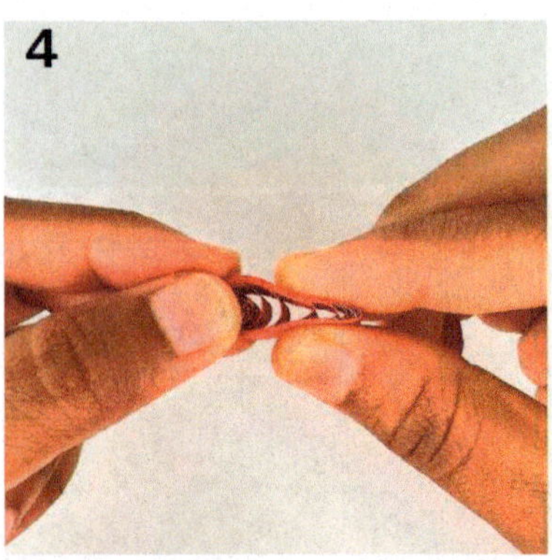

Gently pinch one end of the loose coil to form a teardrop shape

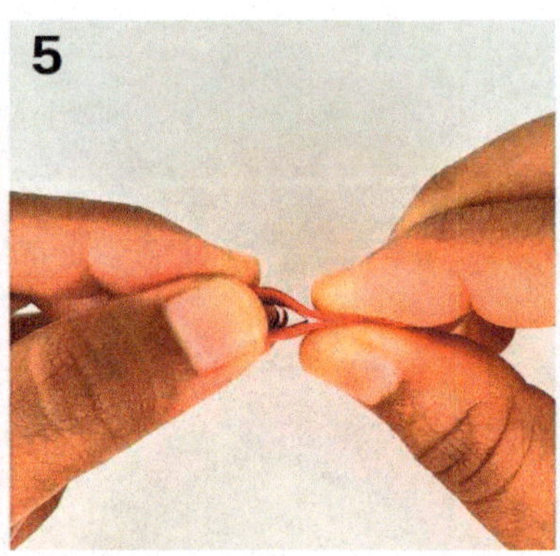

Pinch firmly

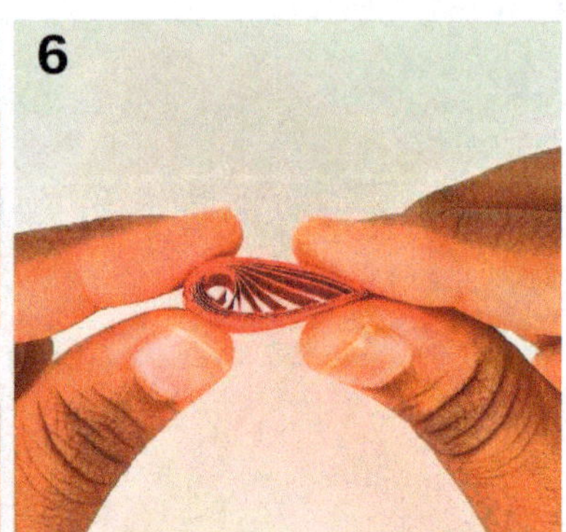

The other end will naturally form a rounded point

MARQUIS (OR MARQUISE) SHAPE

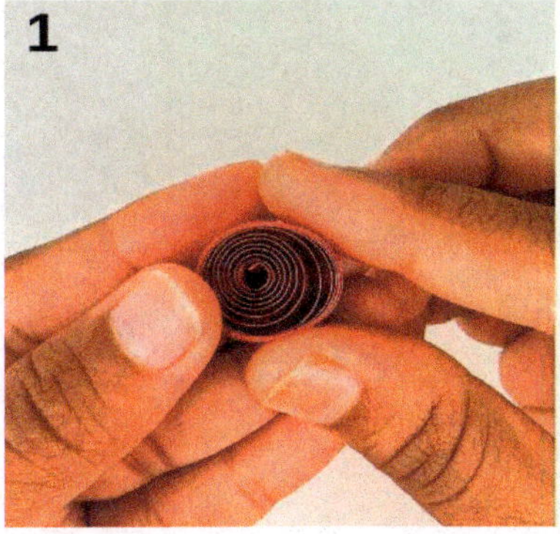

Create a loose coil as before

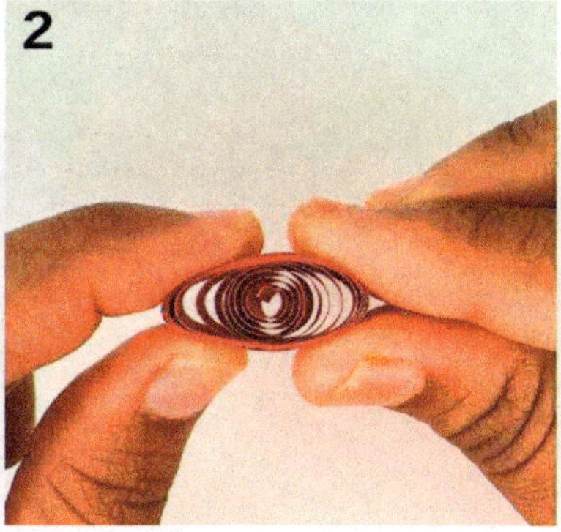

Place the coil between both the fingers

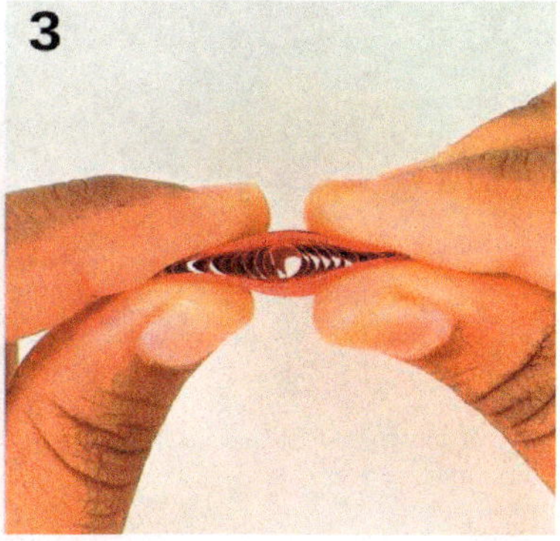

Flatten and pinch the opposite ends

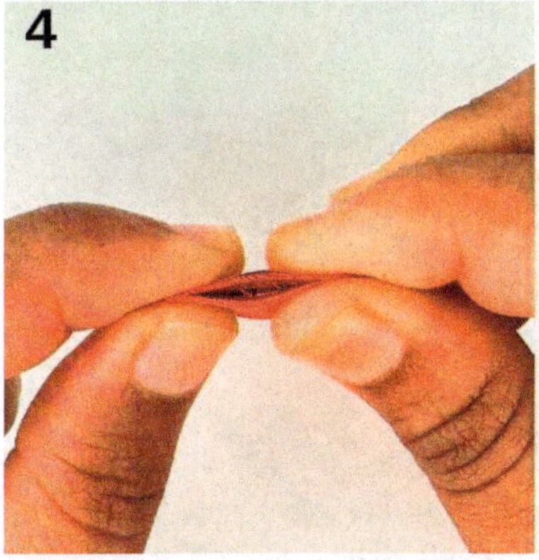

Pinch the edges on both sides to form an elongated oval shape with pointed ends, resembling a marquis

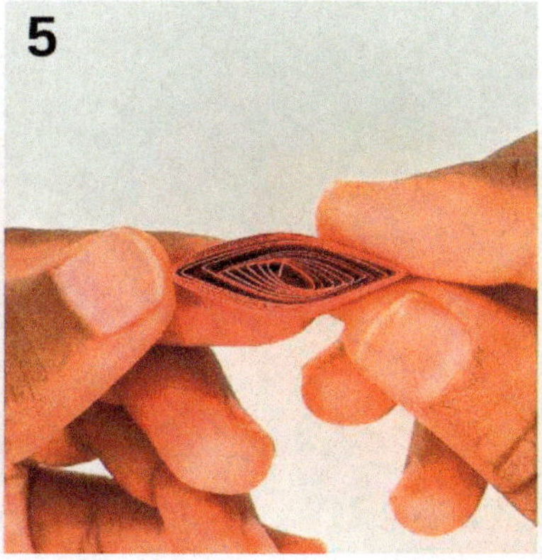

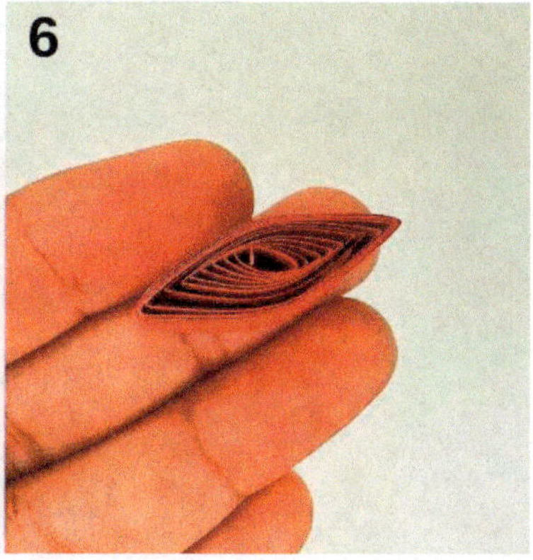

TRIANGLESHAPE

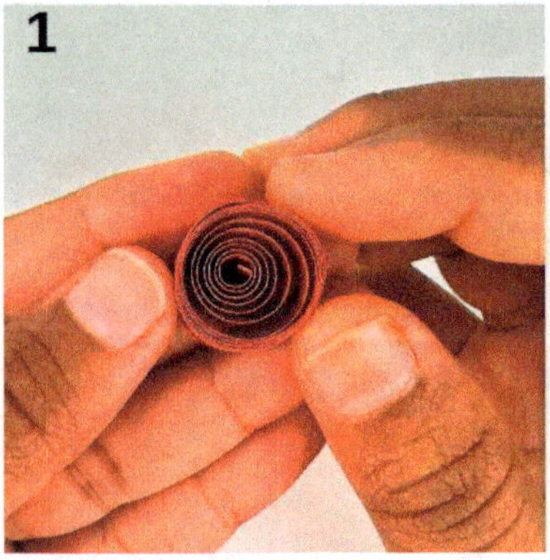

Start with a loose coil

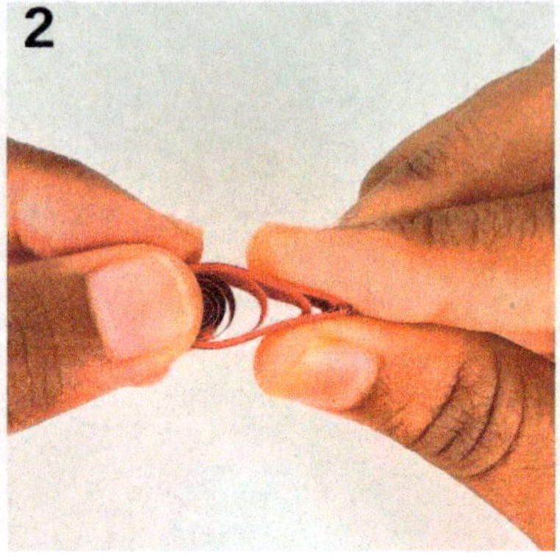

Hold the centre and pinch at one end

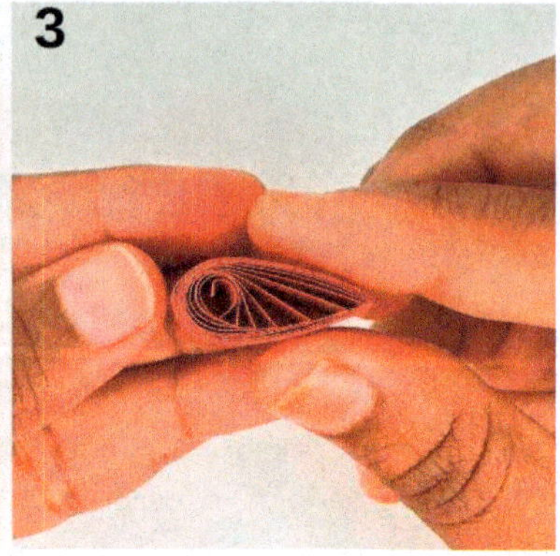

Shape it into a teardrop

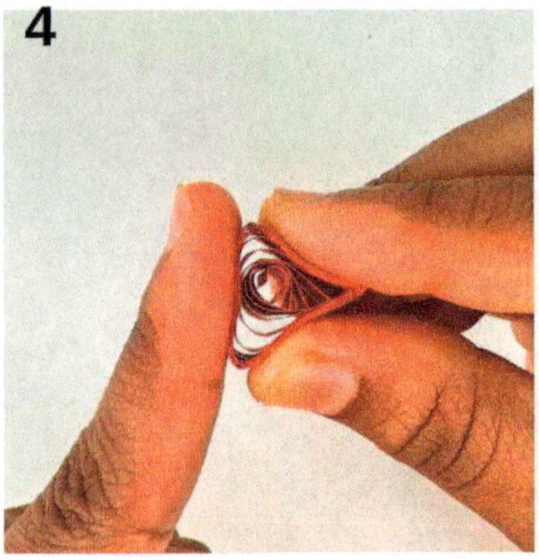

Press the rounded edge of the tear drop against the index finger

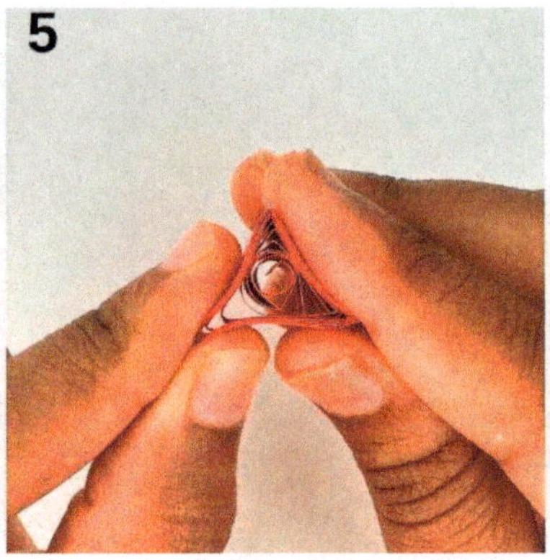

pinch three points of the coil to form a triangle

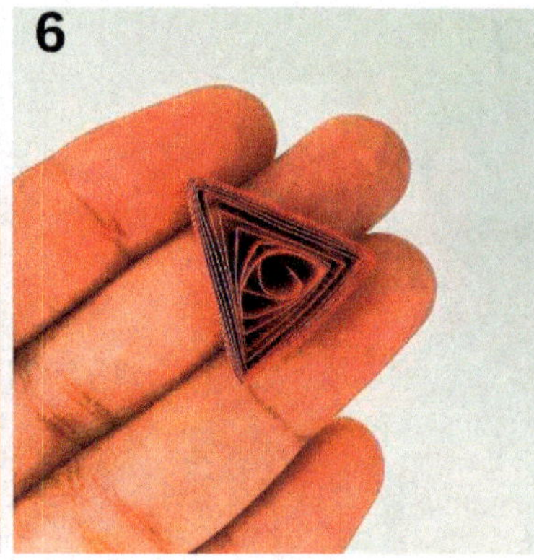

Adjust the size and proportions as needed

SEMI-CIRCLE SHAPE

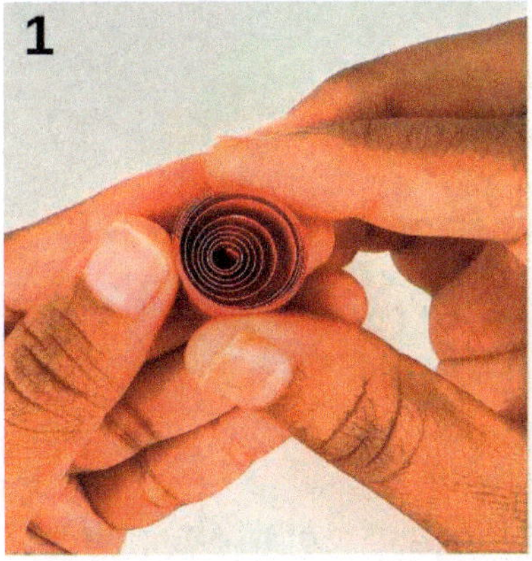

Create a loose coil as before

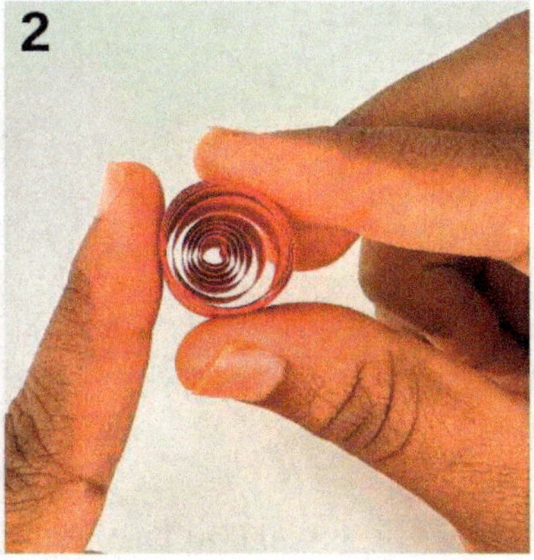

Place the loose coil between the fingers as shown

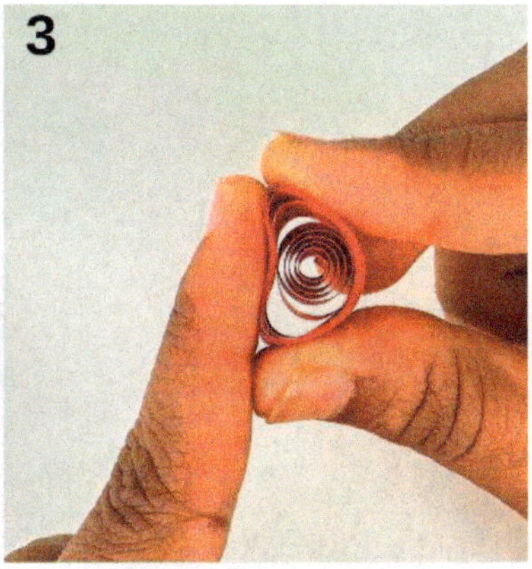

Press the loose coil against the index finger and flatten

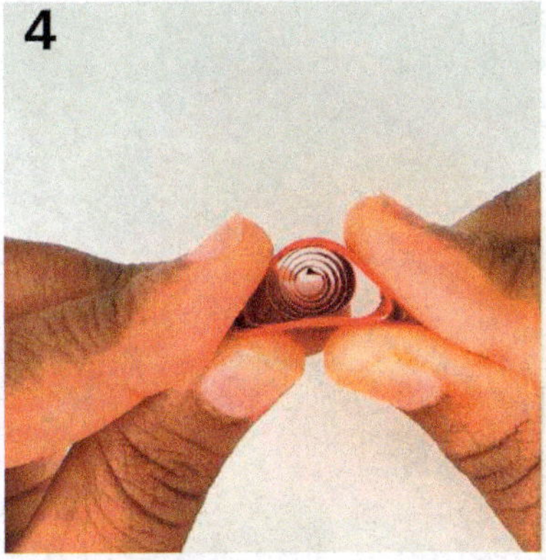

Pinch at two points of the coil to form a semicircle.

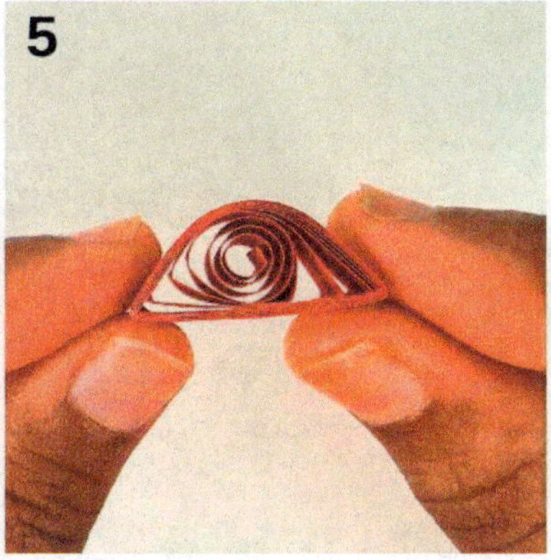

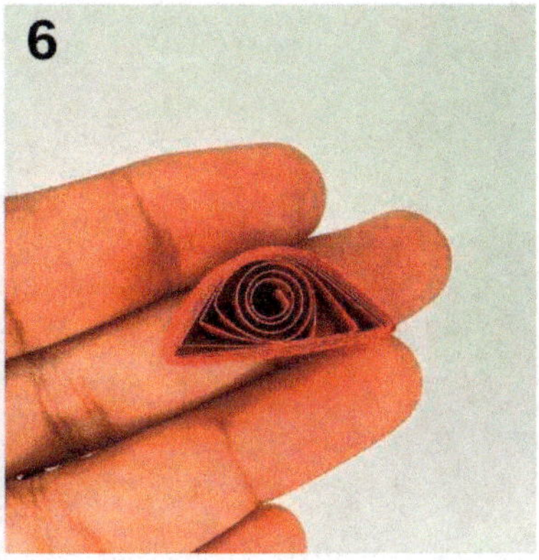

SQUARESHAPE

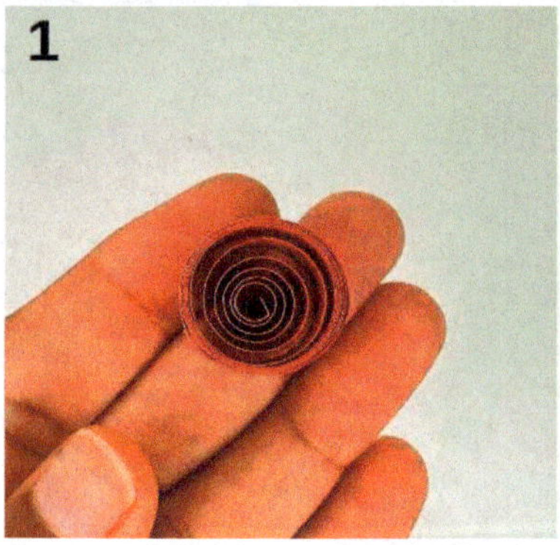

Create a loose coil as before

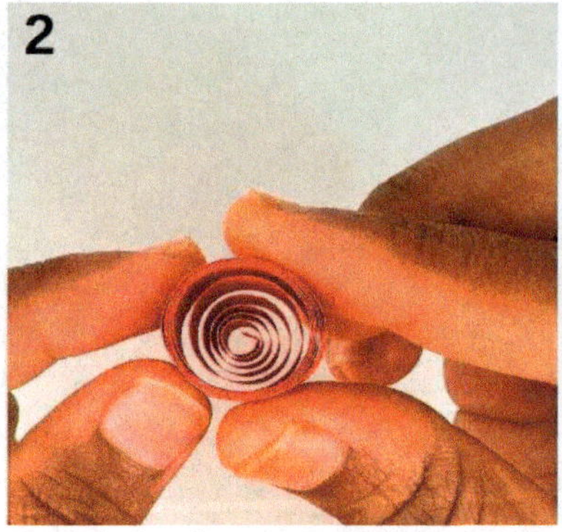

Hold the loose coil between your thumb and index finger

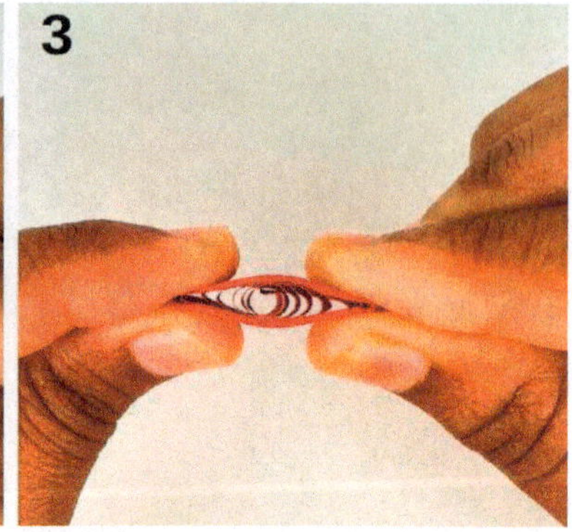

Pinch two opposite points of the coil

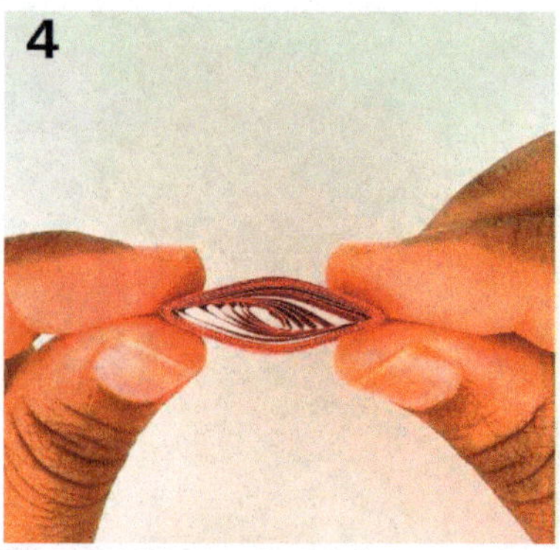

This will result in an eye shape or marquise shape

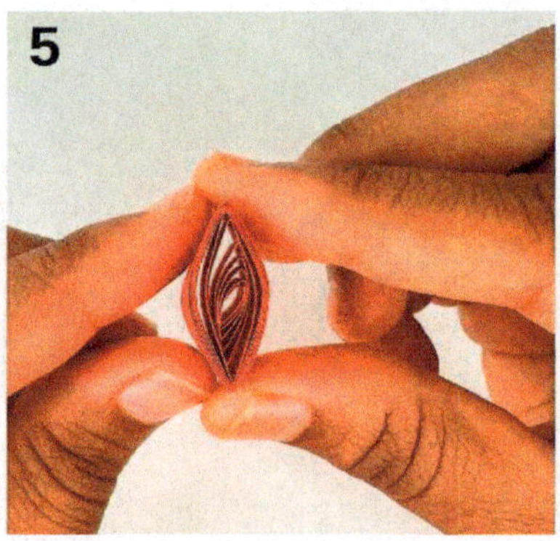

Rotate the coil 90 degrees

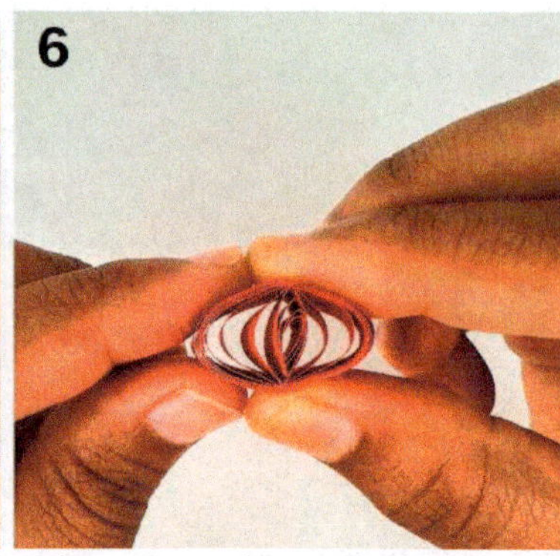

Flatten and pinch the two remaining opposite points

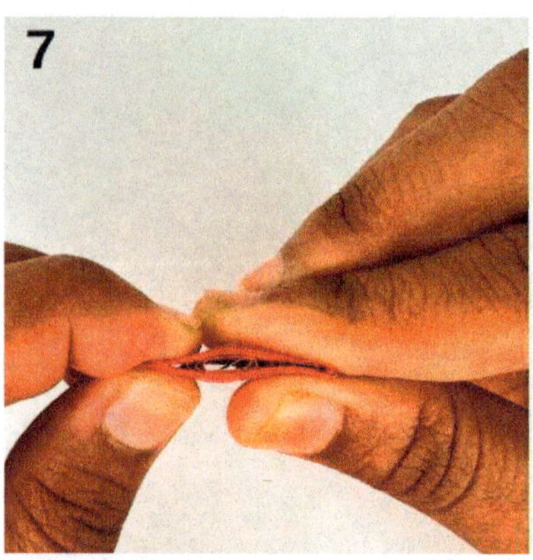

This should result in a square shape with four defined corners and straight edges

If needed, pinch the corners again to sharpen them and make sure they are well-defined

DIAMOND SHAPE

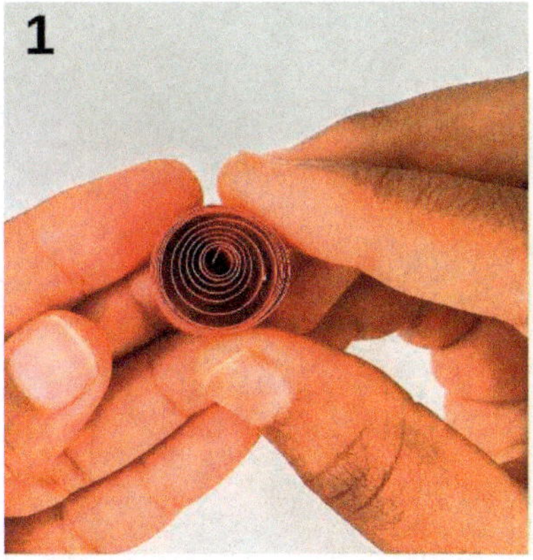

Create a loose coil

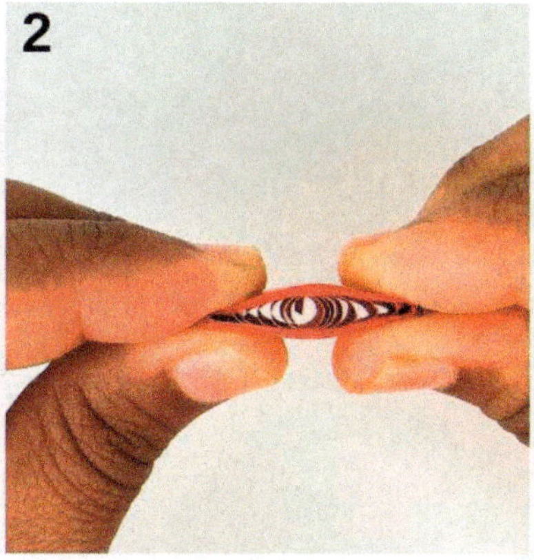

Hold the loose coil between your thumb and index finger and flatten

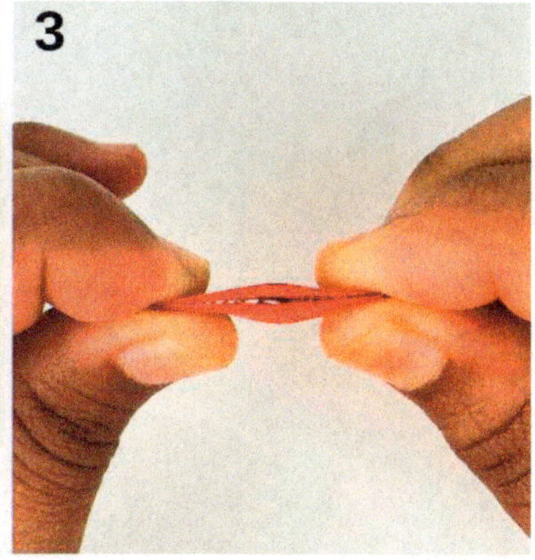

Pinch two opposite points of the coil simultaneously to create an eye shape or marquise shape

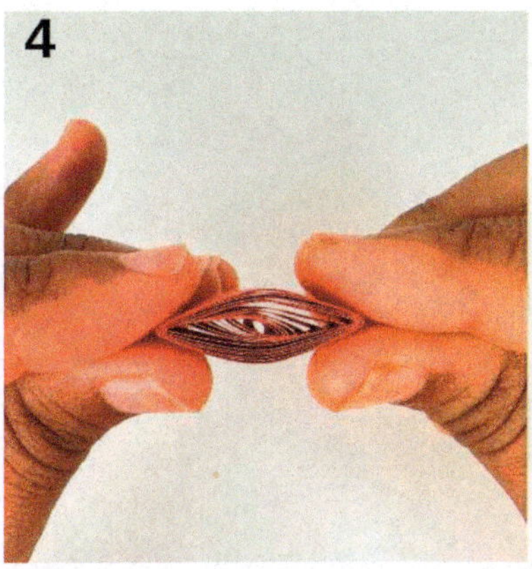

Place the eye shape between the two fingers

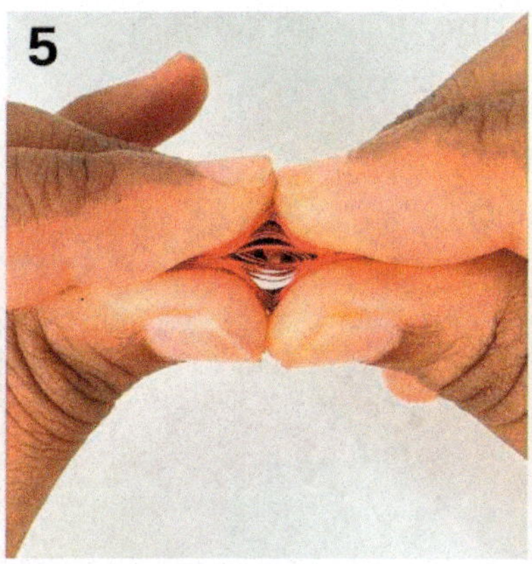

Pinch the other two opposite points, creating a diamond shape

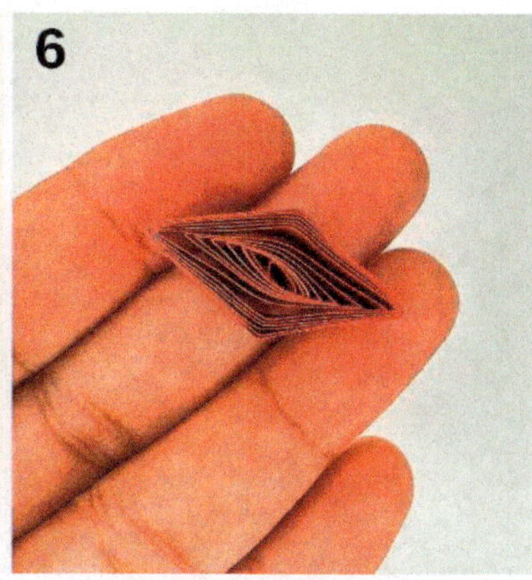

Ensure that all four points are sharply defined and the sides are straight

These basic quilling shapes form the building blocks of more complex designs. By practicing these shapes and understanding their applications, you will gain the skills needed to create diverse and intricate quilled art. Experiment with different sizes, colours, and combinations to develop your unique style and enhance your quilling projects.

JOINING PAPER STRIPS

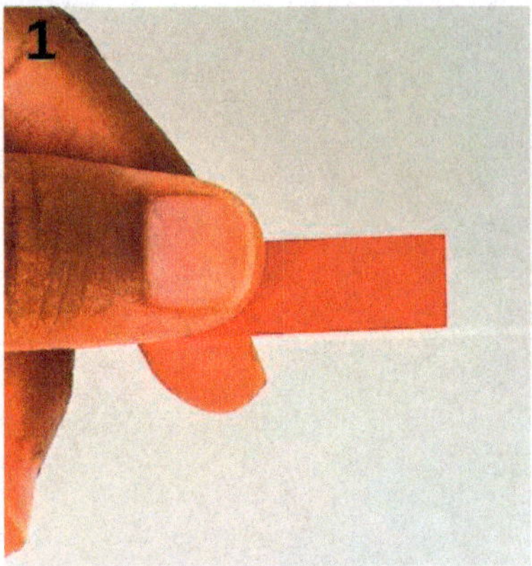

Take the two strips you want to join and ensure their ends are straight. If necessary, trim the ends to ensure a clean edge

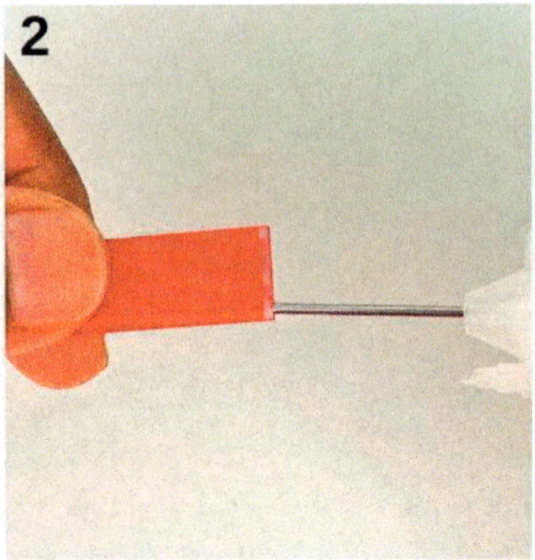

Apply a small dab of glue to the end of one strip. Use a glue that dries clear, such as PVA or craft glue. Be careful not to use too much glue, as it can cause the paper to warp

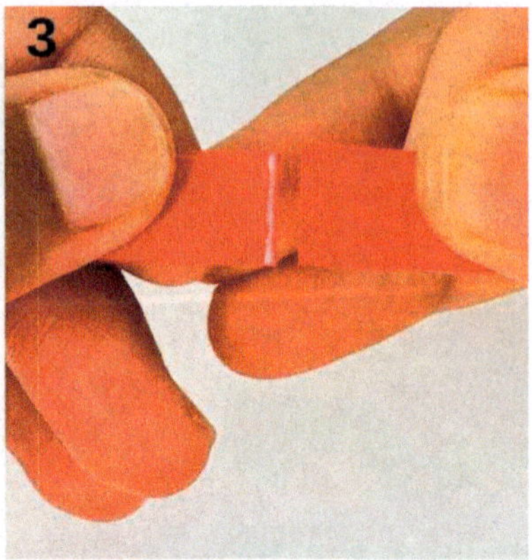

Place the end of the second strip over the glued end of the first strip, aligning them carefully. Press them together gently but firmly

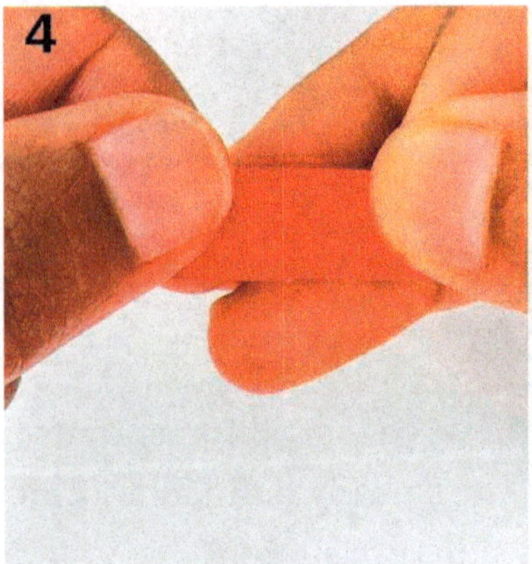

Hold the strips together for a few seconds to allow the glue to set

Once the glue is dry, gently tug the joined area to ensure the bond is secure. The joint should be smooth and not bulky, allowing the strip to be used seamlessly in your quilling project

By following these steps, you can create longer quilling strips that are perfect for any project, whether it's a simple coil or a more complex design.

CLASSIC CHRISTMAS ORNAMENTS

SNOWFLAKE

Paper quilled snowflake is an elegant and intricate craft made by rolling and shaping strips of paper into delicate snowflake patterns. This project beautifully captures the uniqueness of snowflakes, creating a stunning decoration for holiday cards, ornaments, or winter-themed décor. It's a creative and timeless way to add a handmade touch to your seasonal festivities.

Materials and Tools

- Quilling paper strips 10 mm wide in White
- Slotted Quilling tool
- White glue
- Small scissors
- Tweezers
- Quilling board / Circular Ruler
- Fine Brush
- Varnish (Optional)

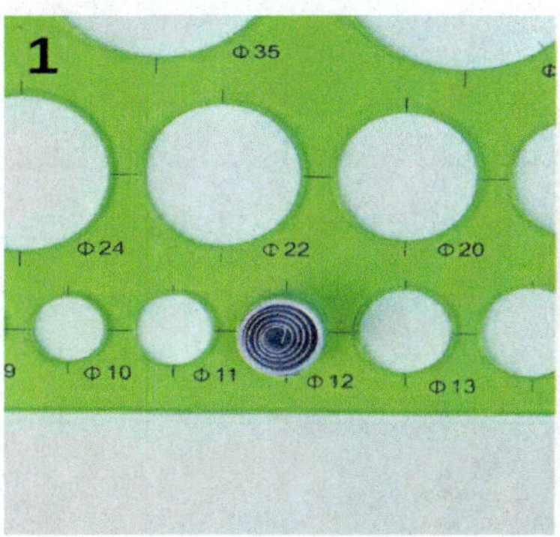

Take a white strip and roll into a coil and allow it to expand using a circular ruler (size 12) to form a loose coil.

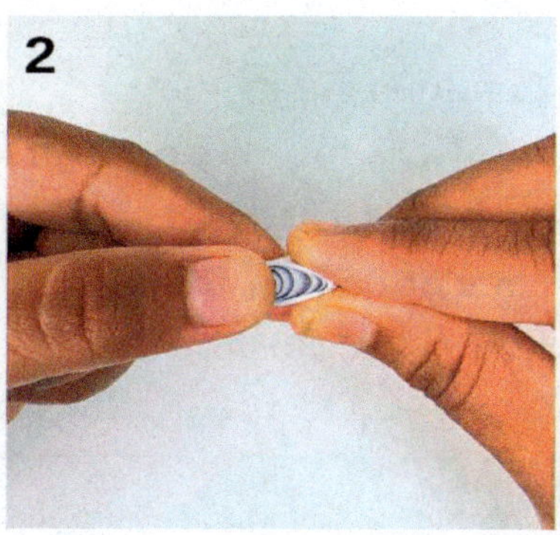

Pinch one end of the coil gently, to form a teardrop shape

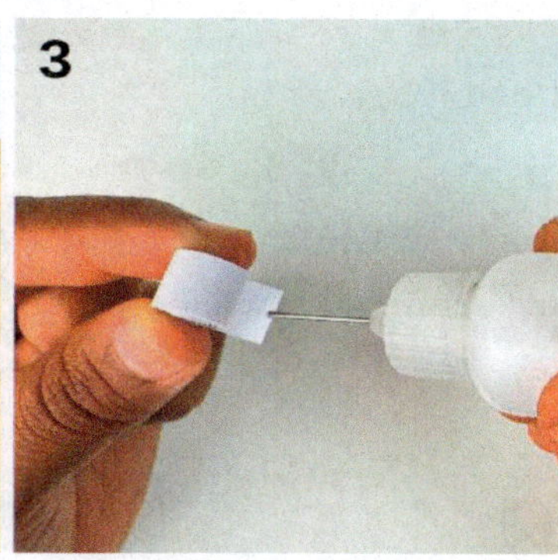

Apply a small amount of glue to the end of the strip to secure the shape

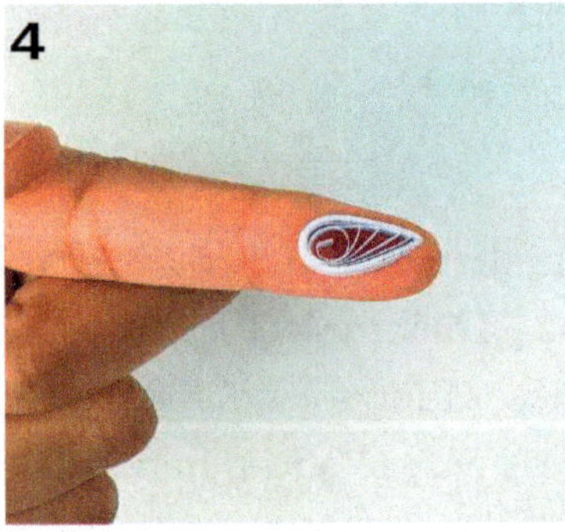

Press the teardrop gently to ensure its refined

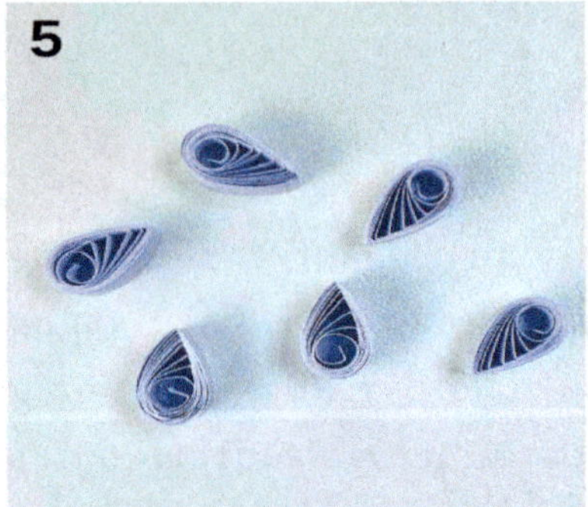

Repeat the above steps to create a total of six teardrop shapes for the snowflake

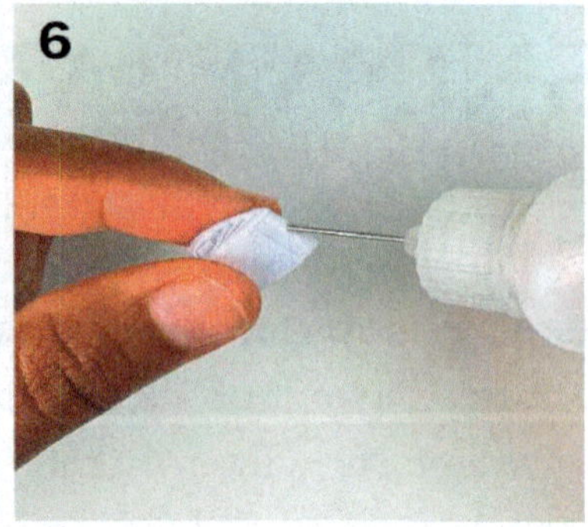

Apply a small amount of glue on the side of one teardrop

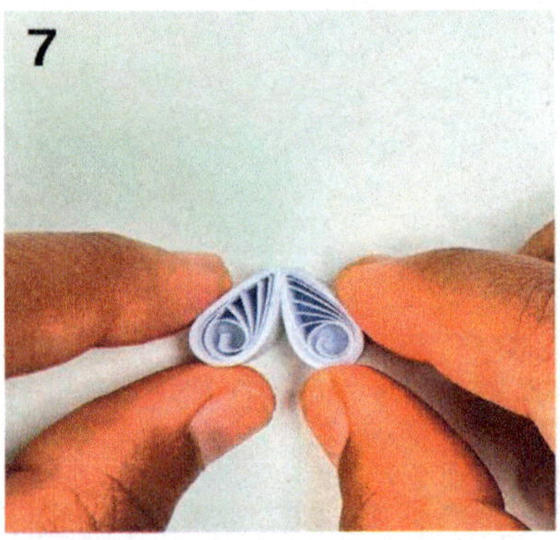

Attach it to another teardrop, aligning them side by side

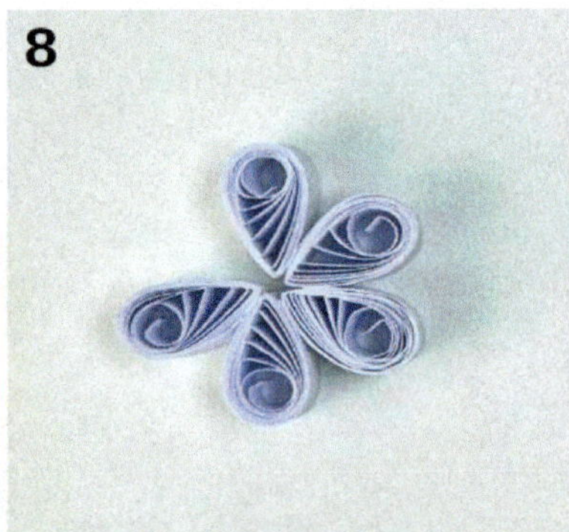

Continue gluing the teardrops together until all six are attached in a circular pattern, forming a flower-like cluster

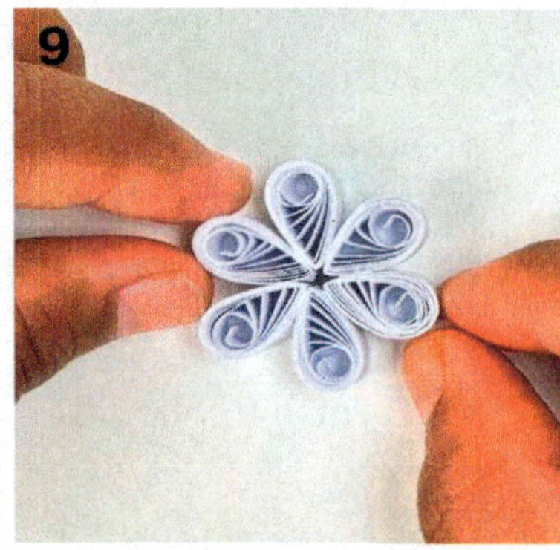

Once all six teardrops are glued together, adjust them as necessary to ensure a neat and symmetrical petal section

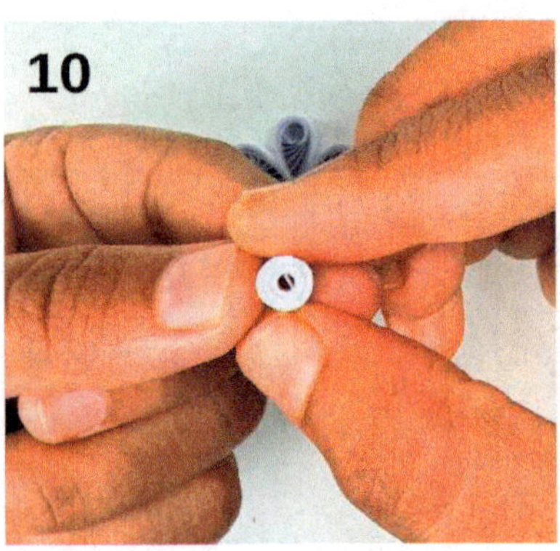

Make a tight coil with 1 white strip

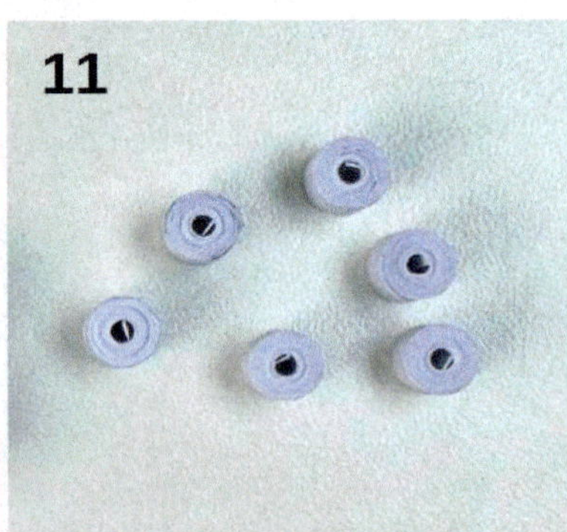

Make 6 similar sized tight coils

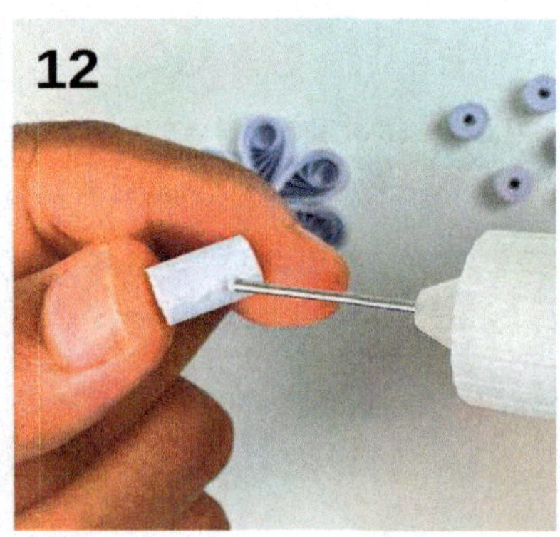

Apply some glue to the tight coil

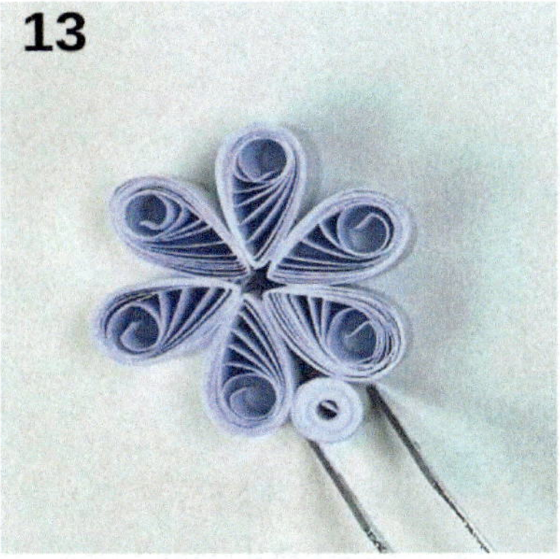

Attach these tight coils in between each of the teardrop shapes on the previously assembled petal cluster

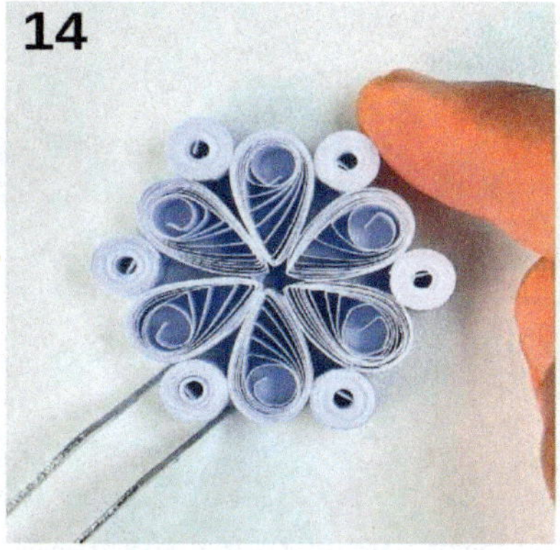

Continue adding the tight coils between each teardrop until you have a complete ring of coils around the petal cluster

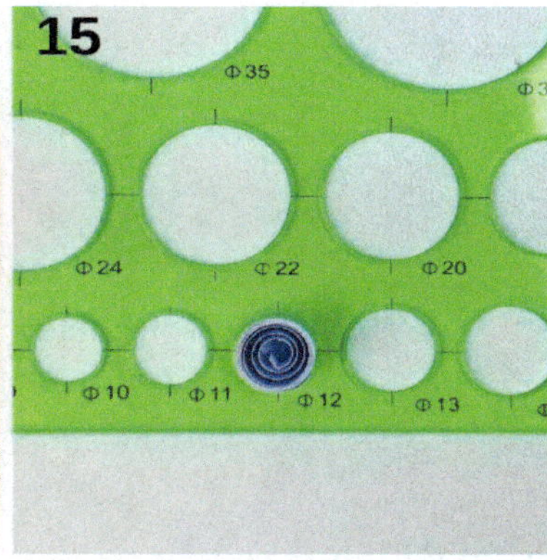

Make a loose coil of size 12 (circular ruler)

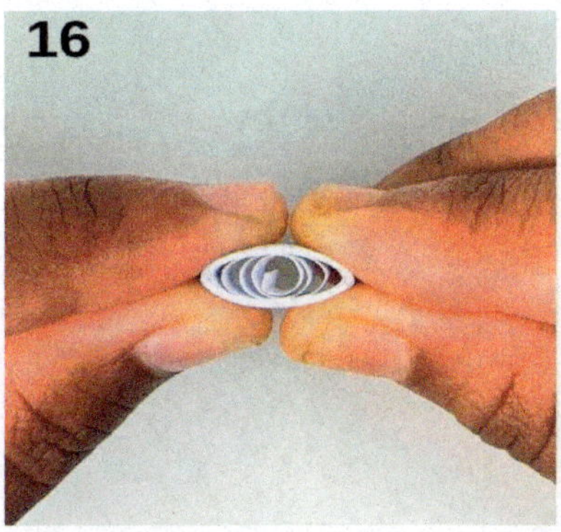

Hold the loose coil between your thumb and index finger and flatten

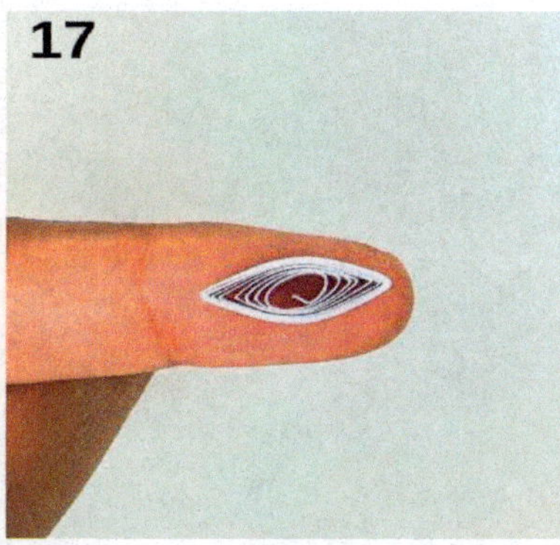

Pinch two opposite points of the coil simultaneously to create an eye shape or marquise shape

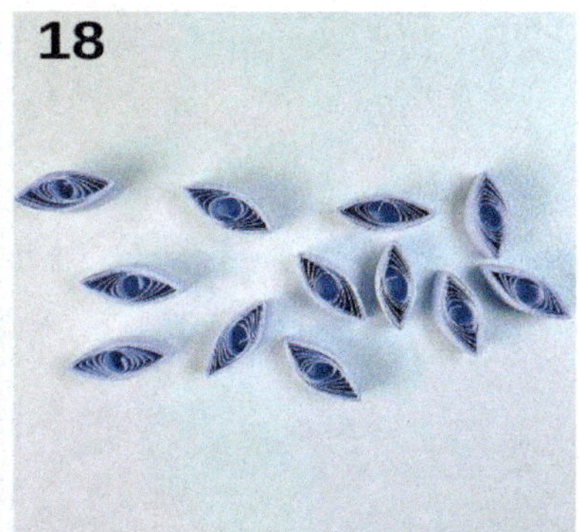

Make 12 similar marquise shape

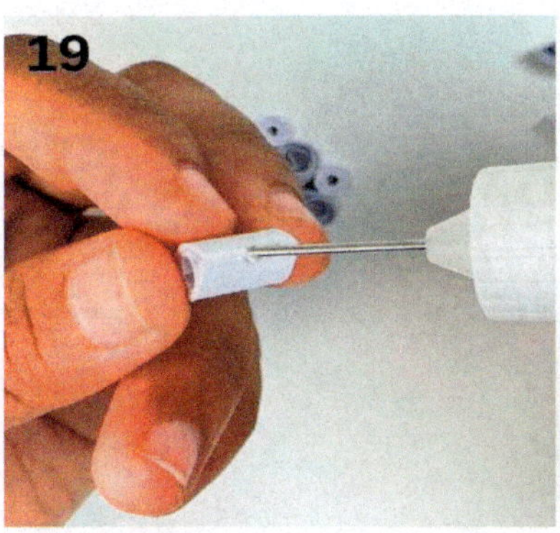

Apply glue in one of the pointed edges of the marquise

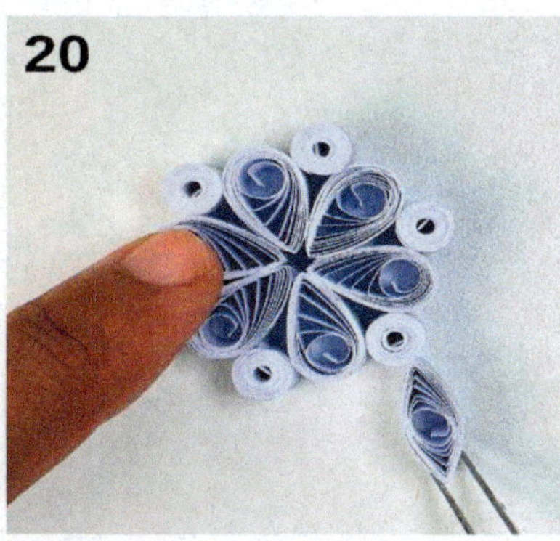

Position it at an angle and attach it to the tight coil

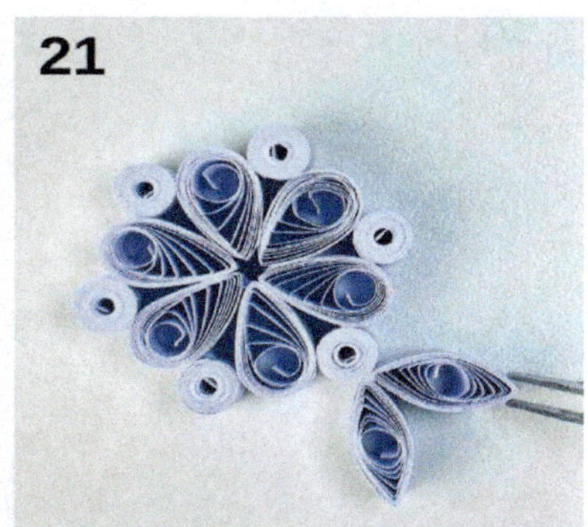

Attach the other marquise shape in a V shape

Arrange them symmetrically to create a balanced look

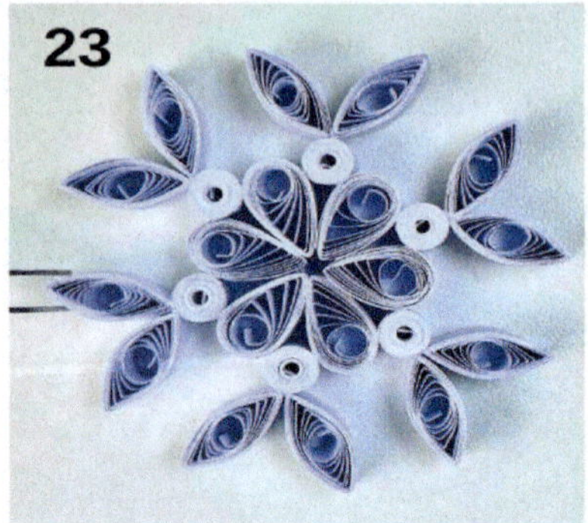

Make sure all elements are aligned and spaced evenly. Adjust any pieces, if necessary, before the glue dries completely

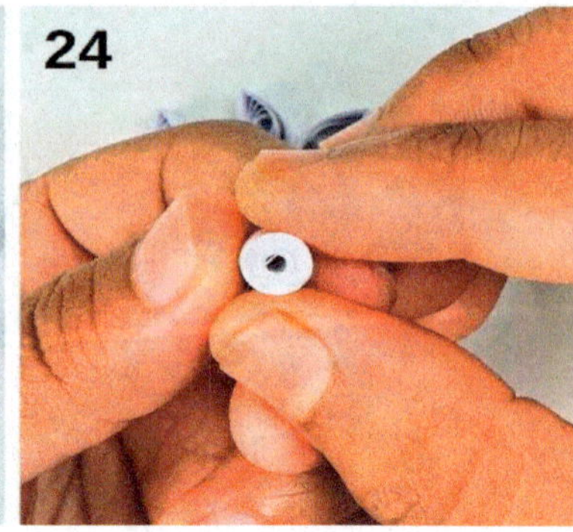

Make a tight coil with a single paper strip

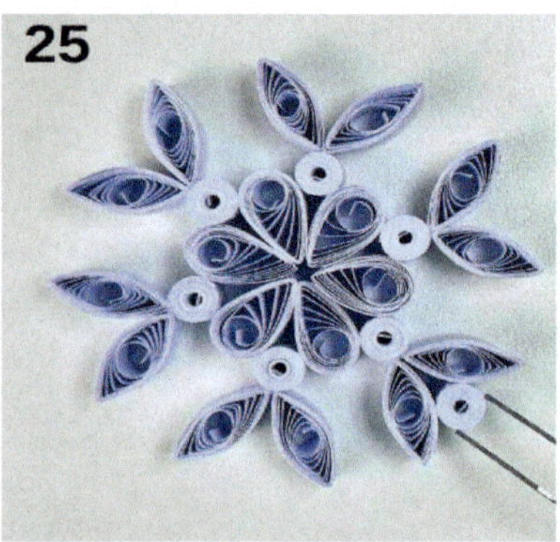

Glue the tight coil in the gap between the two marquis shapes

Glue tight coils in all the gaps around

Once all the tight coils are glued, let it rest for few minutes

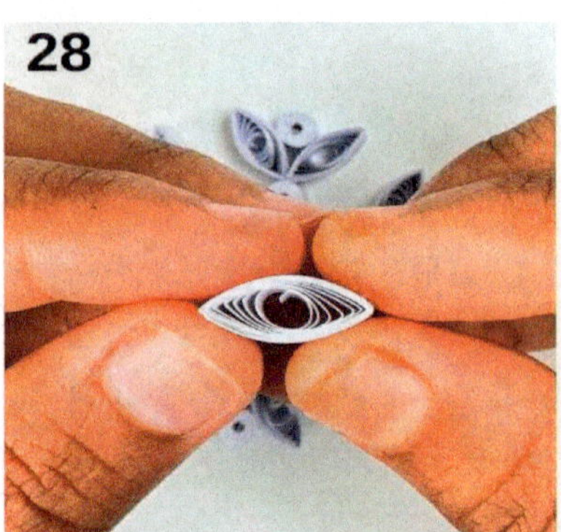

Make a marquise shape by rolling a single quilling strip (Refer steps 15-17)

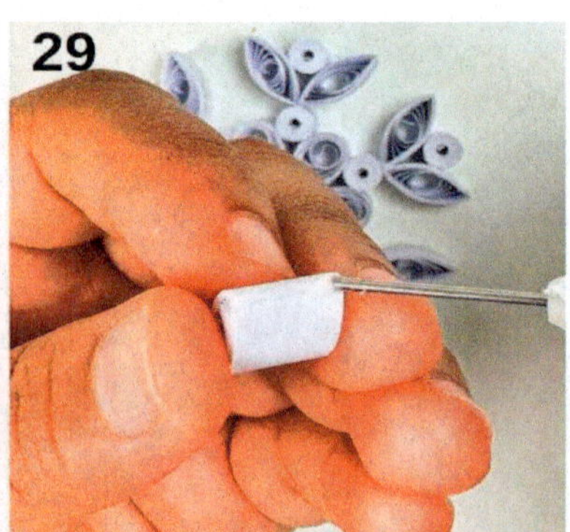

Apply some glue to one of the pointed edges of the marquise shape

Fix it at the centre of the tight coil

Focus on symmetry to ensure the design looks balanced from all angles

Allow the entire snowflake to dry thoroughly. This ensures that all elements are securely attached and prevents shifting

If needed, apply a thin layer of varnish along the front of the snowflake to reinforce its shape

Apply a light coat of clear varnish or sealant to the back of the snowflake

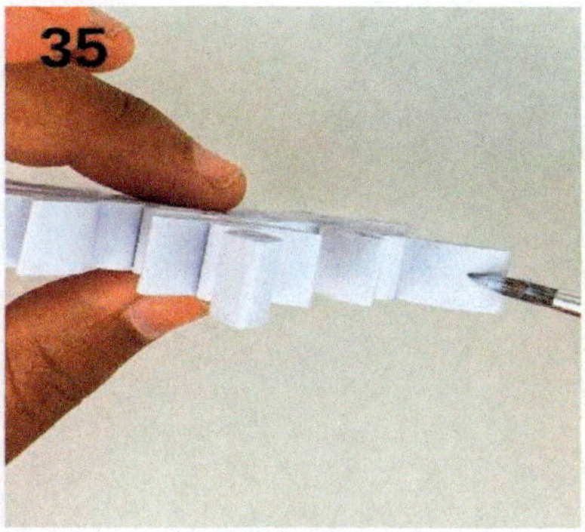

Apply a thin coat of varnish across the sides too

Once dry, you can use your paper quilled snowflake as an ornament, a gift topper, or part of a larger holiday decoration

CHRISTMAS TREE

Paper quilled Christmas tree is a festive and creative craft where strips of paper are rolled and shaped to form a beautiful, intricate tree design. This handmade project adds a unique, decorative touch to holiday cards, ornaments, or seasonal displays. It's a delightful way to showcase your quilling skills and bring holiday cheer into your home.

Materials Needed:

- Quilling paper strips 10 mm wide in green, brown and yellow
- Slotted Quilling tool
- White glue
- Small scissors
- Tweezers
- Quilling board / Circular ruler
- Fine brush
- Varnish (Optional)

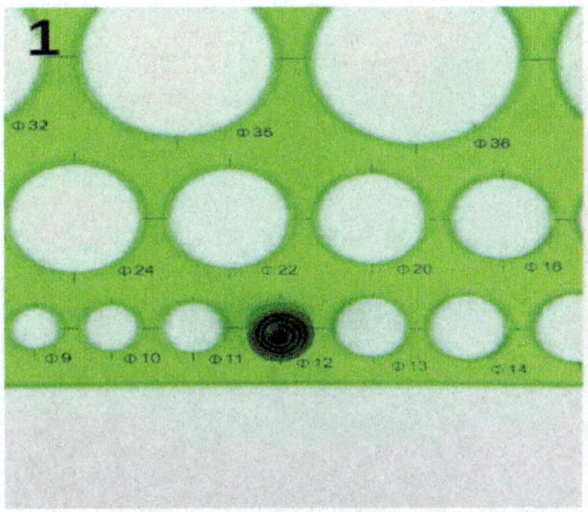

Take a green strip and roll it into a coil and allow it to expand slightly to form a loose coil (Circular ruler - size 12). Secure the end with glue

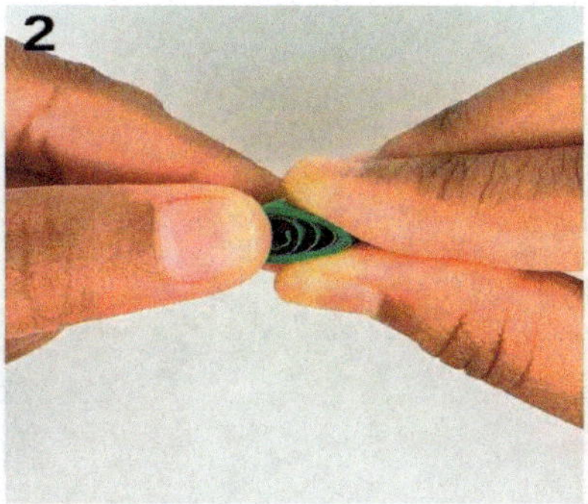

Shape the loose coil into a teardrop by pinching one end

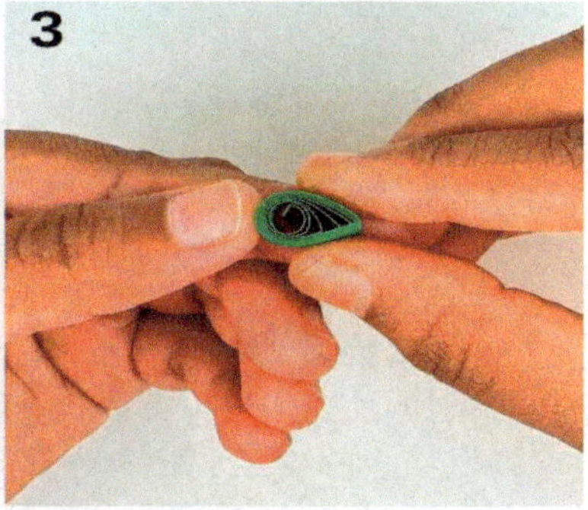

This will be one of the leaves for your Christmas tree

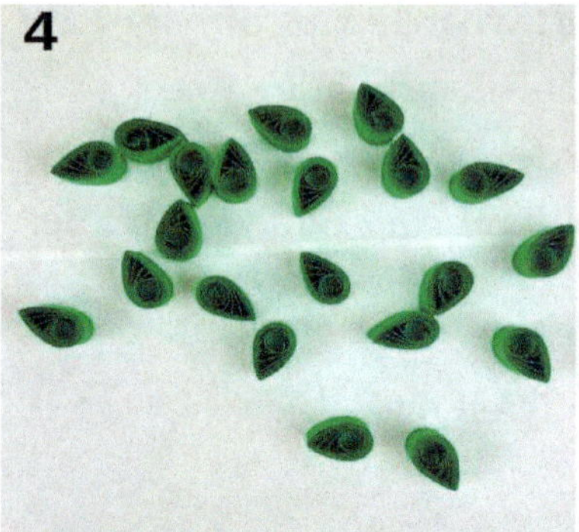

Make 21 similar teardrops

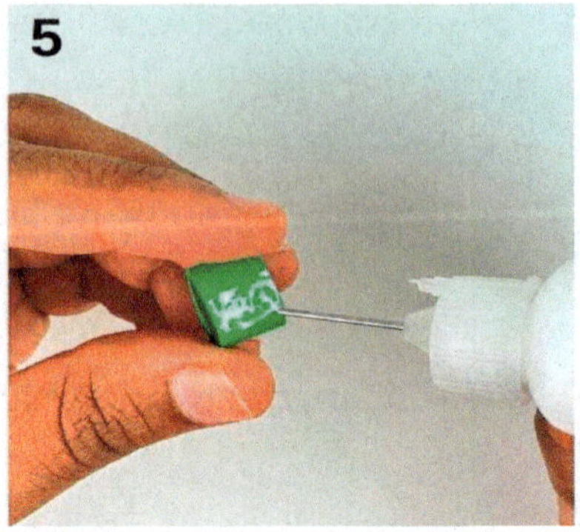

Apply glue to one of the sides of the teardrop

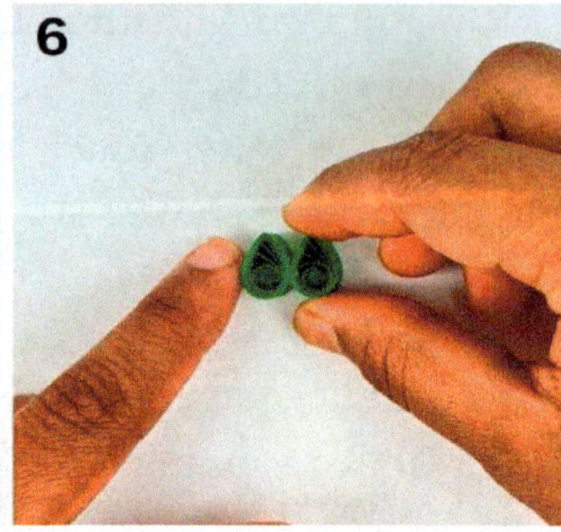

Press the glued side against another teardrop to attach them side by side. Hold them in place for a few seconds until the glue sets

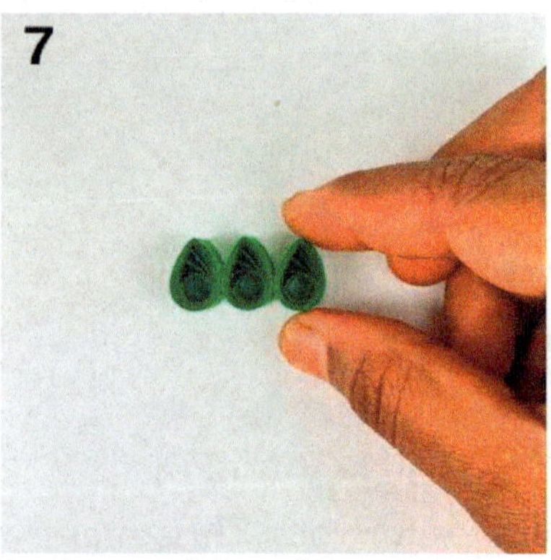

Start attaching the teardrops next to each other

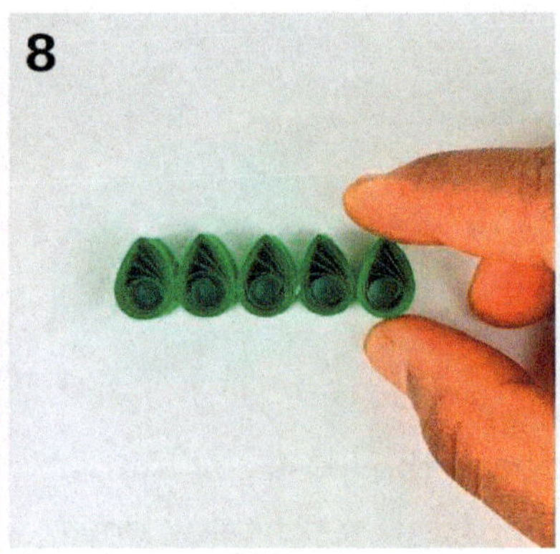

Continue adding more teardrops to create the first row of your Christmas tree

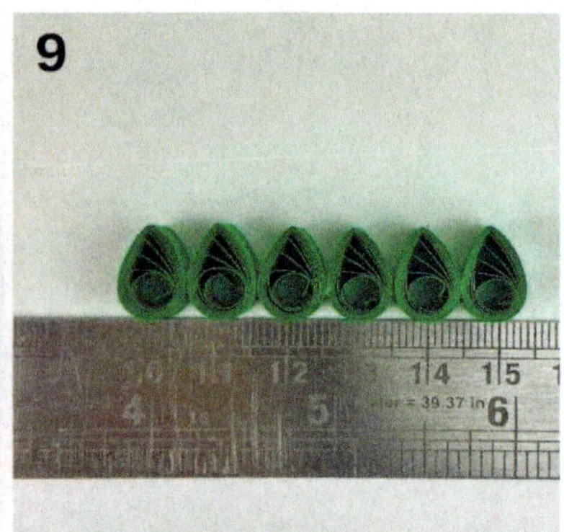

Attach 6 teardrops together. This will be the base row of the tree

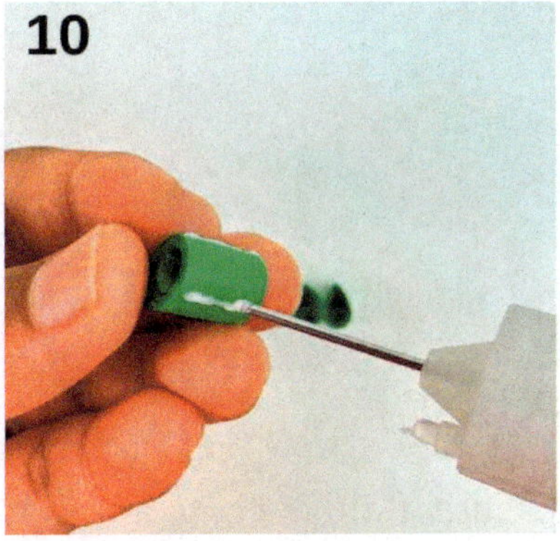

After completing the first row, start a new row by attaching additional teardrops on top of the existing row. Apply glue to the rounded sides of the teardrop

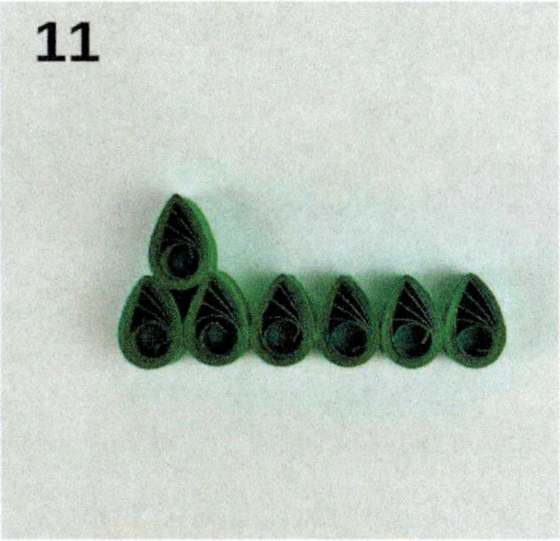

Attach it to the space between the two teardrops

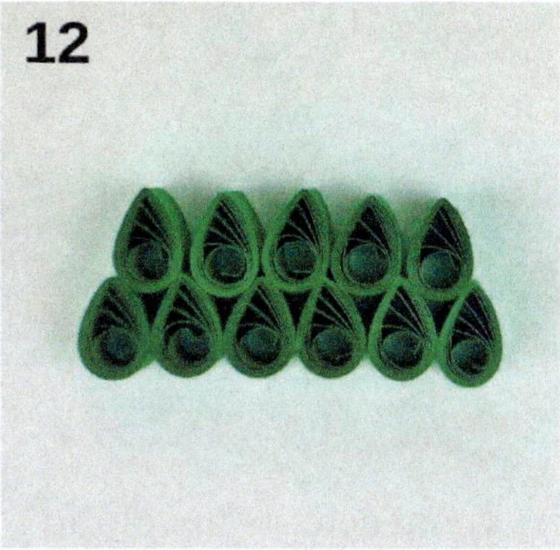

Continue and complete the entire row

Continue adding rows to form the structure of your Christmas tree. Each row should have fewer teardrops as you move up, creating a tapered tree shape

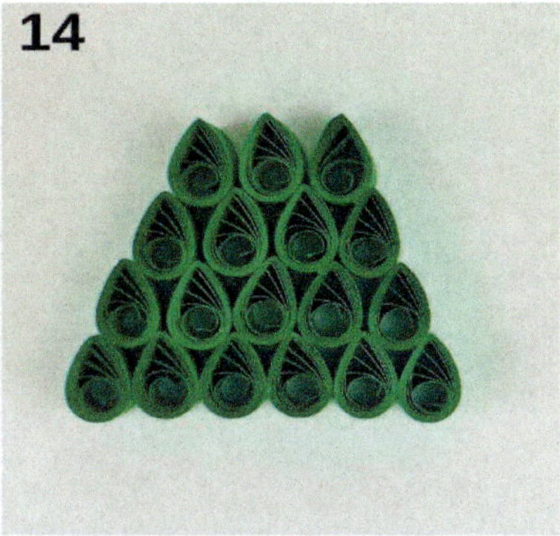

Add another row of teardrop shapes on top of the previous row to continue forming the tree. The new row should have one less teardrop shape than the previous row

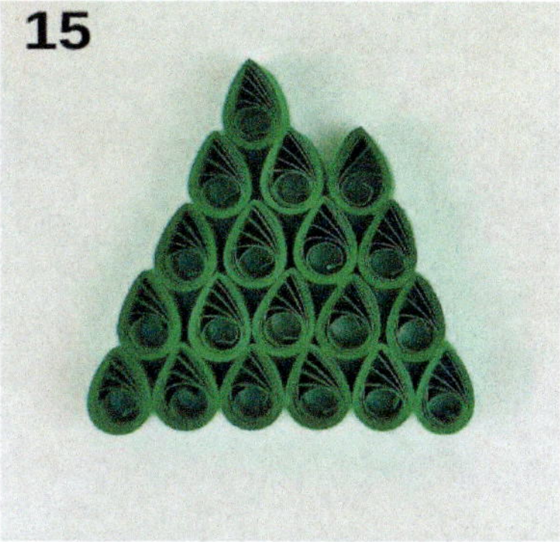

Continue adding rows in this manner, ensuring that each row has one less teardrop shape than the row below it. This will create the triangular shape of the Christmas tree

As you reach the top of the tree, the rows should narrow until you have just one teardrop shape at the top. This final row completes the main structure of your Christmas tree

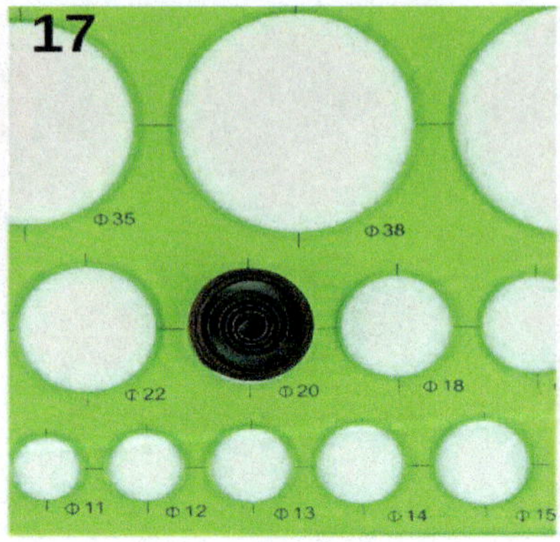

Use 2 brown quilling strips and make into a loose coil of size 20 (circular ruler). Secure the end with glue

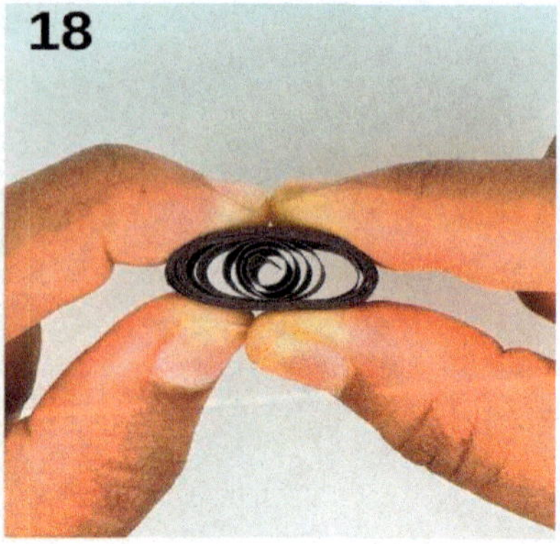

Gently flatten it

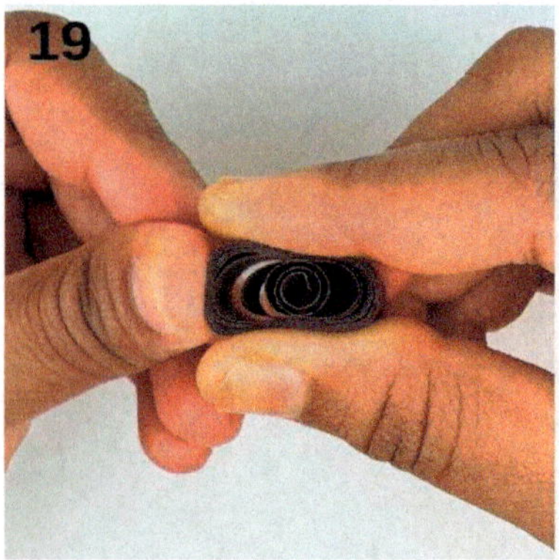

Press the coil slightly on both the sides to form a rectangular shape

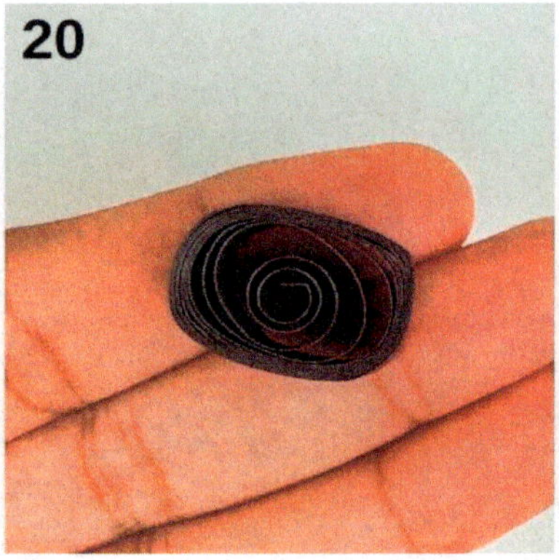

This will be the trunk of your tree

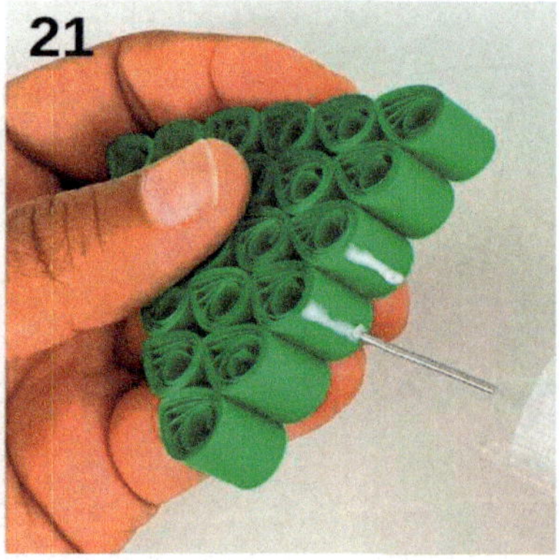

Apply glue in the base of the tree

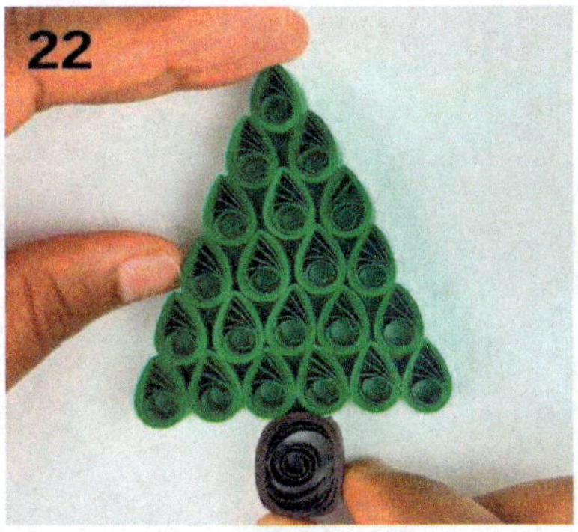

Glue the brown trunk to the bottom of the tree, centring it so that the tree stands upright. Ensure that the trunk is securely attached and the tree is balanced. Make any necessary adjustments to align the trunk with the tree

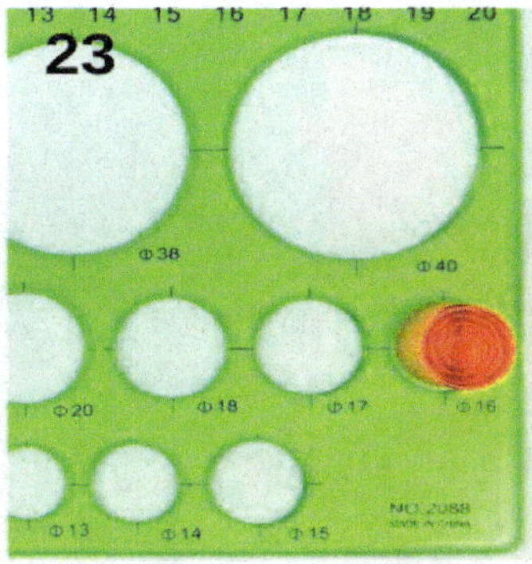

Use 1 yellow quilling strip and make into a loose coil of size 16(circular ruler). Secure the end with glue

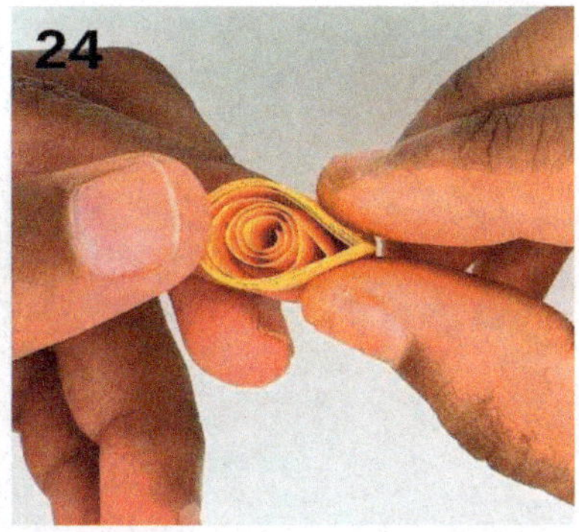

Hold the loose coil between your thumb and index finger. Pinch one point on the coil to create a teardrop that will be the first point of the star

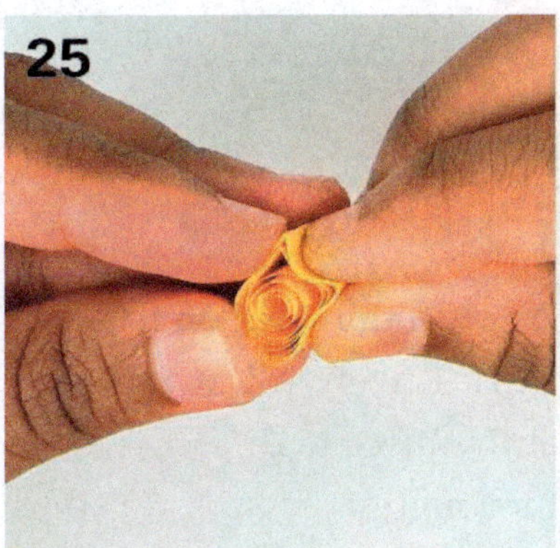

Rotate slightly and pinch the opposite side to create the second and third point

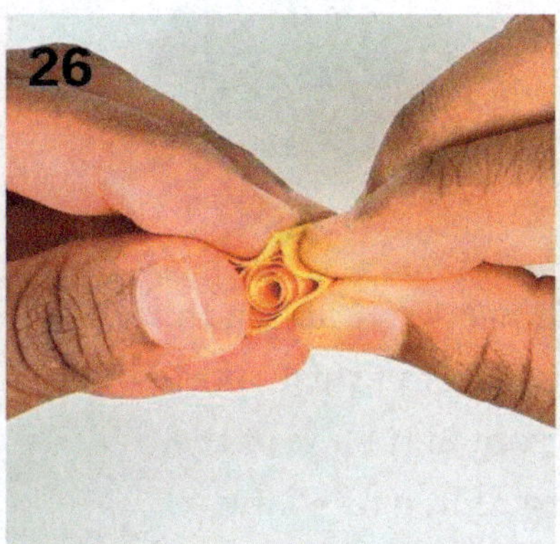

Ensure that the points are evenly spaced around the coil

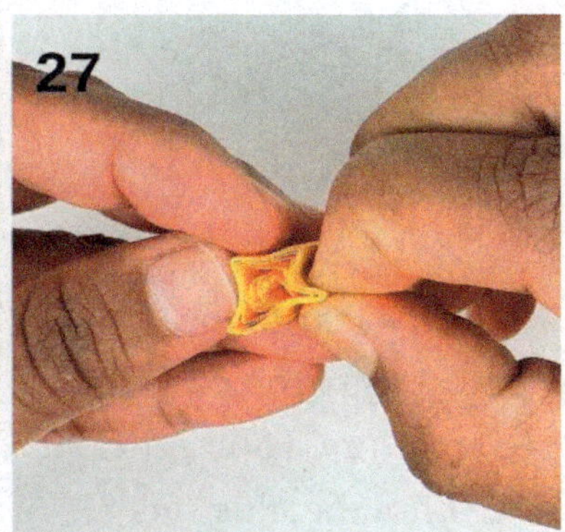

Rotate the coil slightly and pinch a fourth point

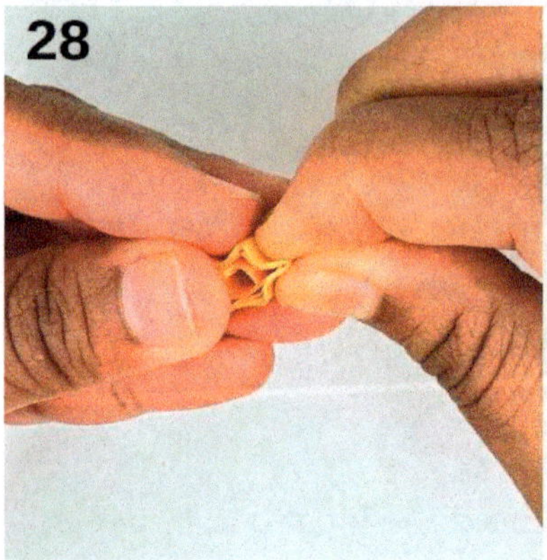

Repeat the process one more time to form the fifth point

Gently adjust the shape by pressing and refining the points to make sure they are sharp

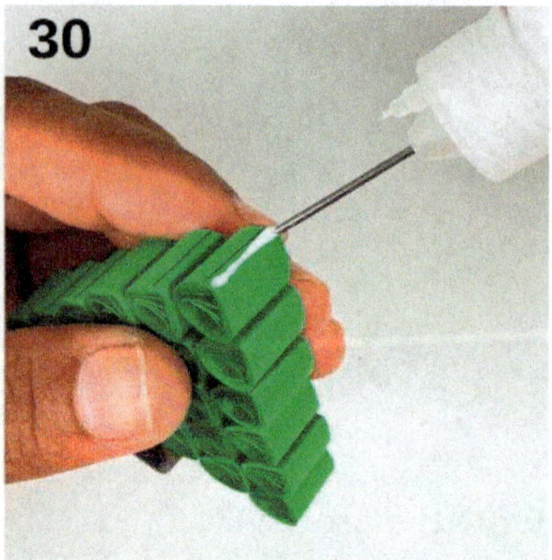

Apply some glue at the top of the tree

Attach the star to the topmost teardrop of the tree structure. Hold it in place until the glue sets

If needed, apply a thin layer of varnish along the front and back of the tree to reinforce its shape

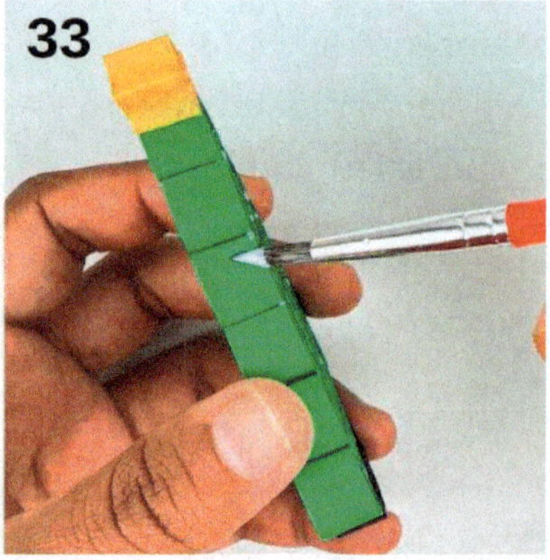

Apply a thin coat on the sides as well. Allow the entire piece to dry thoroughly

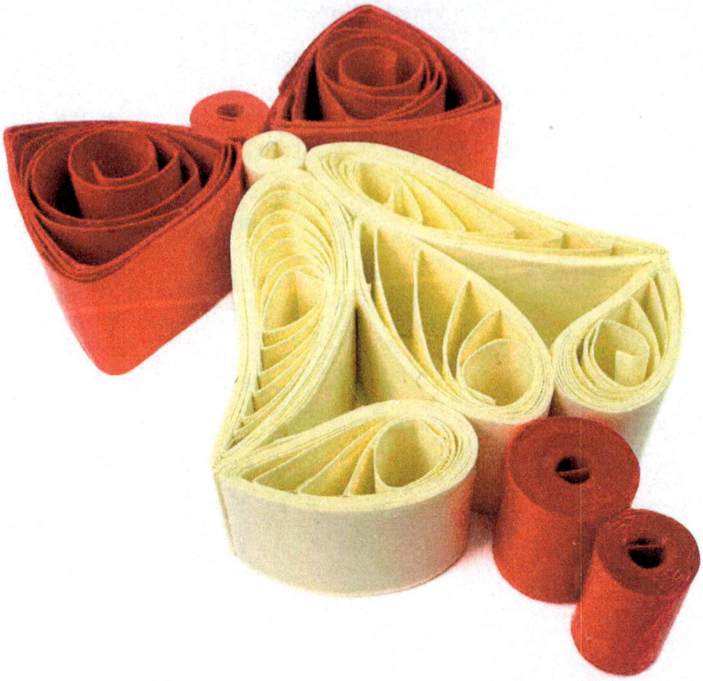

CHRISTMAS BELL

Paper quilled Christmas bell is a festive craft that combines the art of quilling with the traditional holiday bell motif. By rolling and shaping strips of paper, you can create an intricate and delicate bell design perfect for ornaments or seasonal decor. This handcrafted decoration adds a personal, elegant touch to your Christmas celebrations.

Materials Needed:

- Quilling paper strips 10 mm wide in Red and Cream
- Slotted Quilling tool
- White glue
- Small scissors
- Tweezers
- Quilling board / Circular ruler
- Fine brush
- Varnish (Optional)

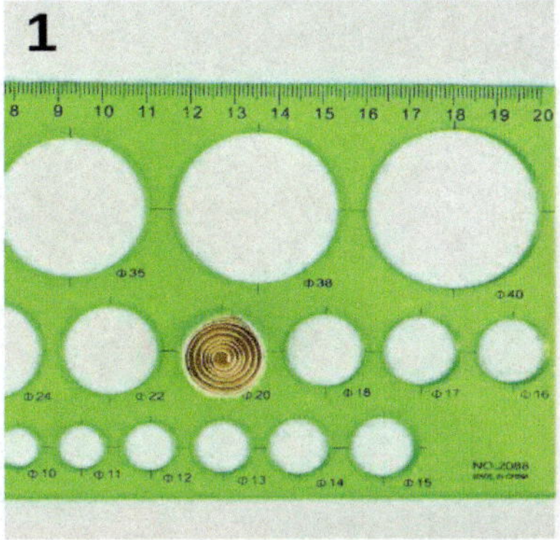

Take a cream quilling strip and roll it into a tight coil using your quilling tool. Place the coil in a circular template (about size 20) and let it expand to form a loose coil. Secure the end of the strip with a dab of glue to keep the coil in shape

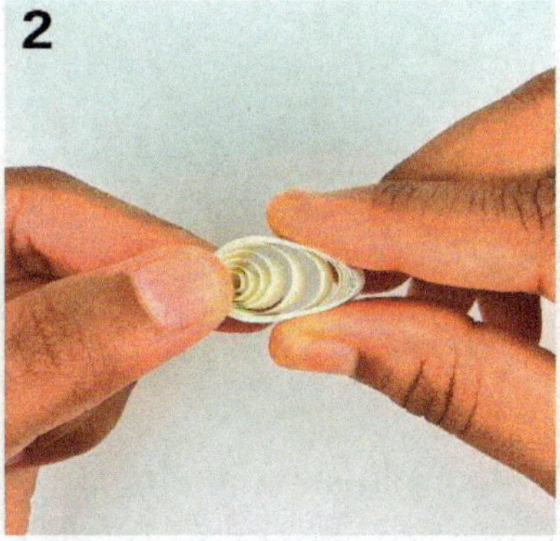

Hold the coil between the fingers as shown

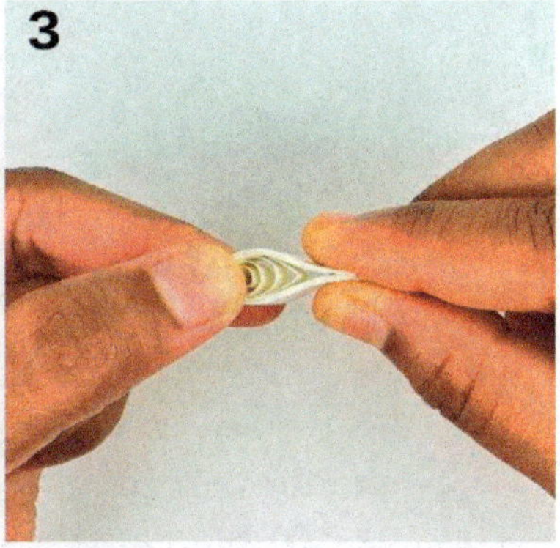

Pinch one side of the loose coil to create a teardrop shape

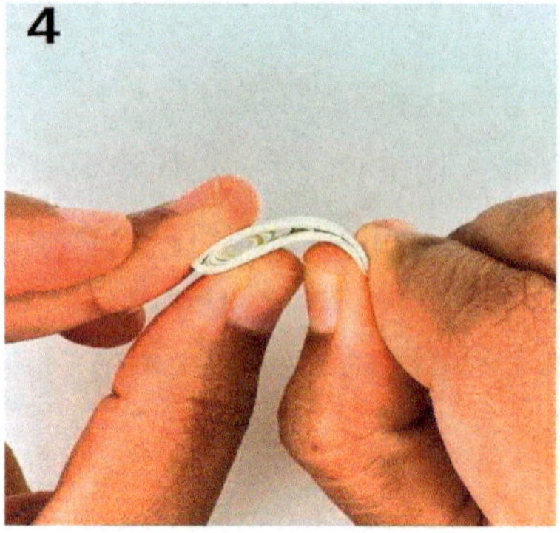

Gently curve the teardrop shape by pushing the centre of one side inward, forming a slightly concave curve

Make another identical shape. You will need two of these shapes to form the main part of the bell

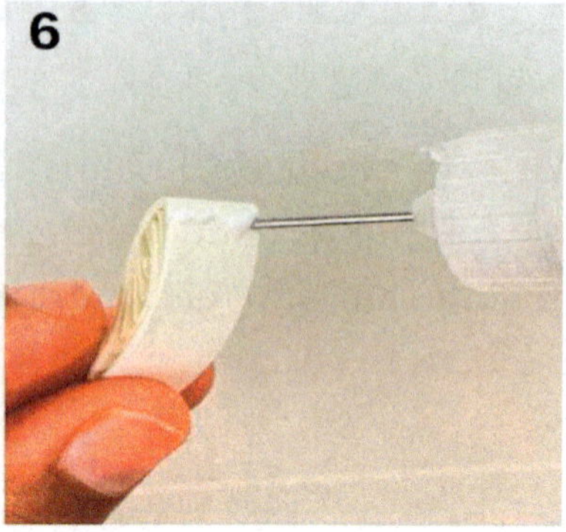

Apply some glue to the curved teardrop shapes

Take two of the curved teardrop shapes and glue them together at the tips, forming a "V" shape

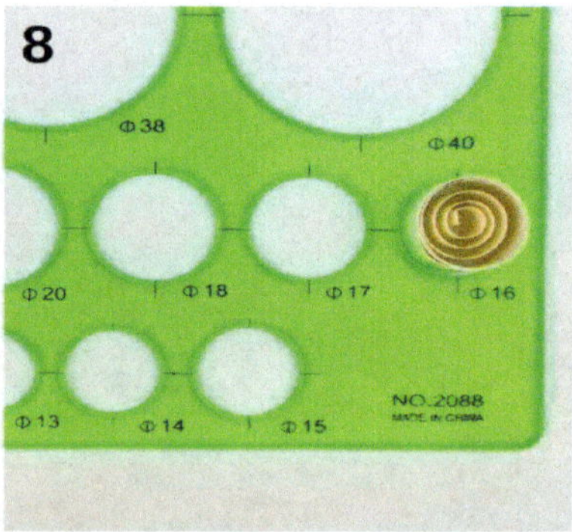

Make a loose coil (circular template about size 16) and secure the end of the strip with a dab of glue to keep the coil in shape

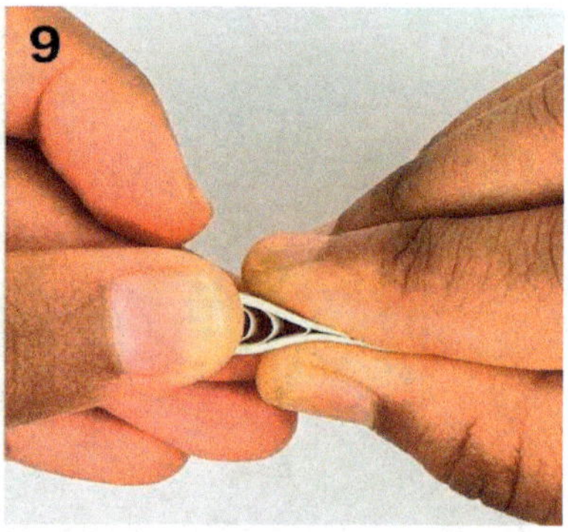

Pinch one side of the loose coil

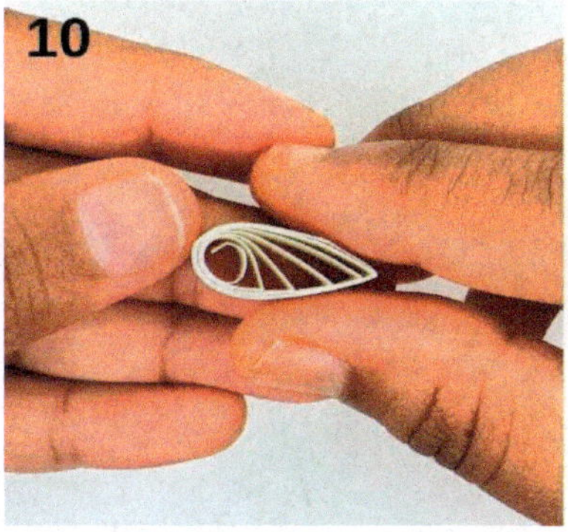

This will result in a teardrop shape

Glue the teardrop shape between the two curved tear drops to complete the bell's body. The three shapes should meet at the top, resembling the structure of a bell

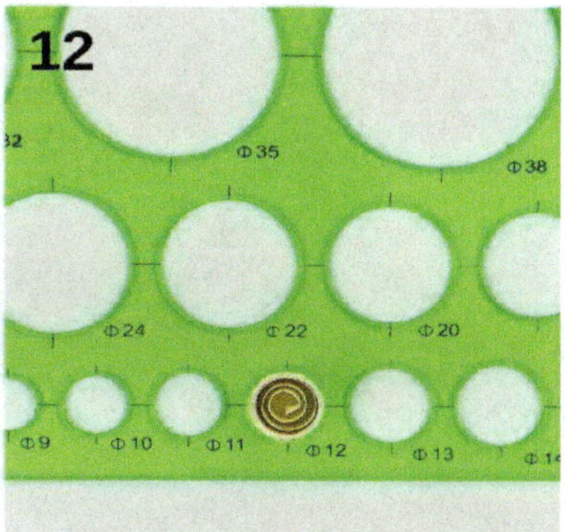

Make a loose coil (circular template about size 12) and secure the end of the strip with a dab of glue to keep the coil in shape

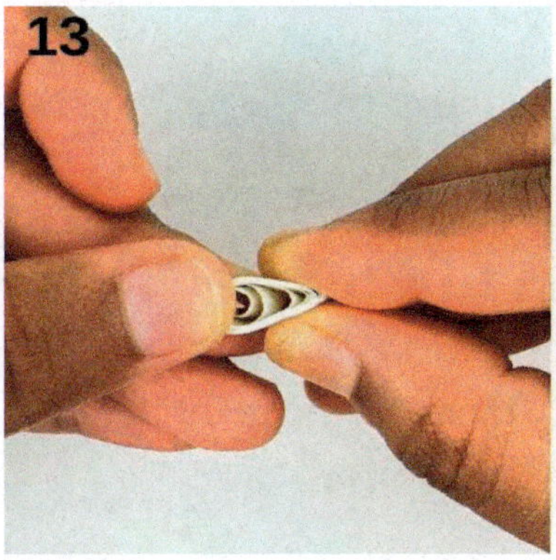

Pinch the coil to make a teardrop shape

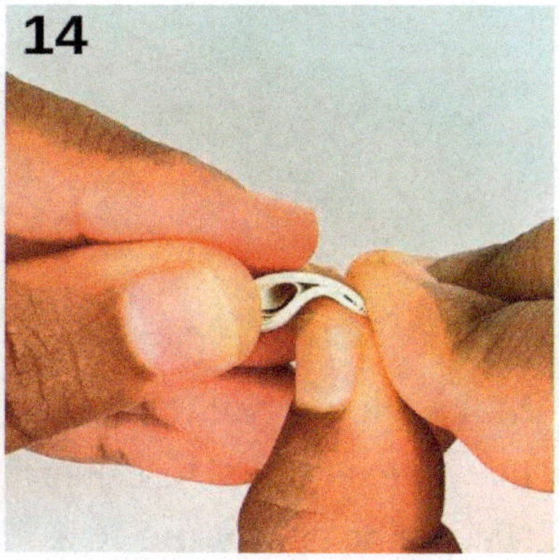

Curve the ends inward slightly to create a more rounded look.

Ensure that each of the teardrop shapes aligns properly to give a smooth curve at the bottom of the bell

Carefully position the shapes and ensure that everything is aligned properly

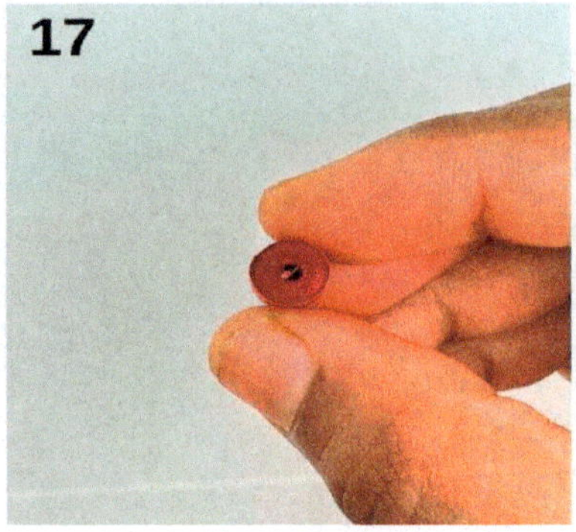

Roll a red quilling strip into a small tight coil to serve as the bell's clapper. Secure the end with a tiny dab of glue

Glue the red tight coil to the centre bottom of the bell

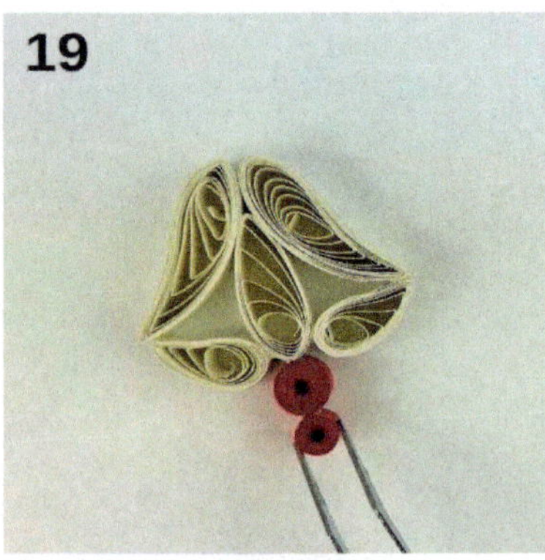

Roll a half cut red quilling strip into a small tight coil. This small coil will dangle from the centre and act as the clapper of the bell. ensure that the clapper is securely attached and centred

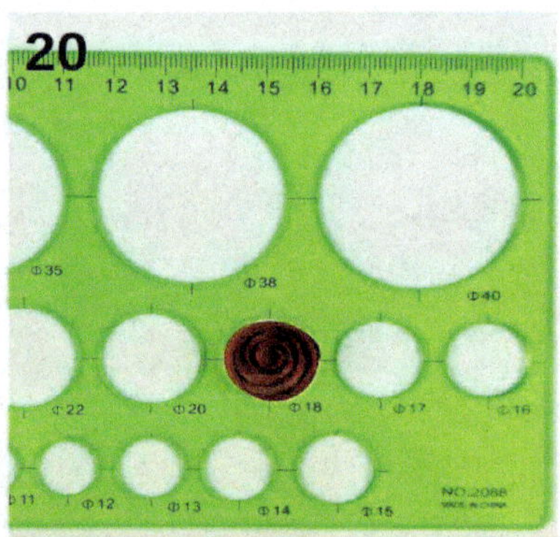

Make a loose coil (circular template about size 18) and secure the end of the strip with a dab of glue to keep the coil in shape

Pinch at one point to make a tear drop

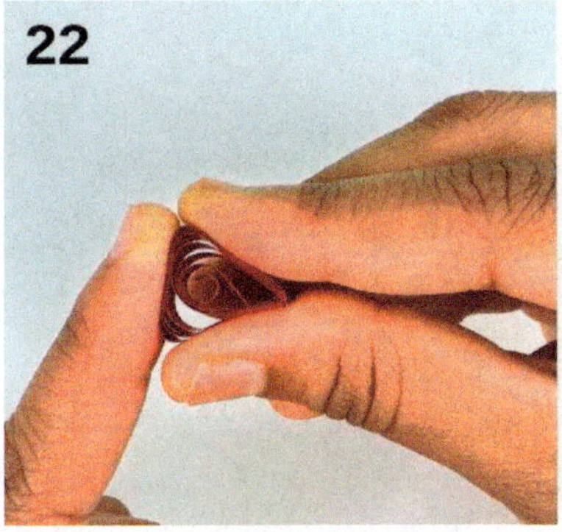

Flatten the rounded side of the tear drop

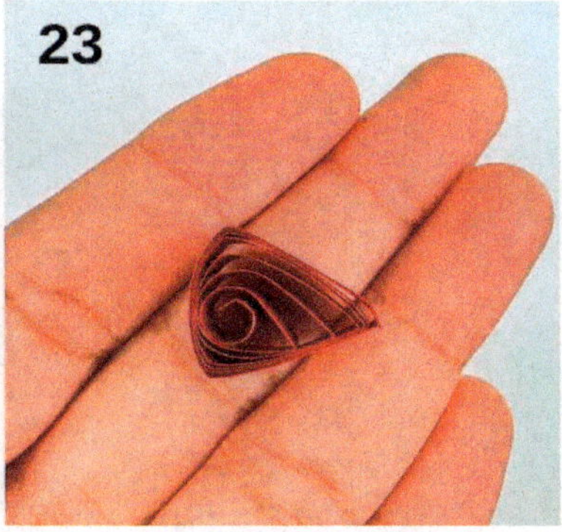

Pinch the three points into triangular shape

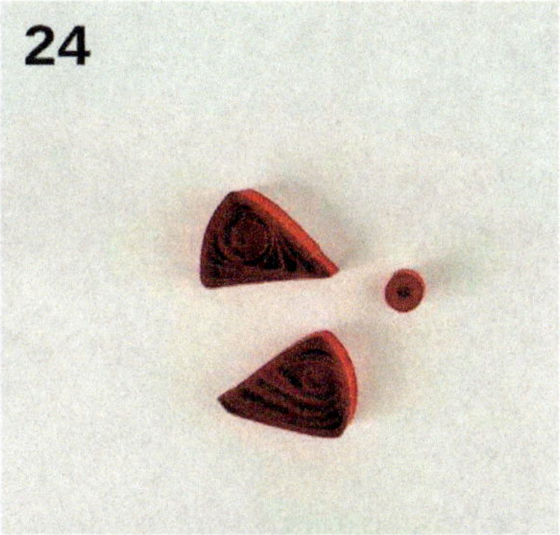

Ensure the triangle shapes are uniform and set them aside. These triangular shapes will form the two loops of the bow. Roll a half cut red quilling strip tightly into a small coil

Glue the two triangular shapes together at the pinched points to form the bow shape. Glue the small tight coil in the centre where the two triangles meet.

Glue the top of the bell to the bottom centre of the bow. Allow the glue to dry completely

If needed, apply a thin layer of varnish along the front and back of the bell to reinforce its shape

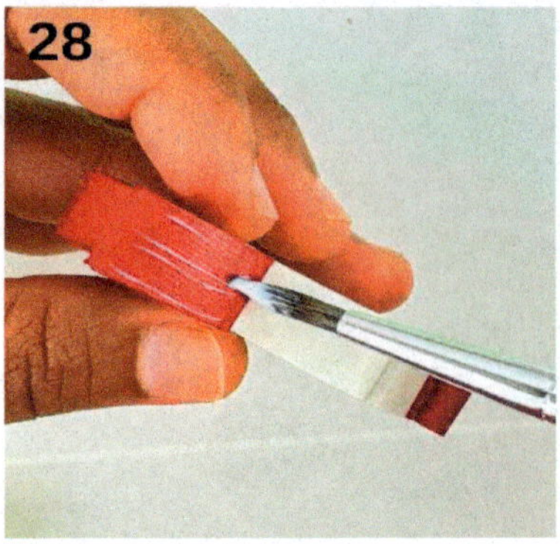

Apply a thin coat of varnish to the sides

Let it dry completely

STAR

A paper quilled Christmas star is a beautiful and intricate craft made by rolling and shaping strips of paper into a delicate star design. This festive project is perfect for ornaments, holiday cards, or seasonal decor, adding a handmade touch to your Christmas celebrations. The elegant quilled star brings a unique blend of creativity and tradition to your holiday decorations.

Materials Needed:

- Quilling paper strips 10 mm wide in Yellow
- Slotted Quilling tool
- White glue
- Small scissors
- Tweezers
- Quilling board / Circular ruler
- Fine brush
- Varnish (Optional)

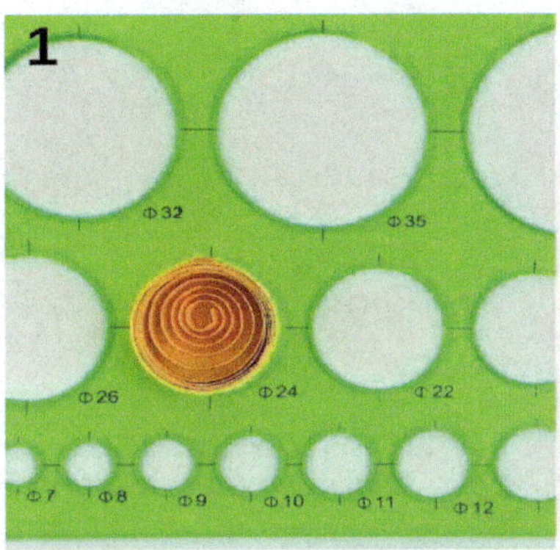

Take a yellow quilling strip and roll it into a coil using the quilling tool. Place the coil in a circular sizing guide (Size 24) to let it expand evenly. Secure the end with glue to maintain the coil's size

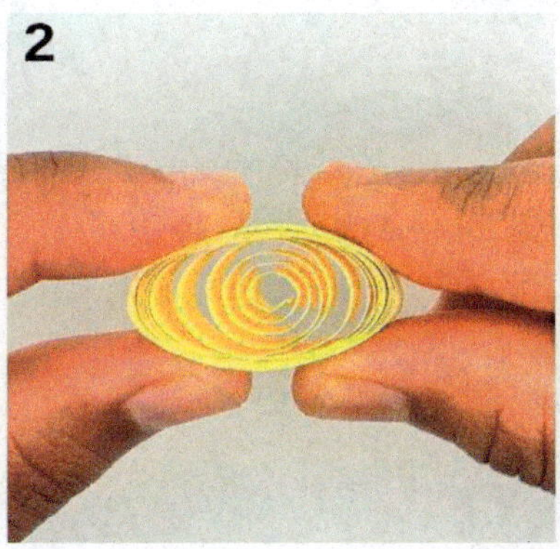

Remove the loose coil from the sizing guide and place the coil between the fingers as shown

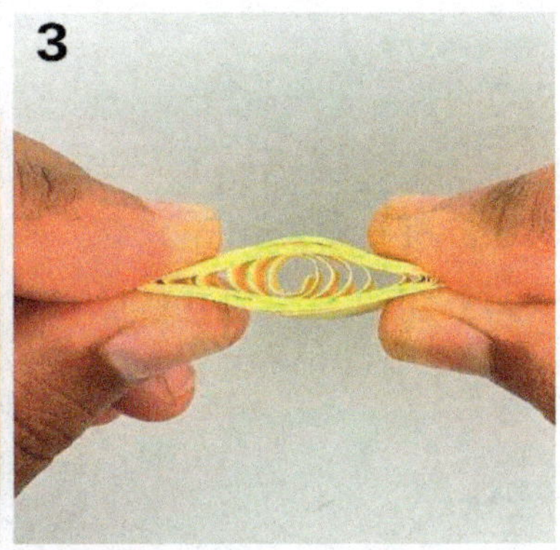

Gently pinch both sides to create a marquise (eye) shape

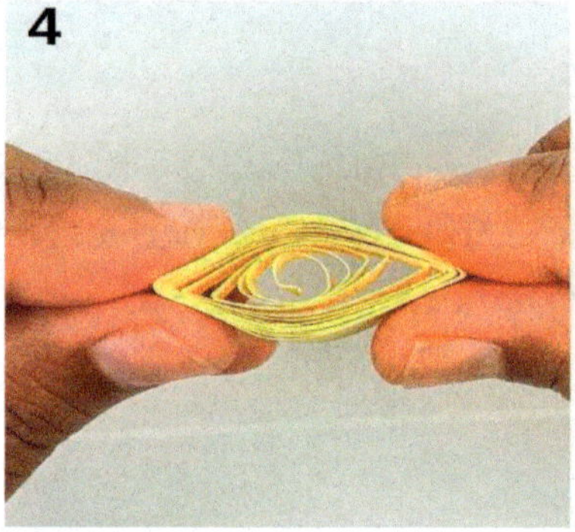

Hold the eye shape between the fingers

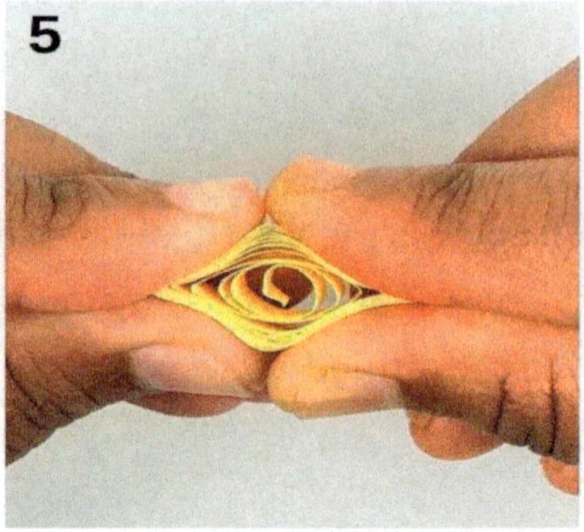

Pinch at two opposite points slightly away from the centre of the marquise

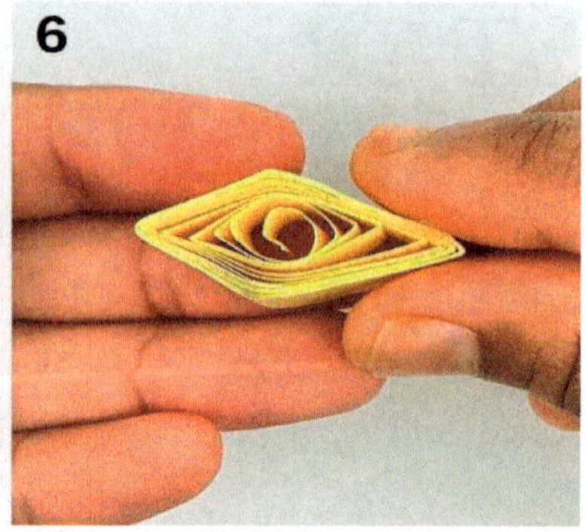

This will result in a kind of diamond shape

Repeat the process to make a total of five similar shapes. These will form the five points of your star

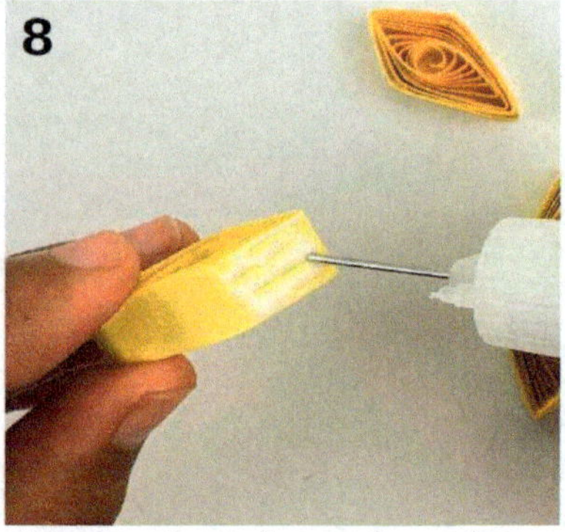

Apply glue along the edge of one of the diamond shapes

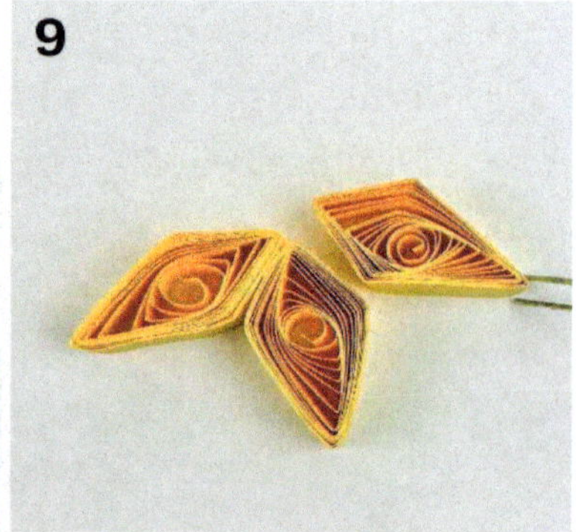

Begin attaching the diamond shapes together at their points, forming a star

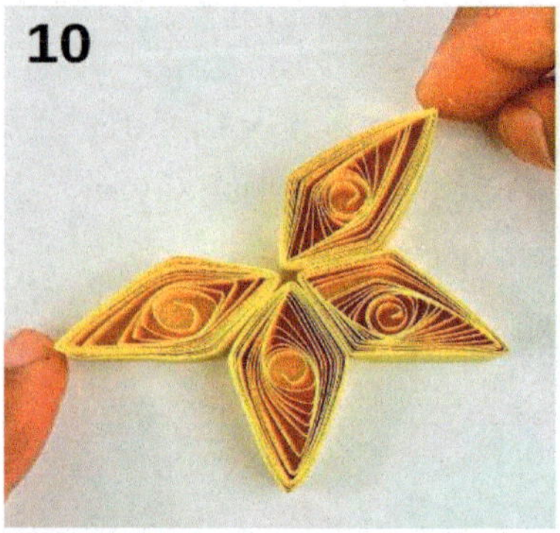

Continue gluing until all five points are attached, creating a complete star shape

Once all the points are glued together, ensure that the star is symmetrical and all points are evenly spaced

Let the glue dry completely before moving on to the next steps

If needed, apply a thin layer of varnish along the front and back of the star to reinforce its shape

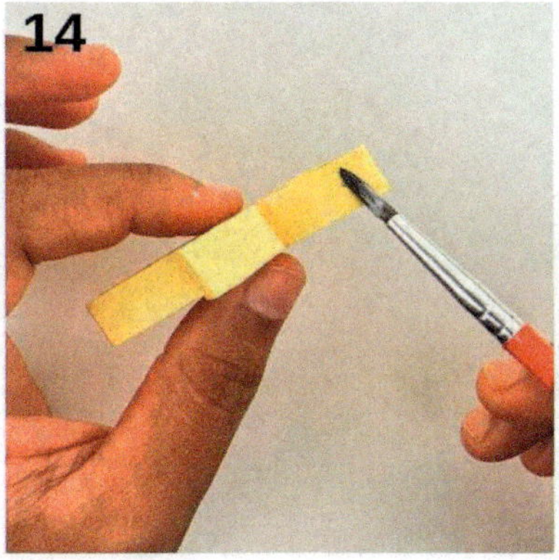

Also apply varnish to the sides of the star. Leave it to dry completely

Your star should now be stable and ready for display

CANDY CANE

Paper quilled Christmas-themed candy cane is a delightful craft that transforms strips of paper into the iconic candy cane shape using quilling techniques. This intricate project adds a festive touch to ornaments, cards, or holiday displays, showcasing the classic red and white twist in a creative, handmade way. It's a fun and unique addition to your seasonal decor.

Materials Needed:

- Quilling paper strips 10 mm wide in Red and Cream
- Quilling paper strips 3 mm wide in Red and Green
- Slotted Quilling tool
- White glue
- Small scissors
- Tweezers
- Quilling board / Circular ruler
- Fine brush
- Varnish (Optional)

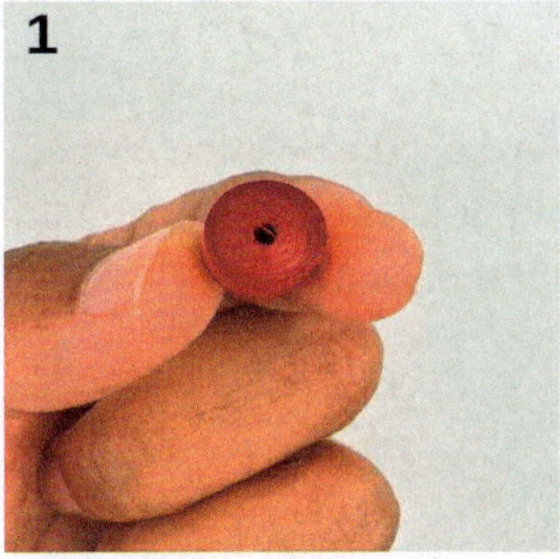

Glue the ends of 2 red quilling strips and roll into a tight coil

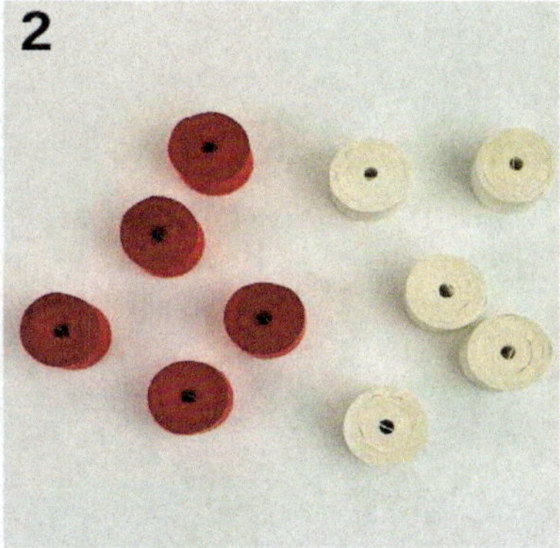

Roll 5 tight coils using red and 5 using cream quilling strips. Each coil will form one segment of the candy cane. Secure the ends of the coils with a dab of glue to ensure they stay tightly wound

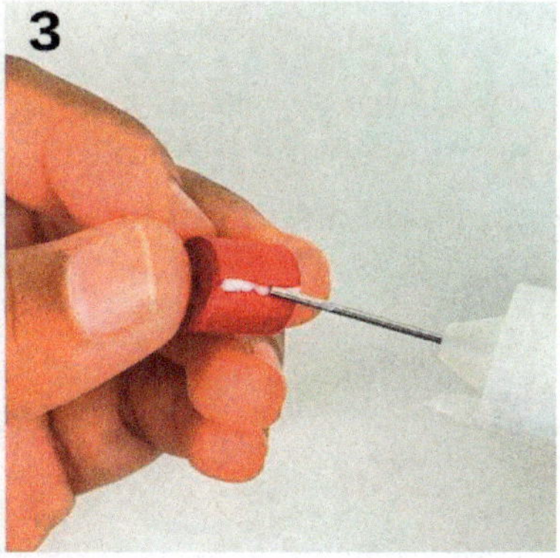

Apply some glue to one point of a tight coil

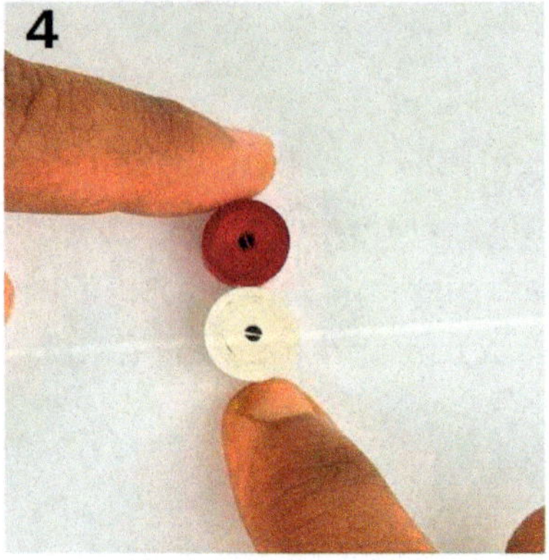

Start gluing the coils together

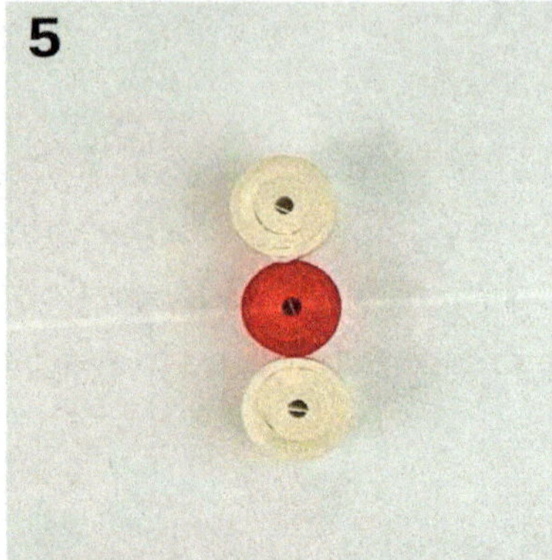

Alternate between red and white coils

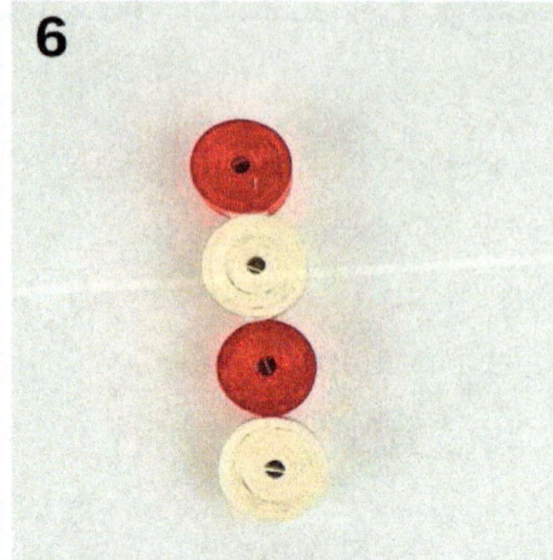

This will create the traditional striped appearance of a candy cane

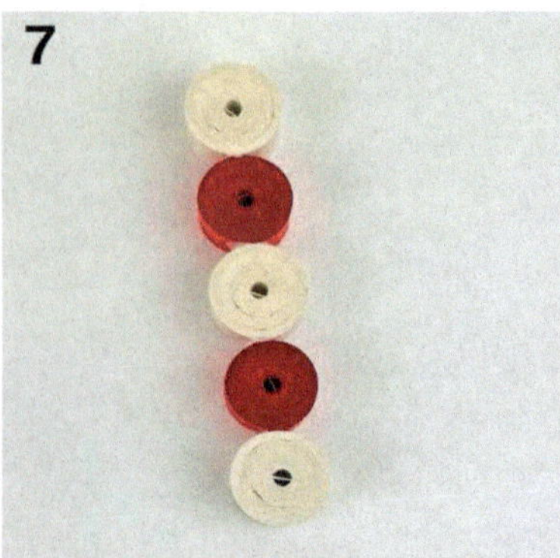

Continue gluing the coils together in a straight line

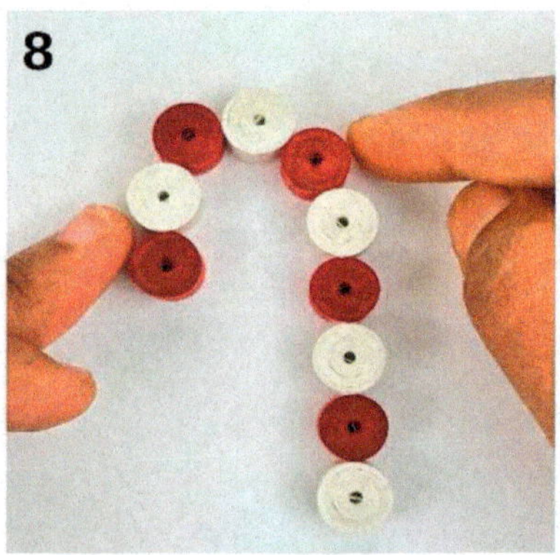

Gently bend the line to form the hooked shape of the candy cane

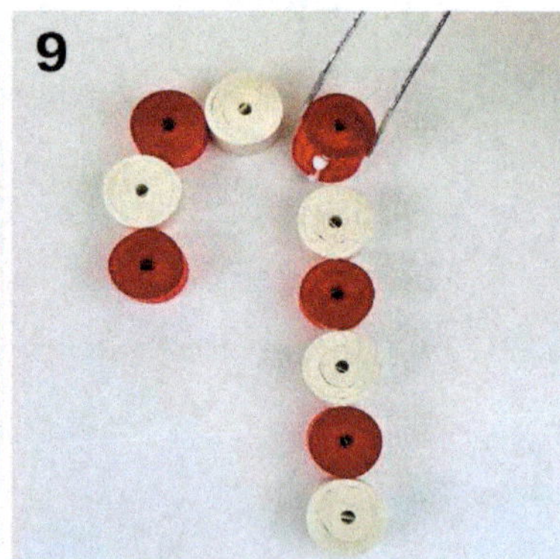

Adjust the position of the coils as needed to maintain the curved shape

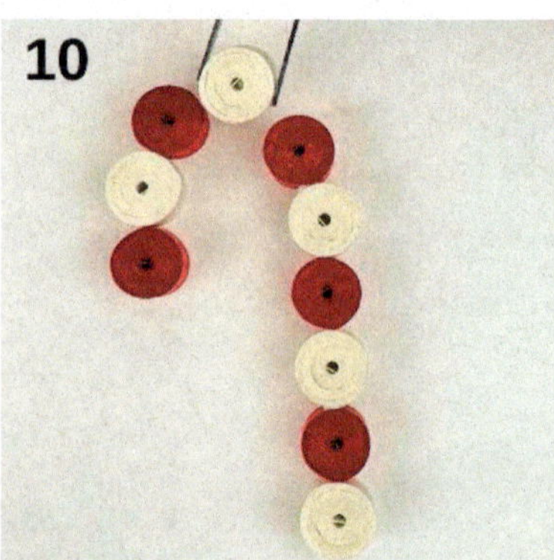

Once the desired curve is reached, glue each of the tight coils in place

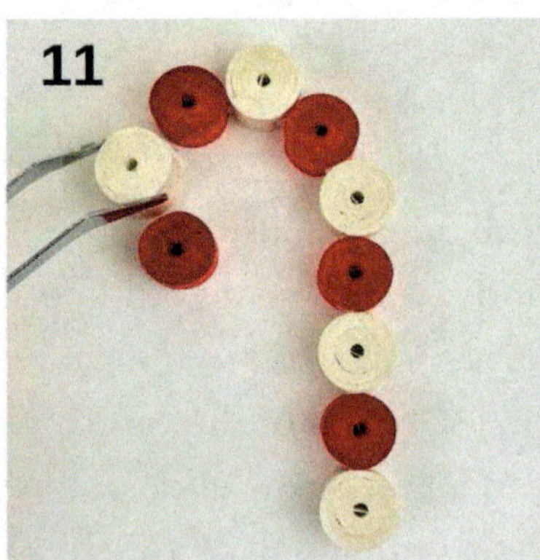

Use tweezers to easily position the coils in place

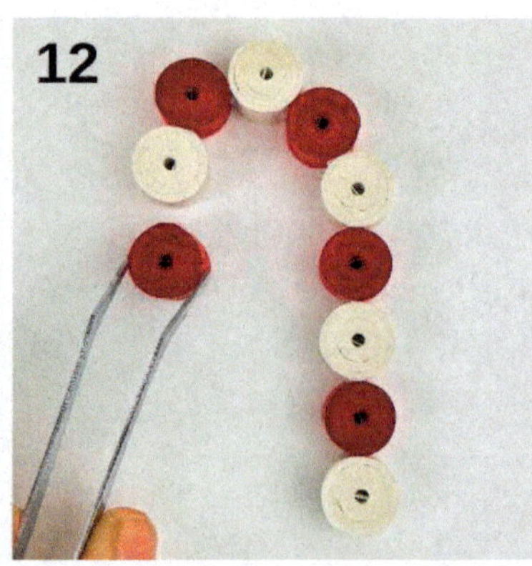

Glue the last coil and let it rest

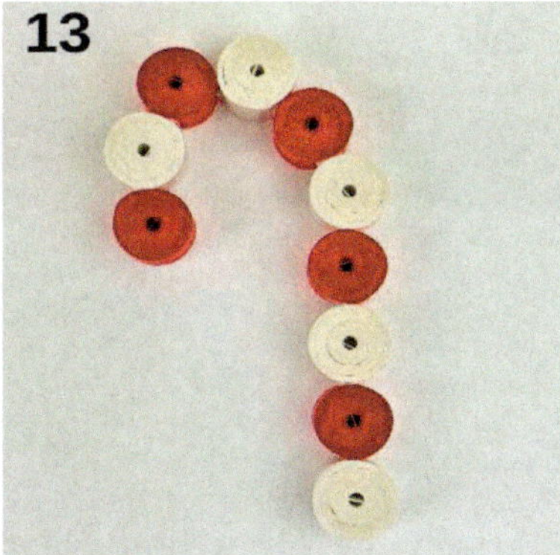

Leave it undisturbed till the glue is completely dried

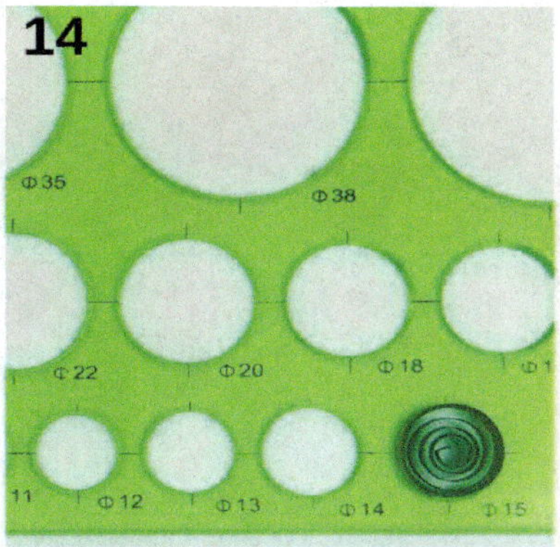

Roll a 3mm green quilling strip into a loose coil (size 15 in circular ruler). Secure the end with glue

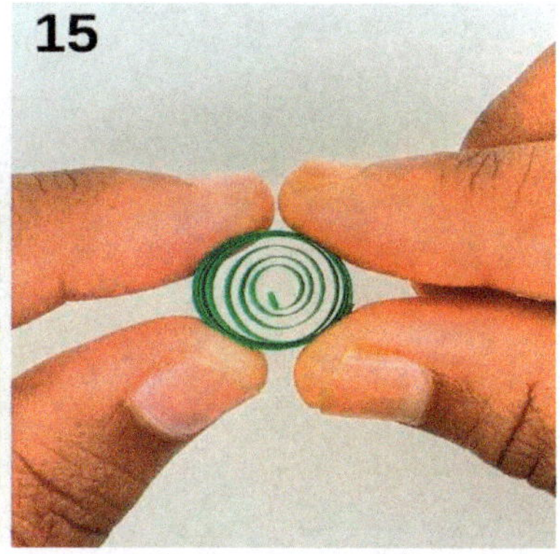

Place the loose coil between the thumb and index finger

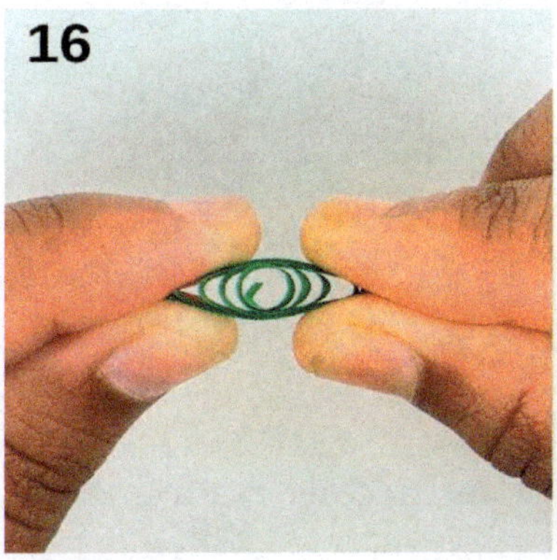

Flatten it gently

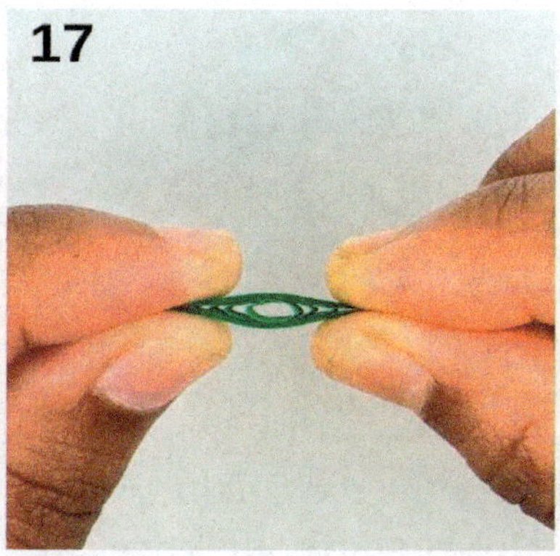

Pinch two opposite sides of the coil to create a marquise (eye) shape

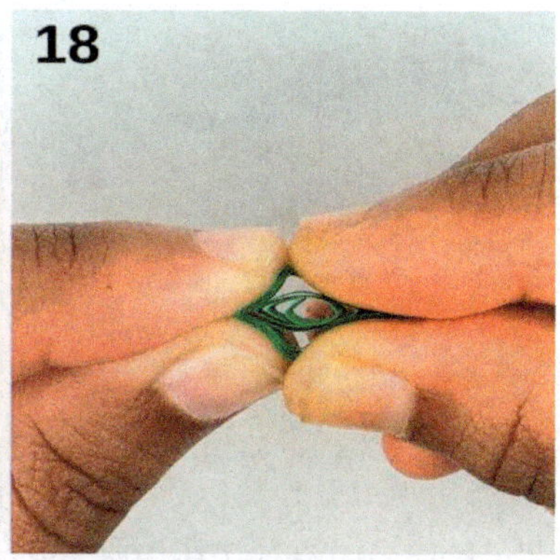

Continue pinching and shaping the marquise to create the pointed, jagged edges of a holly leaf

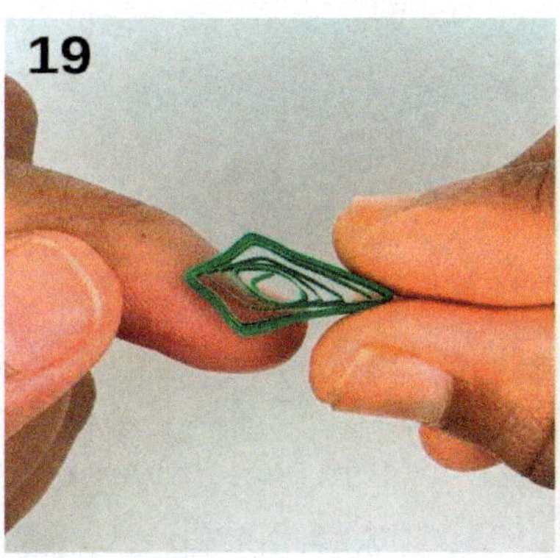

This will be one end of the holly leaf

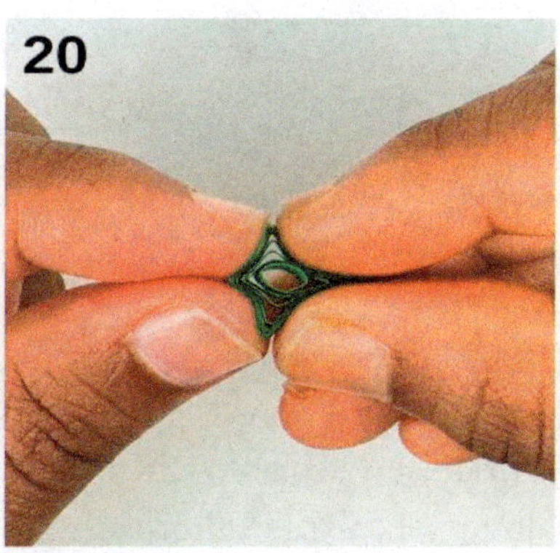

Repeat the process on the other end of the marquise

Holly leaf is done

Repeat the process to create additional leaf

Apply glue to the bottom of the holly leaf and attach them to the candy cane at the bend.

Attach the other holly leaf. Use tweezers to position the leaves carefully

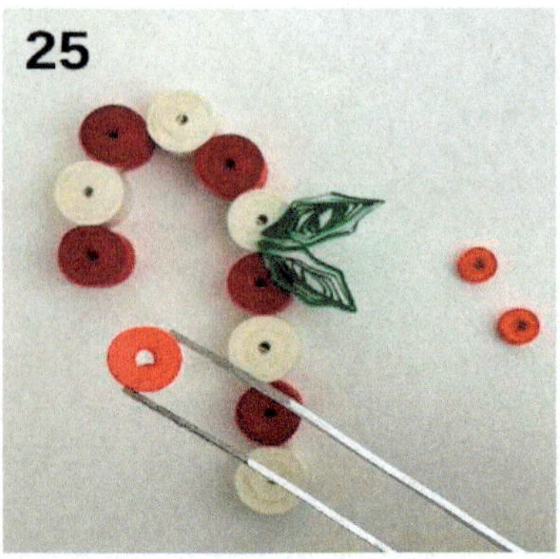

Create small tight coils using 3 mm red quilling strips to represent holly berries

Glue the red coil (berries) close to the holly leaves to complete the decoration.

Glue to coils in a triangular position

Ensure everything is well attached and allow the candy cane to dry completely

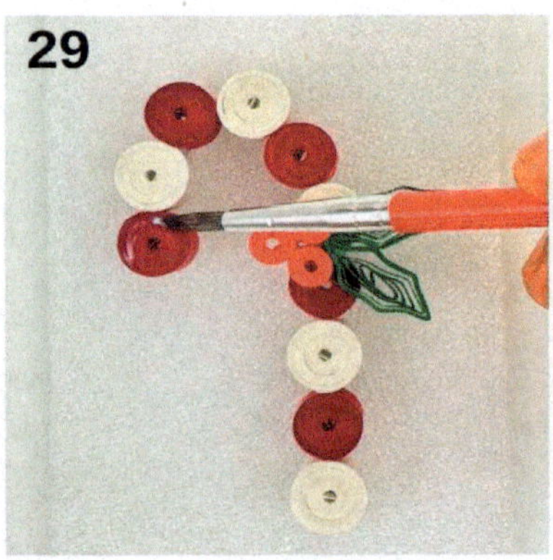

If needed, apply a thin layer of varnish along the front and back of the candy cane to reinforce its shape

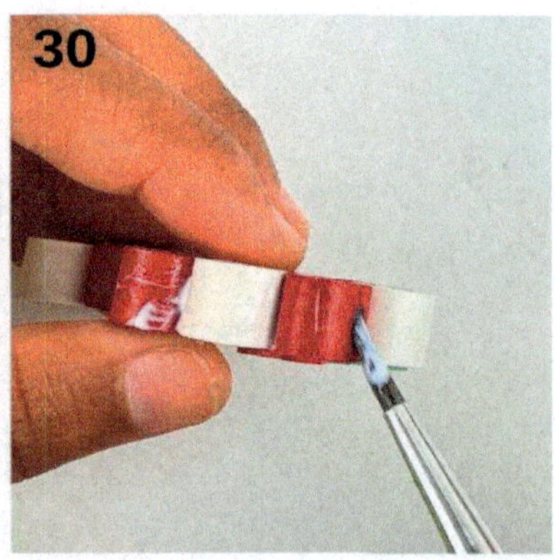

Apply thin coat of varnish to the sides as well

HOLIDAY SYMBOLS

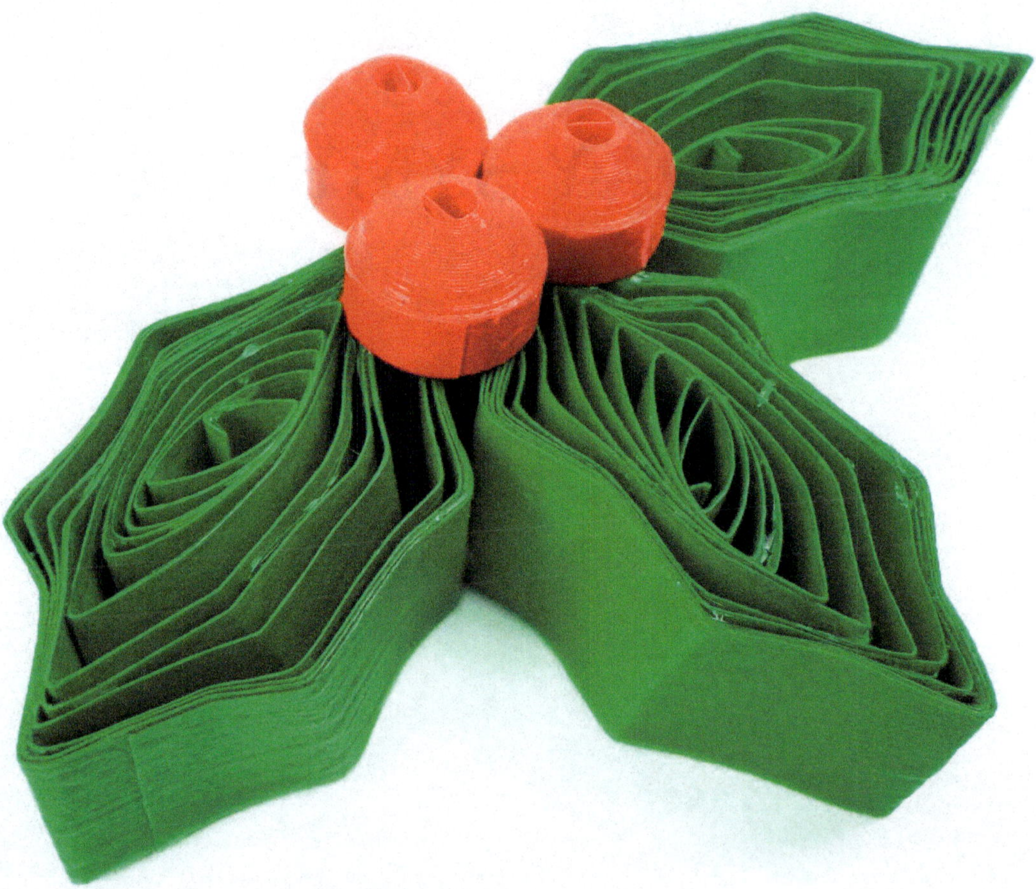

HOLLY LEAVES AND BERRIES

Paper quilled holly leaves and berries design is a festive craft that uses rolled and shaped paper strips to create the classic holiday motif. This intricate project captures the vibrant green leaves and red berries, perfect for adding a handmade touch to cards, ornaments, or seasonal decor. It's a creative and elegant way to celebrate the holiday season.

Materials Needed:

- Quilling paper strips 10 mm Green
- Quilling paper strips 3 mm wide in Red
- Slotted Quilling tool
- White glue
- Small scissors
- Tweezers
- Quilling board / Circular ruler
- Fine brush
- Varnish (Optional)

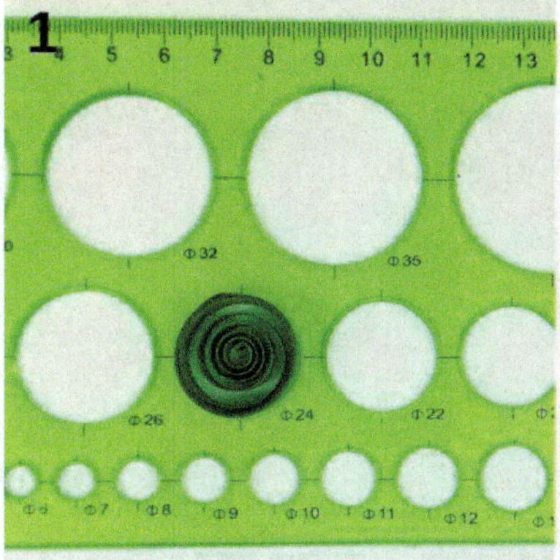

Take a green quilling strip and roll into a loose coil using the quilling tool. Place the coil in a circular sizing guide (size 24) to let it expand evenly. Secure the end with glue to maintain the coil's size

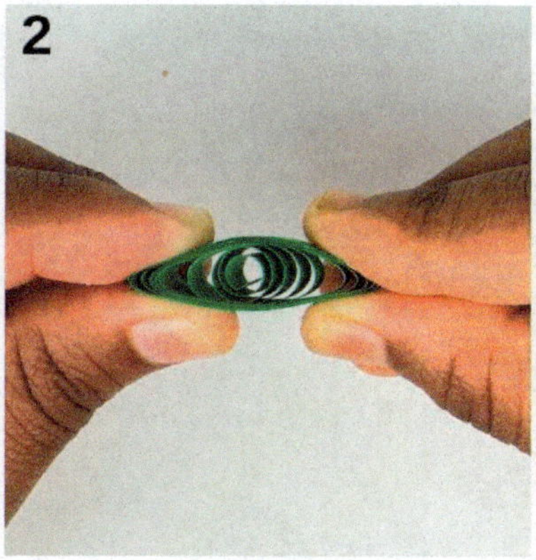

Flatten it slightly by placing between the fingers

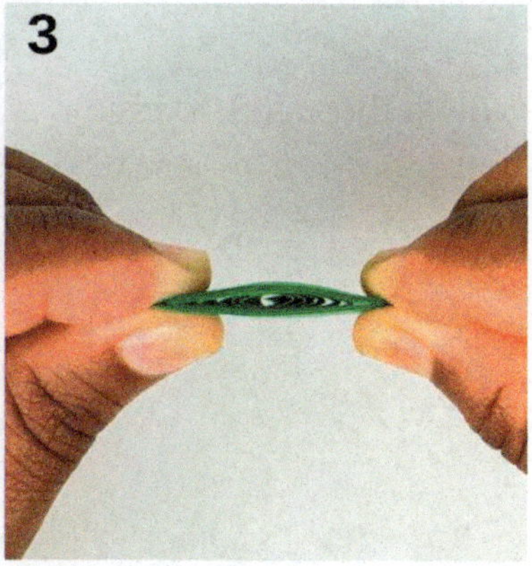

Pinch two opposite sides of the coil to create a marquise (eye) shape

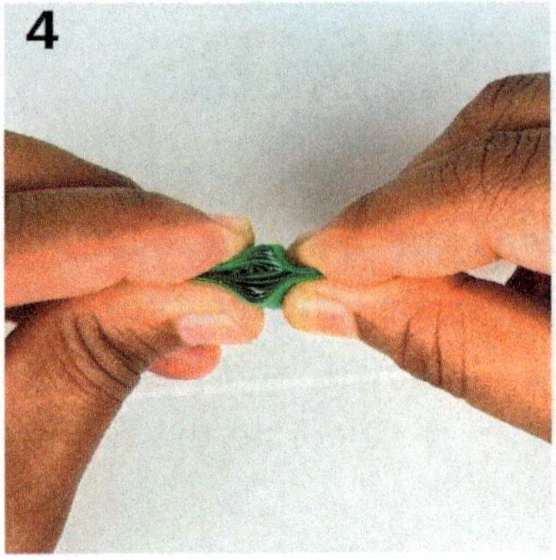

Continue pinching and shaping the marquise to create the pointed, jagged edges of a holly leaf

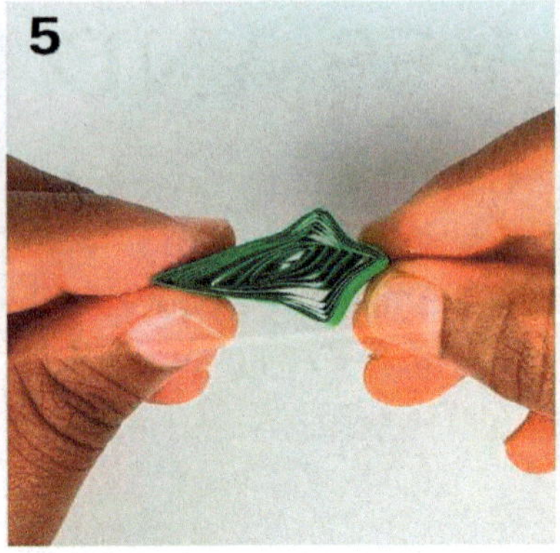

This will be one end of the holly leaf

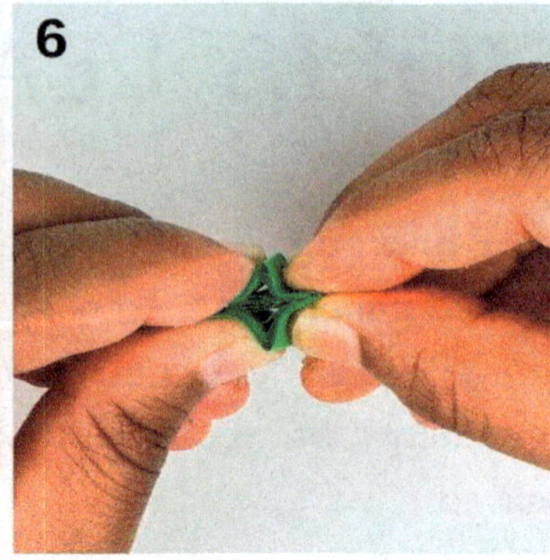

Repeat the process on the other end of the marquise

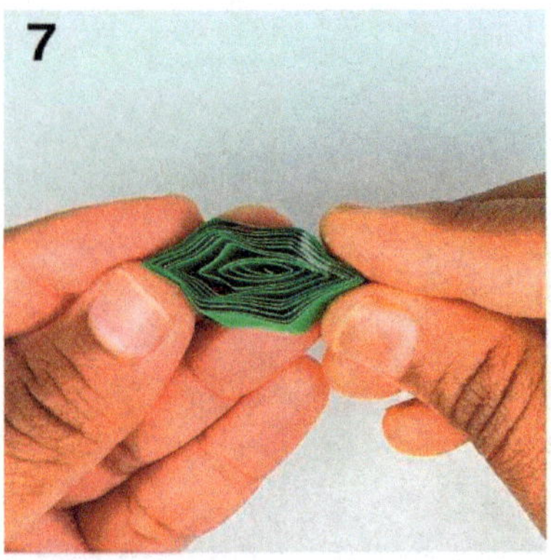

Adjust the shape to give it a natural, wavy appearance

Create two more leaves using the same technique, so you have a total of three holly leaves.

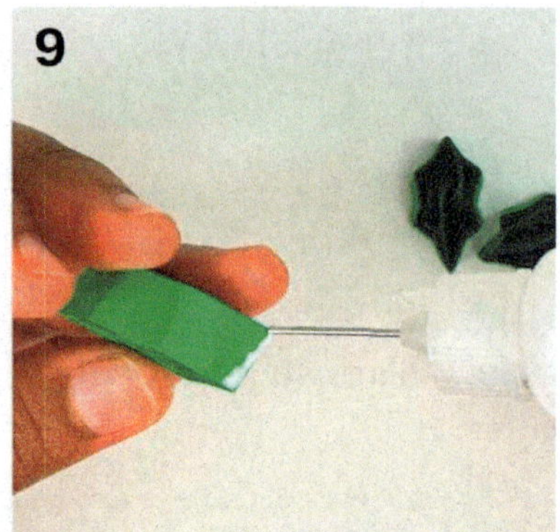

Apply glue to one end of the holly leaf

Glue the second holly leaf

Glue the third leaf at the base to form the holly leaf cluster.

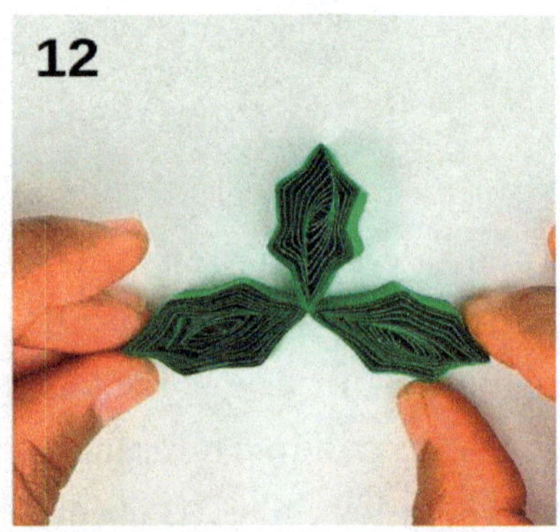

Ensure they are securely attached and well-aligned

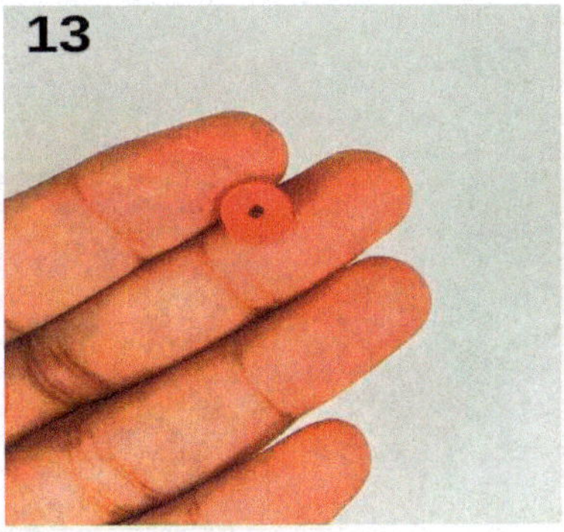

Roll small tight coils using 3mm red quilling strips. These coils will represent the holly berries

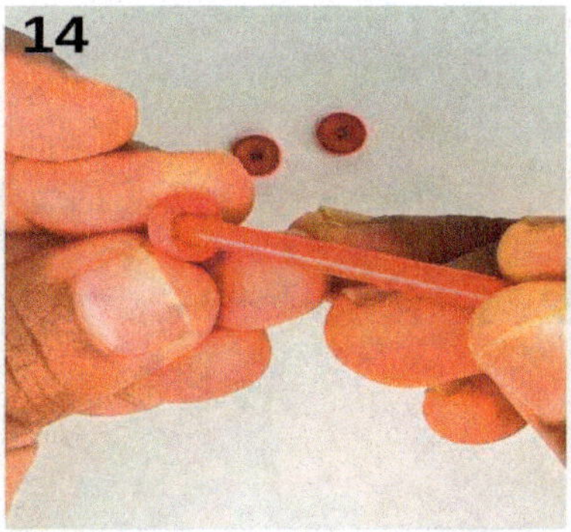

Secure the ends with glue and slightly shape them into a dome by pressing the centre gently

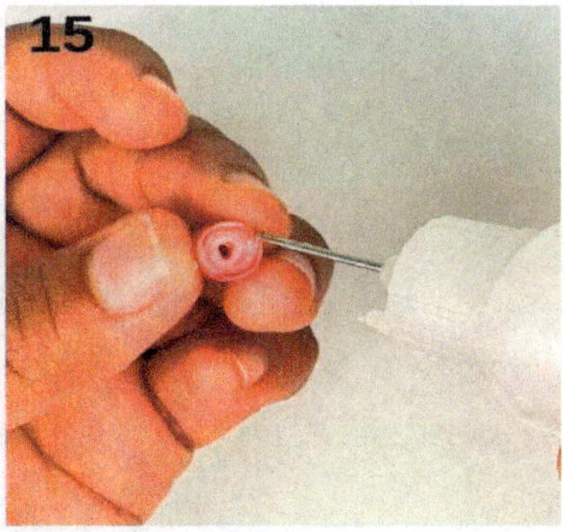

Spread glue to the inner side of the dome to retain its shape

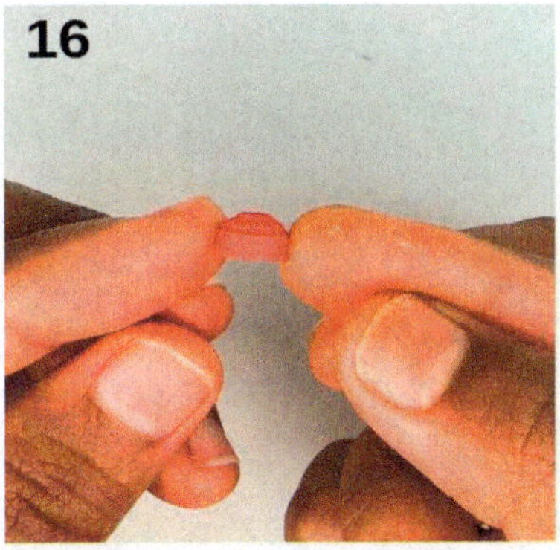

Let the glue dry completely

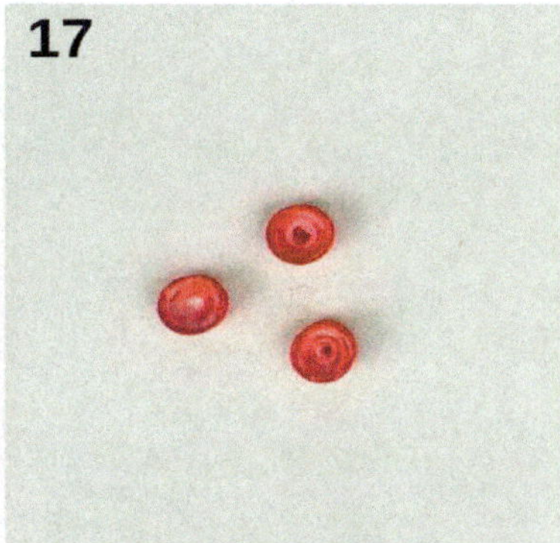

Repeat the process to create at least three berries

Apply a small amount of glue to the centre of the holly leaf cluster

Attach the berries to the centre of the holly leaf cluster

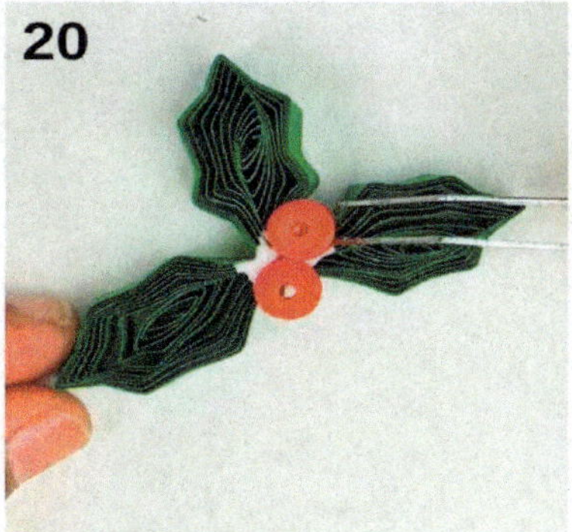

Use tweezers to position them accurately. Apply more glue where needed to ensure all elements are securely attached

Let the assembled holly leaves and berries dry completely before handling

If needed, apply a thin layer of varnish along the front and back of the holly leaf and berries to reinforce its shape

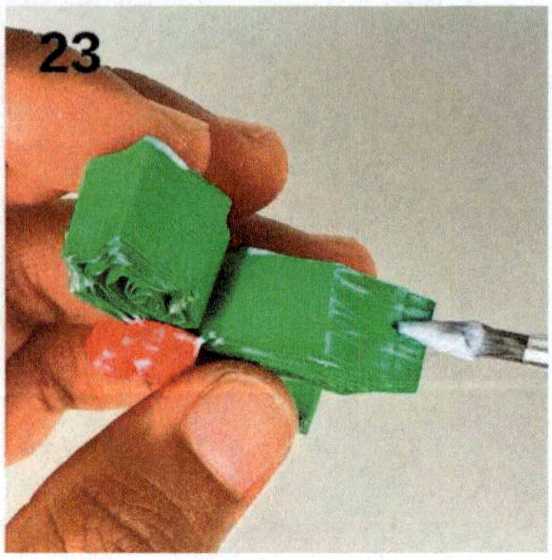

Apply thin coat of varnish to the sides of the leaves and berries

Let the varnish dry completely before using them in your decorations

CHRISTMAS WREATH

Paper quilled Christmas wreath is a festive and intricate craft made by rolling and shaping strips of paper to form a decorative holiday wreath. This handmade project features delicate details like leaves and berries making it perfect for ornaments, cards, or seasonal decor. It's a creative way to bring holiday cheer and a personal touch to your decorations.

Materials Needed:

- Quilling paper strips 10 mm wide in Red and 2 shades of Green
- Slotted Quilling tool
- White glue
- Small scissors
- Tweezers
- Quilling board / Circular ruler
- Fine brush
- Varnish (Optional)

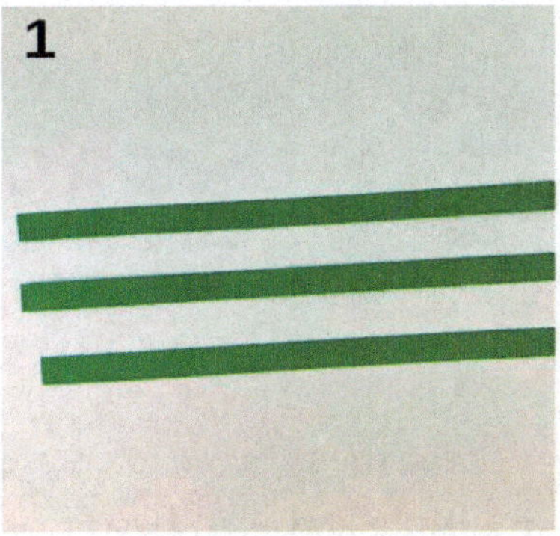

Take 3 green quilling strips

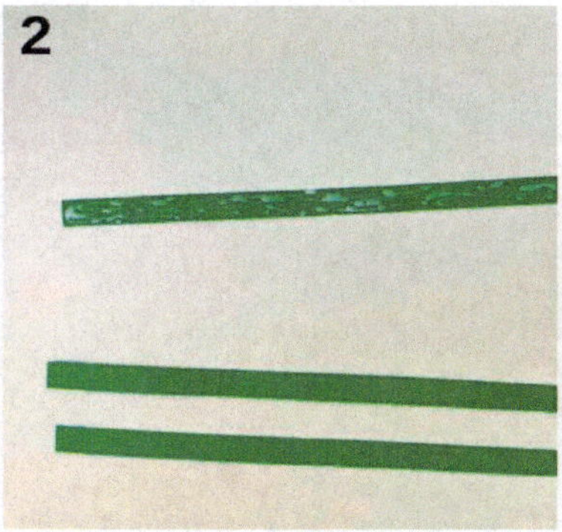

Apply a thin layer of glue along one side of the quilling strip

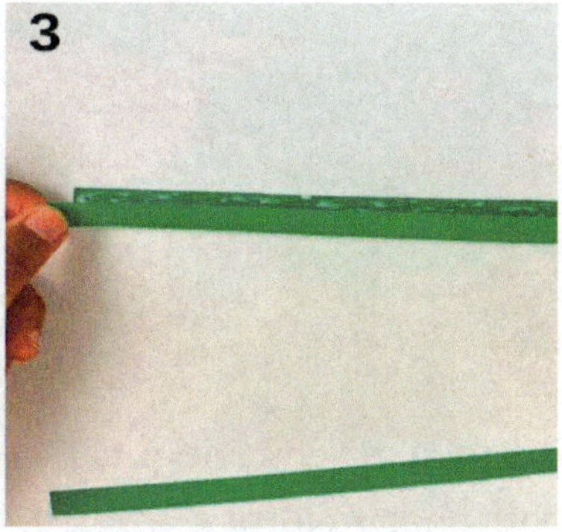

Layer the strips by gluing them together

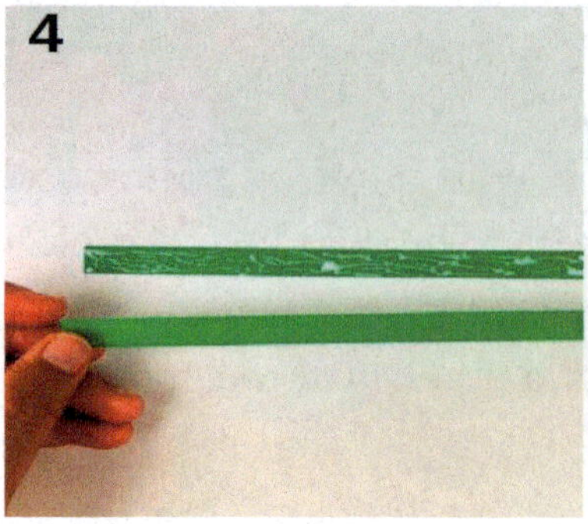

Repeat the same and glue the third strip on the top

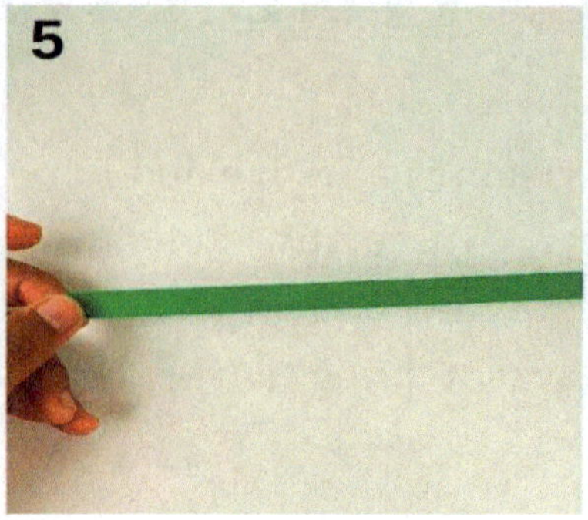

This process will create a thicker and stronger base for the leaves

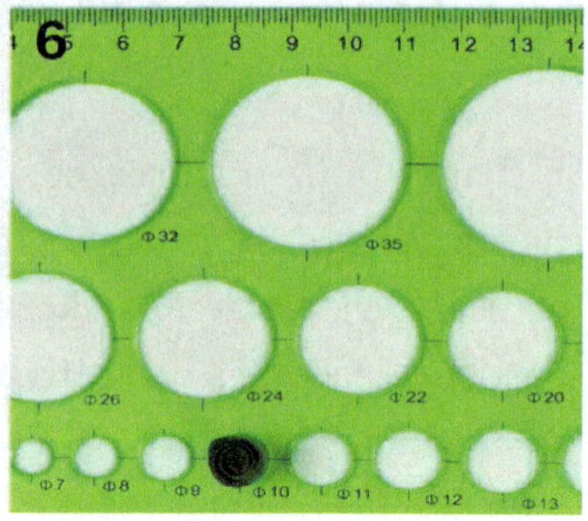

Roll the green colour strip into a coil and place it into a circular template (size 10) to let it expand slightly. Secure the end with some glue

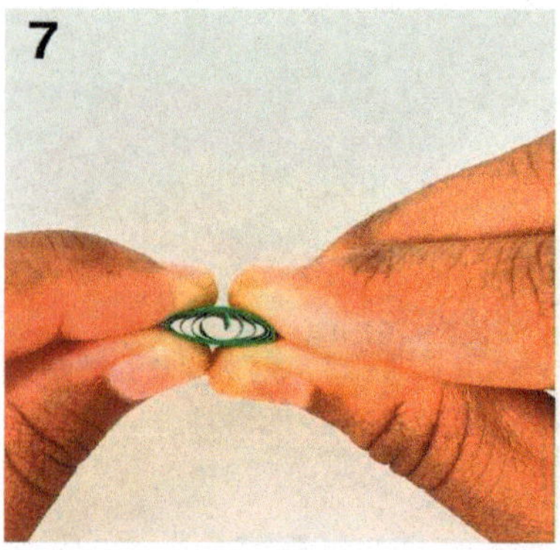

Remove the coil and pinch both ends to form a marquise (eye) shape.

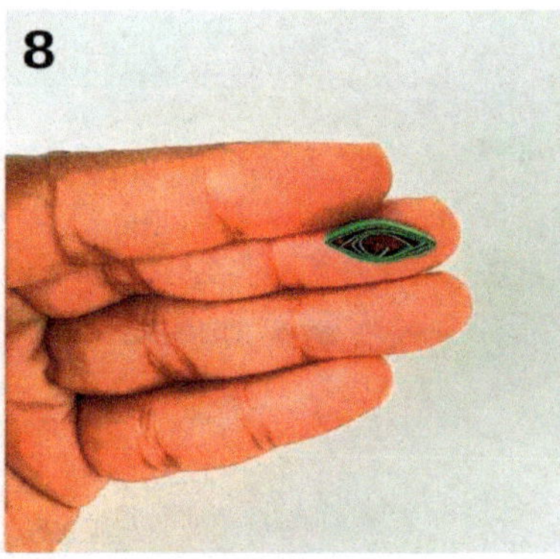

This will be the leaf

Repeat the process to create multiple leaves in two shades of green. You'll need several leaves for the wreath

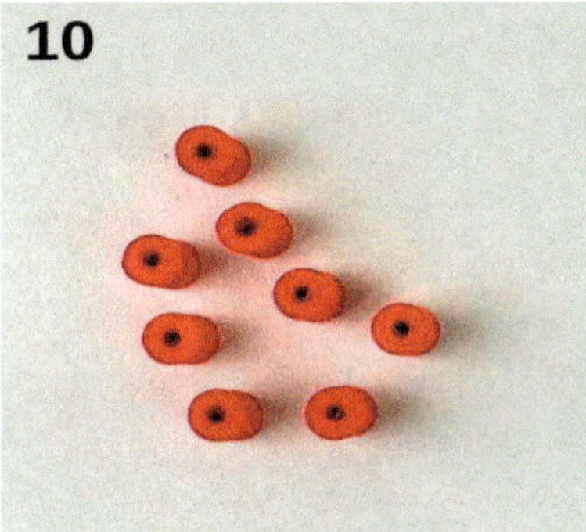

Roll single red quilling strips into tight coils to form the berries

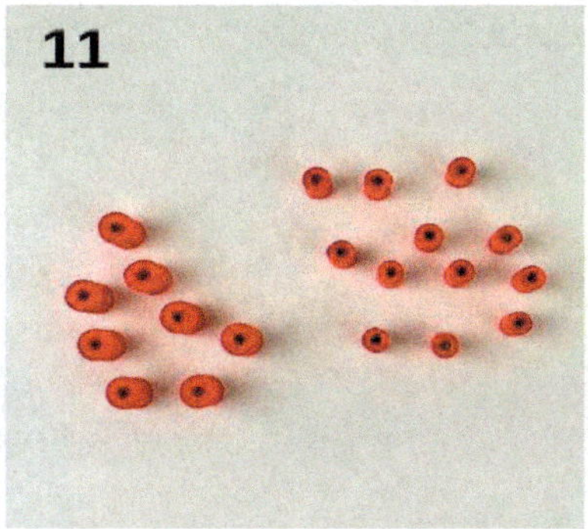

Roll half cut red quilling strips into tight coils to form smaller berries. Create several berries to add to your wreath

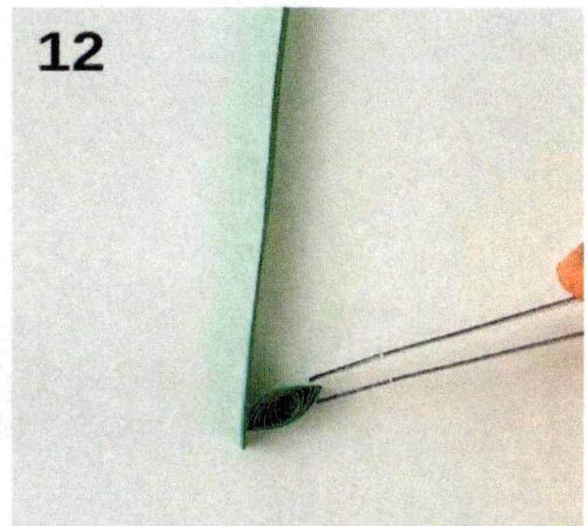

Begin by attaching the first set of leaf to a green quilling strip that will serve as the base for your wreath

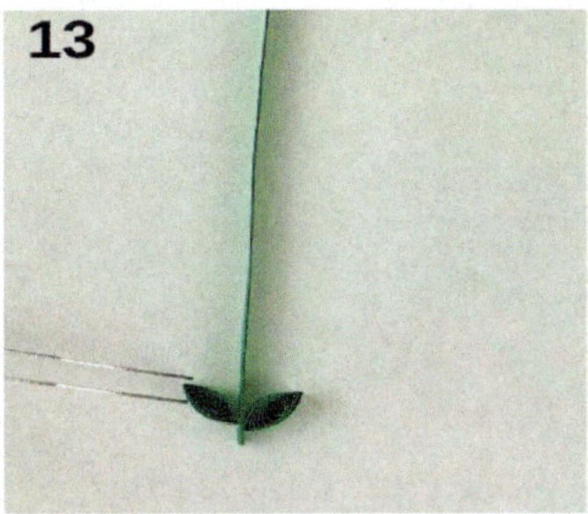

Attach the second leaf on the other side of the base

Continue adding leaves, alternating their direction slightly to give the wreath a natural look

Start adding the berries between the leaves as you go

Use tweezers to position them accurately

Attach the second batch of leaves in different shades of green

Attach one large and two small berries

Continue with attaching around 5 to 6 leaves

Change the position of the large and small berries by not making it uniform all over

Continue adding leaves and berries

Repeat the process along the strip until you have a long, fully decorated piece

Leave a small portion at the end of the strip without attaching any leaves or berries

Once your strip is fully decorated, gently bend it into a circular shape to form the wreath.

Ensure the ends meet and attach them securely with glue

Complete the wreath by adjusting any leaves or berries that may need repositioning

Fill the joint with more berries

Attach some leaves to the gaps

If needed, apply a thin layer of varnish along the front and back of the wreath to reinforce its shape

Allow the wreath to dry completely

ANGEL

Paper quilled angel is a delicate and beautiful craft that uses rolled and shaped paper strips to create an intricate angel design. This handmade project is perfect for ornaments, holiday cards, or seasonal displays, adding an elegant and festive touch to your Christmas decor. It's a creative way to celebrate the season with a personal and artistic flair.

Materials Needed:

- Quilling paper strips 10 mm wide in Purple, Cream and Skin-Tone
- Slotted Quilling tool
- White glue
- Small scissors
- Tweezers
- Quilling board / Circular ruler
- Fine brush
- Varnish (Optional)

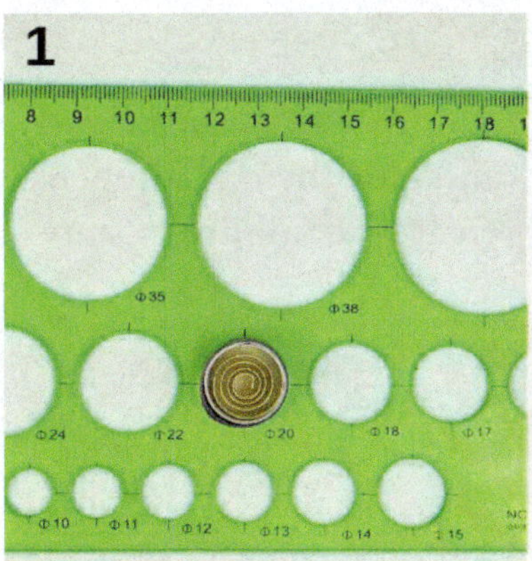

Attach the end of purple and cream paper strip and start rolling from the cream strip into a loose coil and place the coil into a circular template (Size 20) to allow it to expand. Secure the end with a dab of glue.

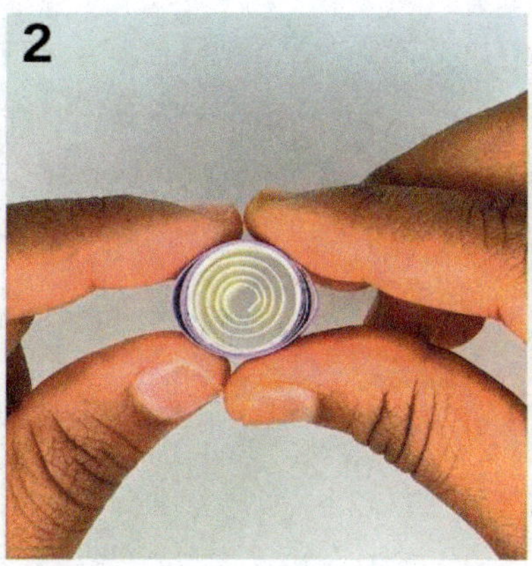

Place the loose coil between the fingers

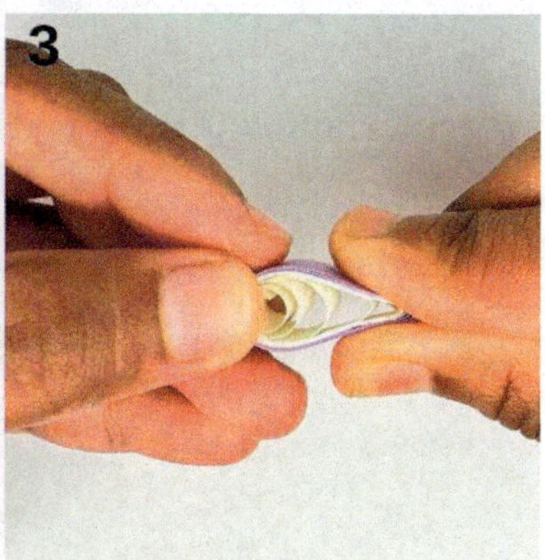

Pinch one side of the loose coil to create a teardrop shape

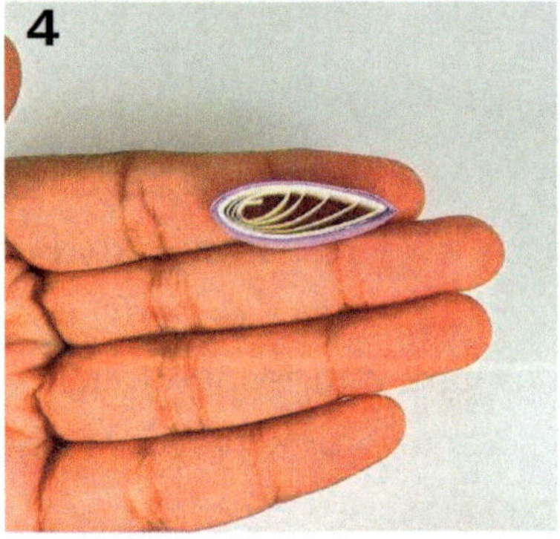

Ensure the teardrop shape is well-defined and symmetrical

Repeat this process to create four teardrop shapes. These will form the base of the angel's dress

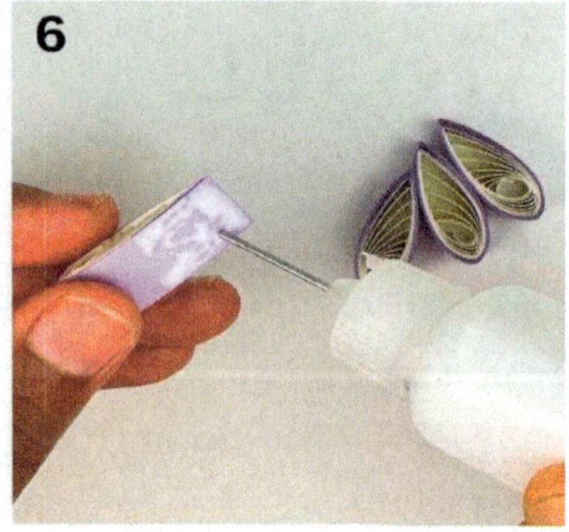

Apply glue to the sides of the teardrop

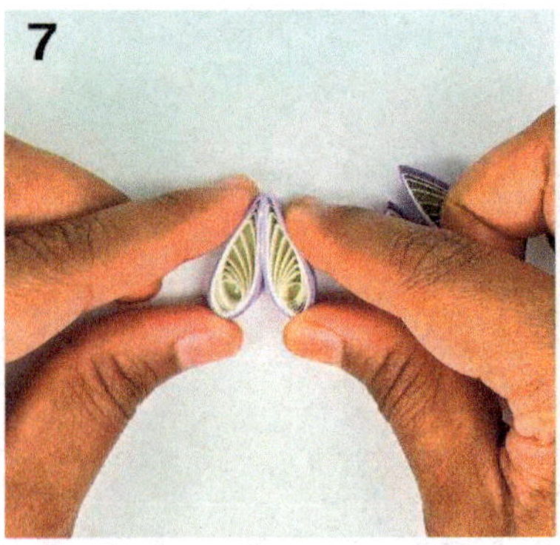

Attach the other tear drop

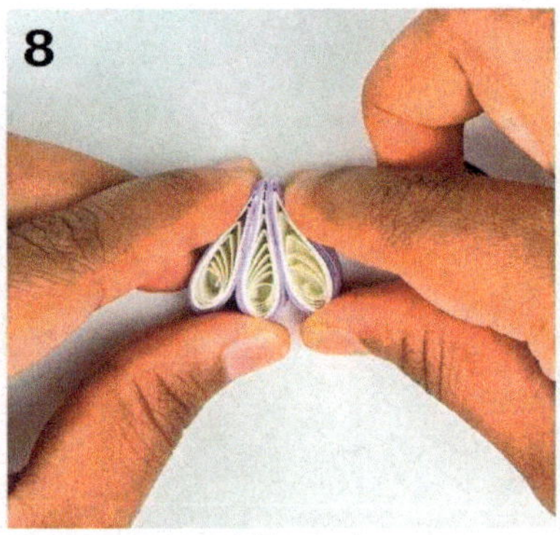

Start assembling them together to form the lower part of the angel's dress.

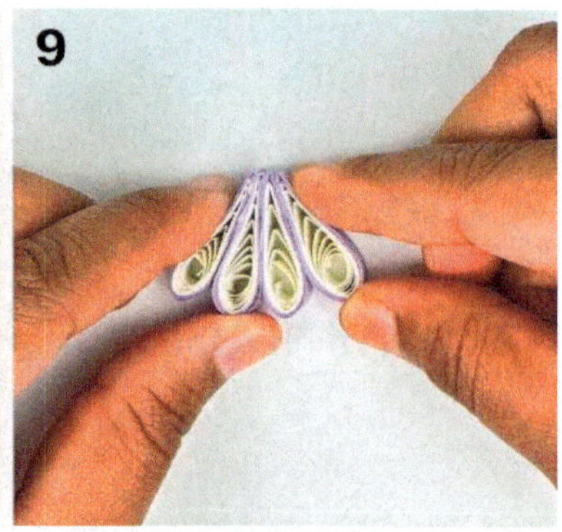

Align the teardrops closely and glue them securely to create the full-dress shape

Roll a small tight coil using a purple quilling strip. This coil will be used as a connector between the dress and the upper body

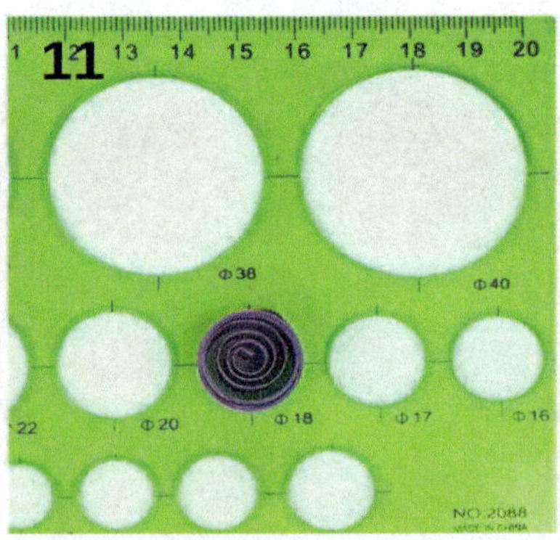

Roll a purple strip into loose coil and place them into a circular template (Size 18)

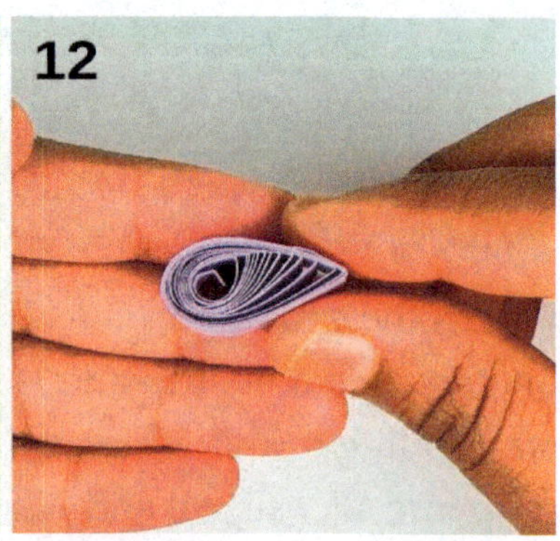

Pinch one end of the loose coil to form a tear drop shape

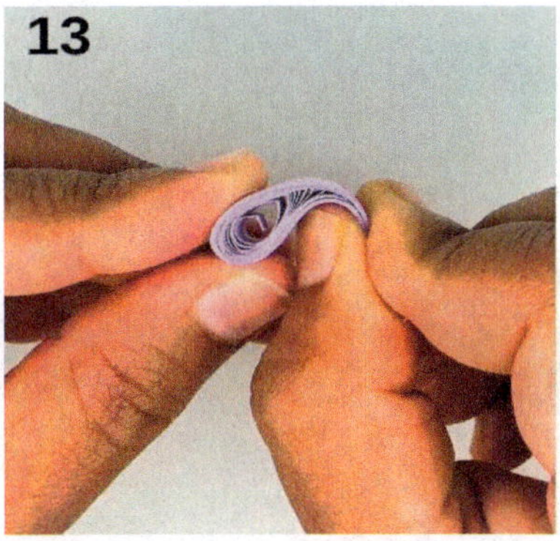

Slightly curve the pointed end of the tear drop

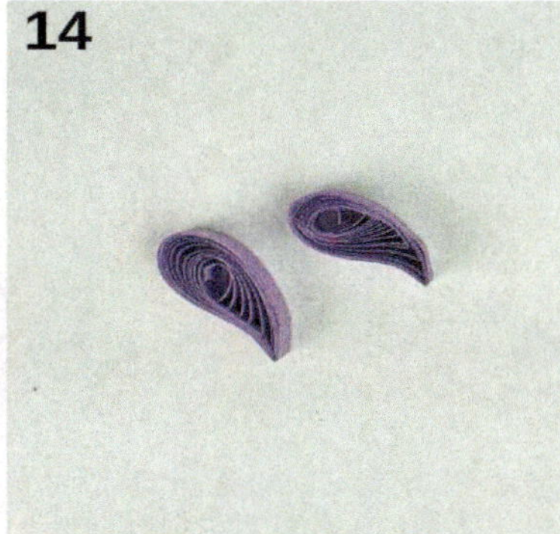

Make two similar shapes for the wings

Apply glue to the sides of the curved teardrop shapes and attach them to the top of the dress, creating the angel's wings

Ensure that the wings are symmetrically aligned and securely attached

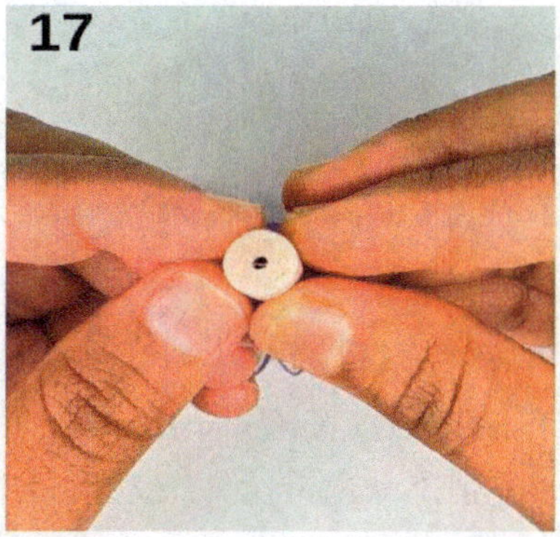

Roll 2 skin-toned quilling strip into a tight coil to form the angel's head. Ensure the coil is slightly larger than the tight coil used for the dress connector

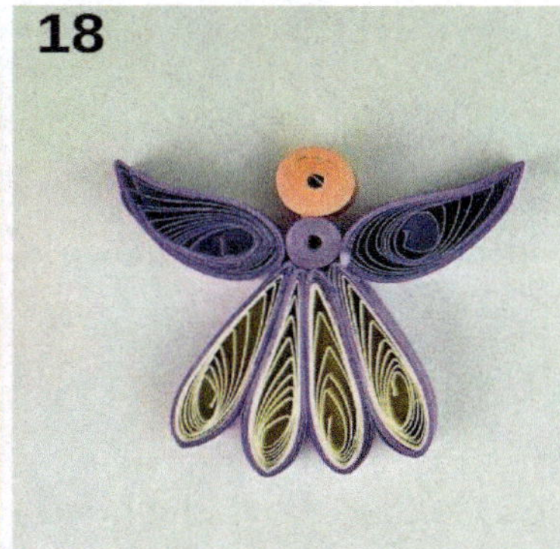

Apply glue to the bottom of the head coil and attach it to the top centre of the dress and wings assembly.

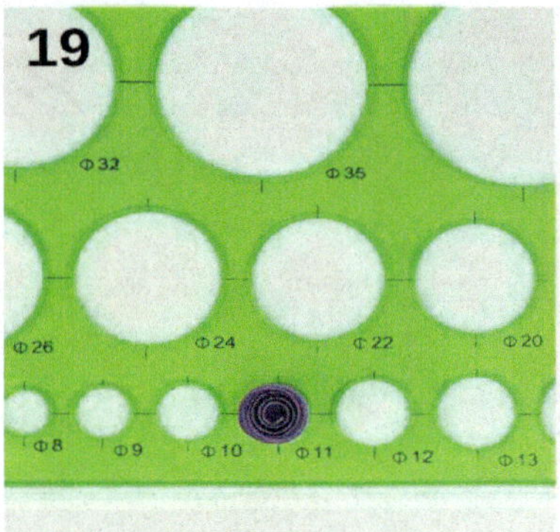

Roll a small purple strip into a coil and place it in a circular template (Size 11). Secure the end with a glue

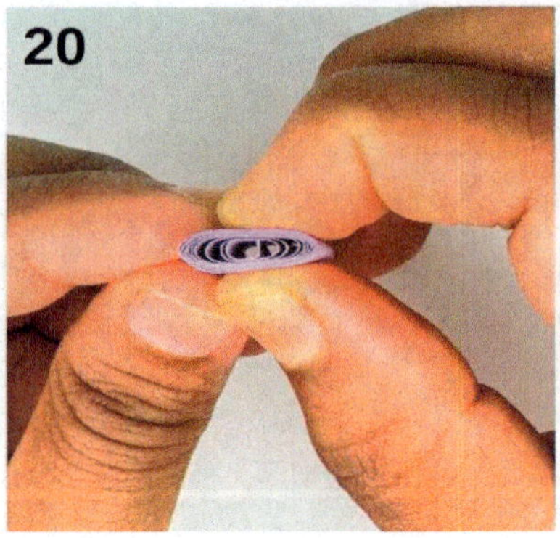

Flatten the coil slightly

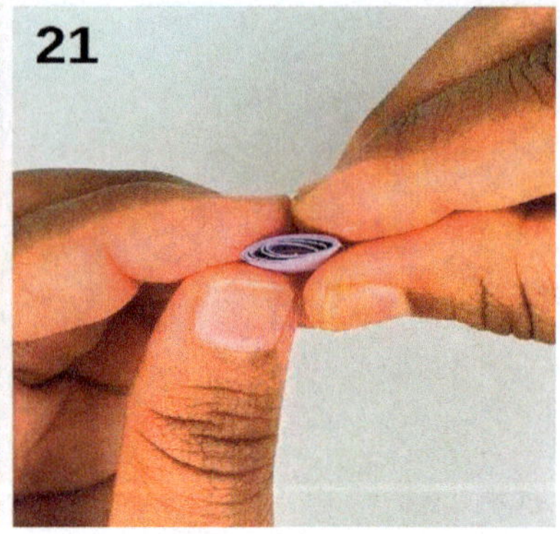

Gently pinch the sides of the coil to give it a slight oval shape, which will form the angel's halo

Use tweezers to position the halo just above the head and apply a small amount of glue to secure it. Adjust the halo to ensure it is properly centred and balanced above the head.

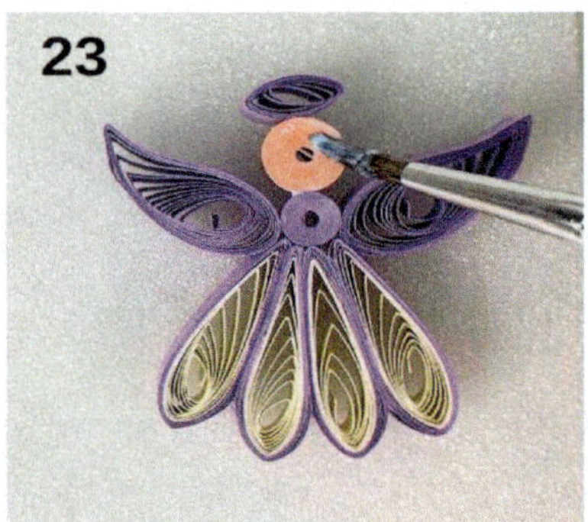

If needed, apply a thin layer of varnish along the front and back of the angel to reinforce its shape

Allow all the pieces to dry completely before handling

CHRISTMAS PRESENTS

Paper quilled Christmas present is a festive craft that transforms rolled and shaped paper strips into the shape of a beautifully wrapped gift. This intricate design adds a charming, handmade touch to holiday cards, ornaments, or seasonal decor. It's a creative and unique way to celebrate the joy of gift-giving during the Christmas season.

Materials Needed:

- Quilling paper strips 10 mm wide in Red, Green and Cream
- Quilling paper strips 3 mm wide in Cream
- Slotted Quilling tool
- White glue
- Small scissors
- Tweezers
- Quilling board / Circular ruler
- Fine brush
- Varnish (Optional)

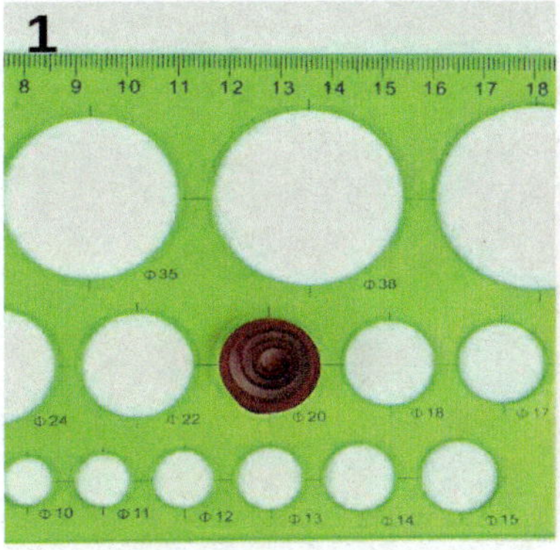

Start by rolling a red quilling strip into a loose coil and place the coil into a circular template (Size 20) to allow it to expand evenly. Secure the end with the glue

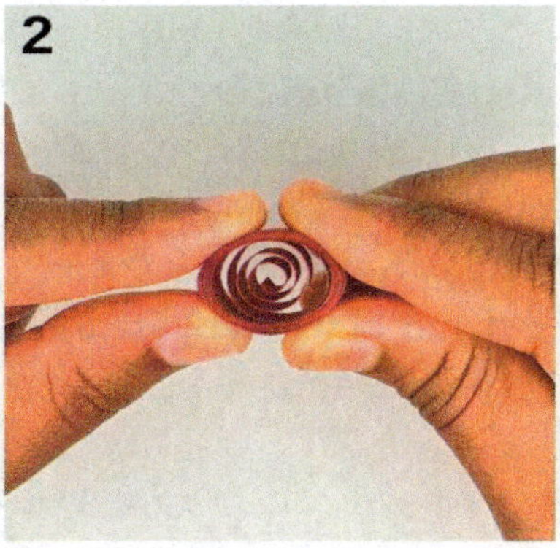

Place the coil between the fingers

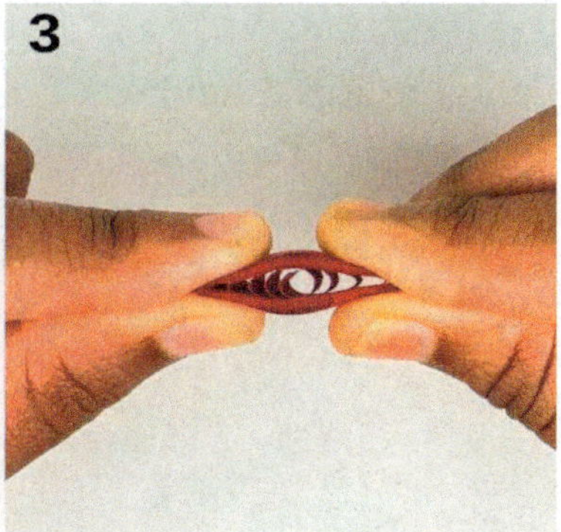

Pinch both sides of the coil to create a marquise (eye) shape

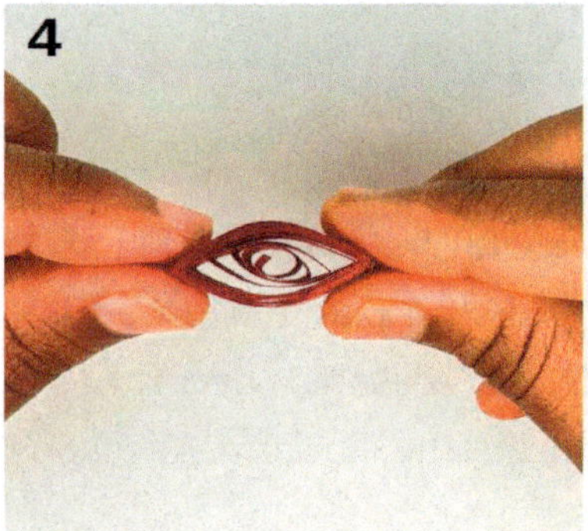

This will be 2 points of the square

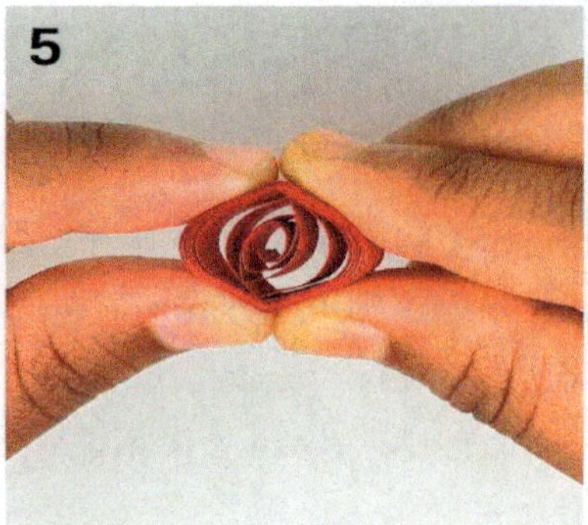

Rotate the eye shape to 90 degrees

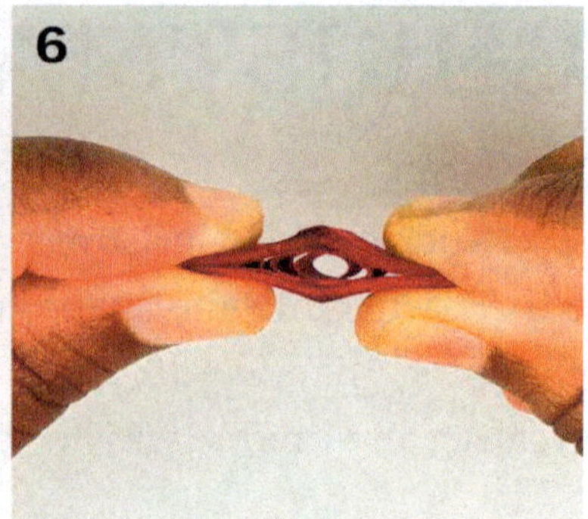

Pinch the two opposite points again to turn the marquise shape into a diamond shape

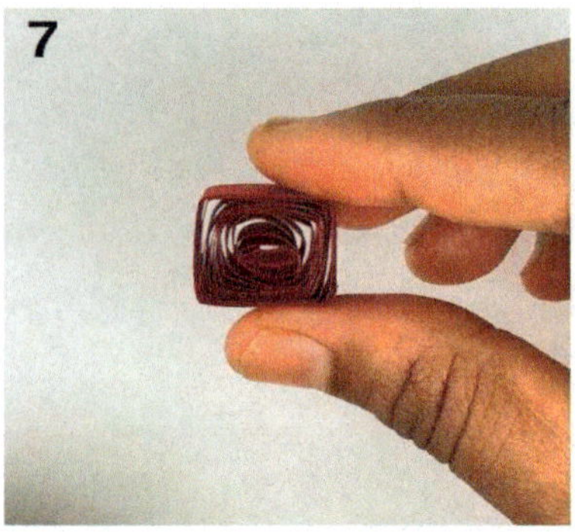

Continue adjusting the shape until it forms a square

Repeat the process to make four squares—two in red and two in green. Ensure that all four squares (two red and two green) are the same size and shape

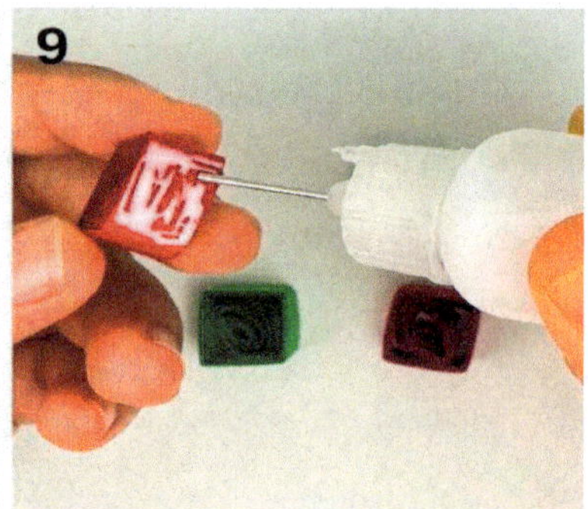

Apply glue to the edges of one square

Attach another square to the glued edge, aligning them carefully.

Repeat the process to attach the remaining squares, forming a 2x2 square grid

Ensure that all squares are securely attached and form a uniform block

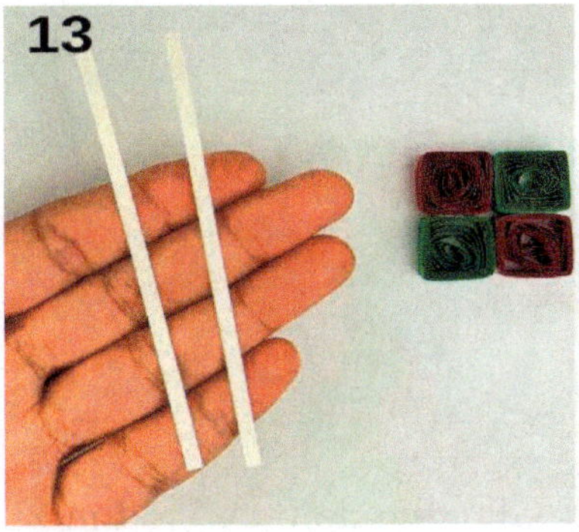

Cut two strips of 3mm wide cream quilling paper

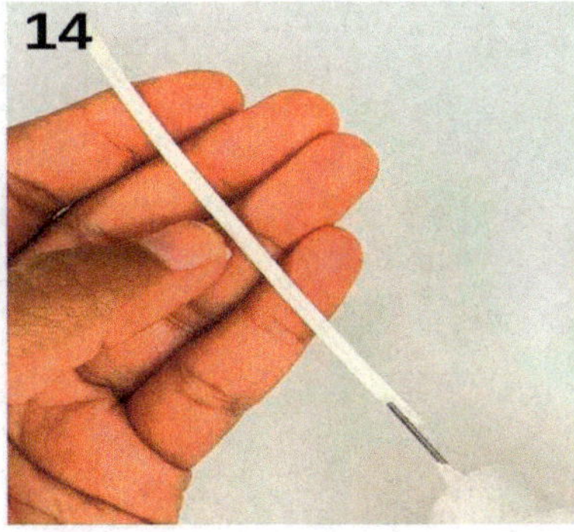

Apply glue along one edge of a white strip

Attach the strip across the centre of the present block, as if wrapping a ribbon around it.

Repeat with the second white strip, wrapping it around the other side to create a cross pattern on the present.

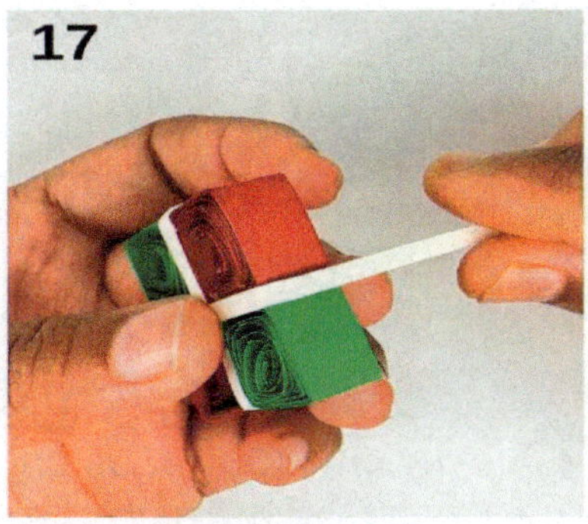

Wrap the ribbon strip around the present block, securing it with glue as you go

Ensure that the ribbon is securely glued and neatly aligned

Leave it to dry completely

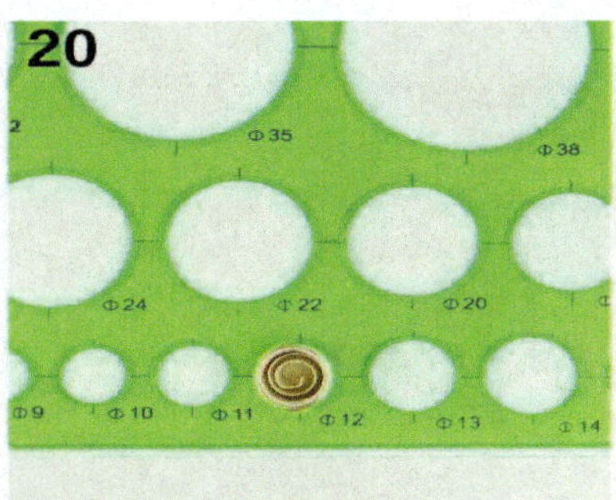

Roll a cream quilling strip into a loose coil and place the coil into a circular template (Size 12) to allow it to expand evenly. Secure the end with the glue

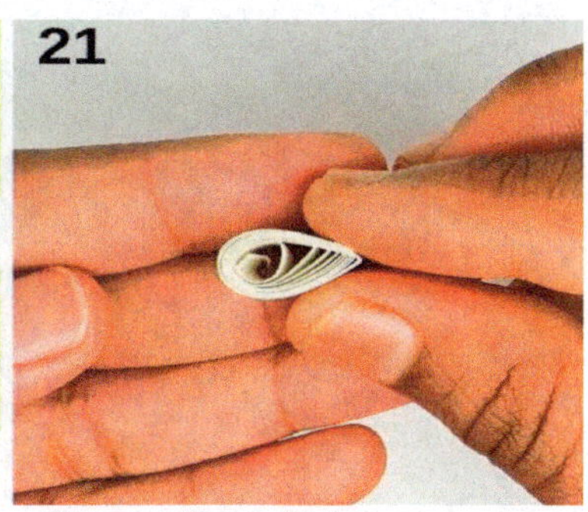

Shape the coil into a teardrop shape to form the bow's loops

Repeat the process to make another loop for the bow

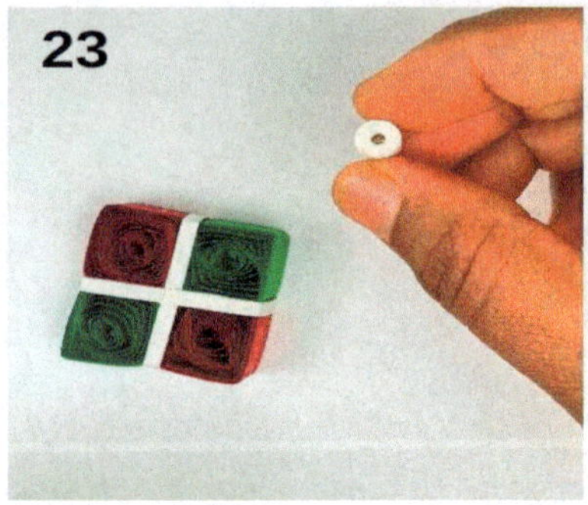

Roll a half-cut cream colour strip into a tight coil

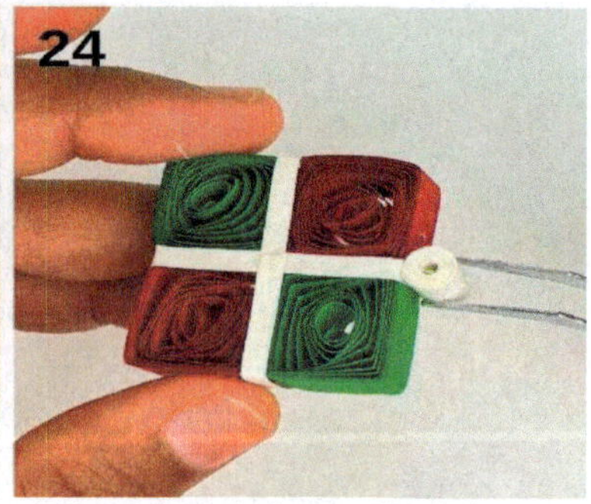

Glue the tight coil to the top of the present block

Glue the bow loop to the right side of the tight coil

Glue the other bow loop on the left side of the tight coil. Use tweezers to position the bow accurately and ensure its securely attached

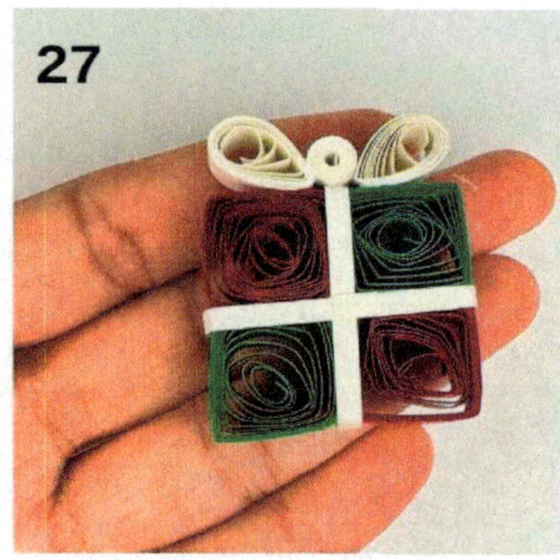

Allow the glue to dry completely and make any final adjustments to ensure the present looks neat and symmetrical

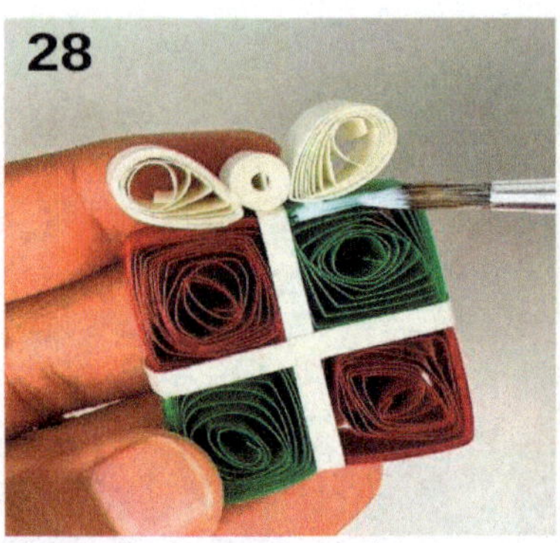

If needed, apply a thin layer of varnish along the front and back of the present to reinforce its shape

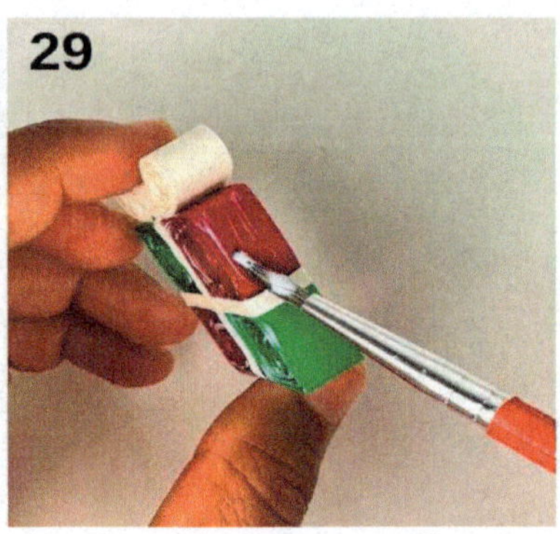

Apply a thin coat on the sides of the present

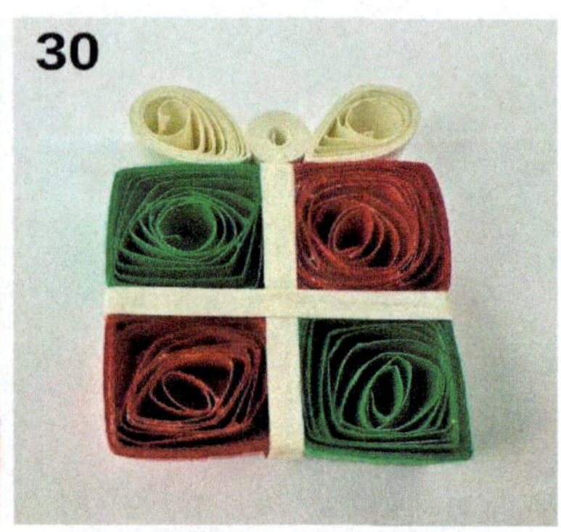

Allow all the pieces to dry completely before handling

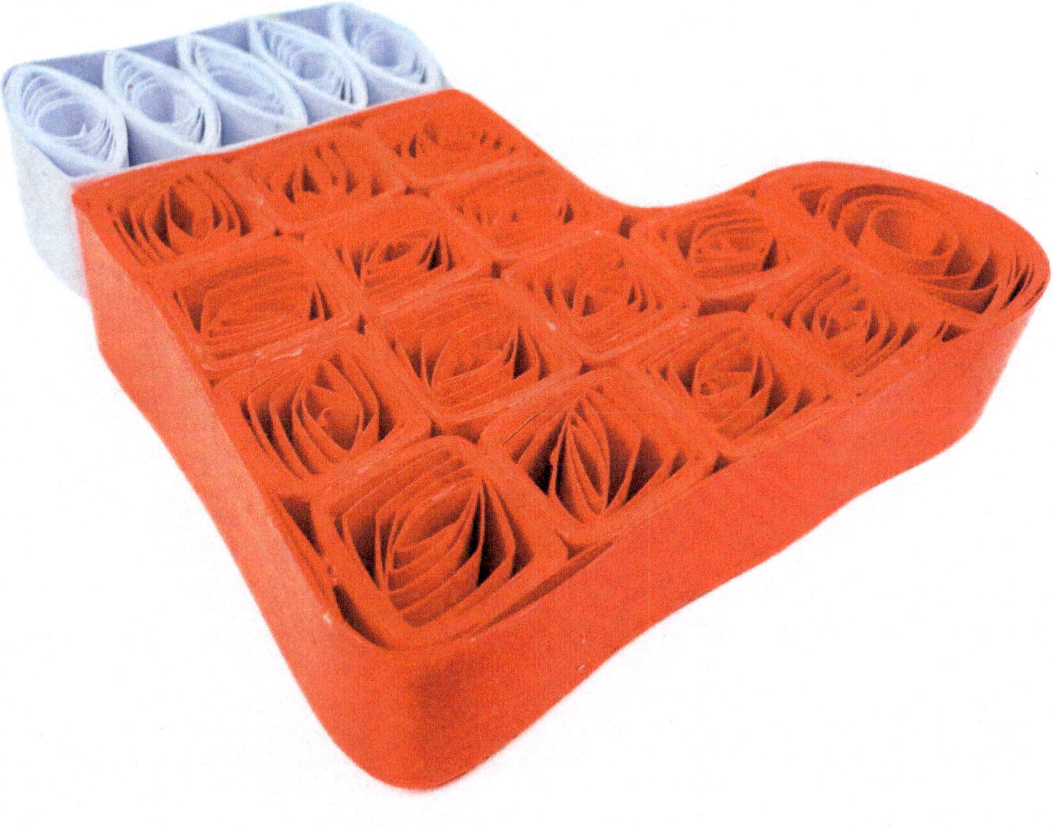

STOCKING

Paper quilled Christmas stocking is a fun and festive craft where rolled and shaped paper strips form the iconic holiday stocking. This intricate design makes a charming addition to holiday cards, ornaments, or seasonal decor, adding a handmade and personalized touch. It's a creative way to capture the joy of Christmas in your decorations.

Materials Needed:

- Quilling paper strips 10 mm wide in Red and White
- Slotted Quilling tool
- White glue
- Small scissors
- Tweezers
- Quilling board / Circular ruler
- Fine brush
- Varnish (Optional)

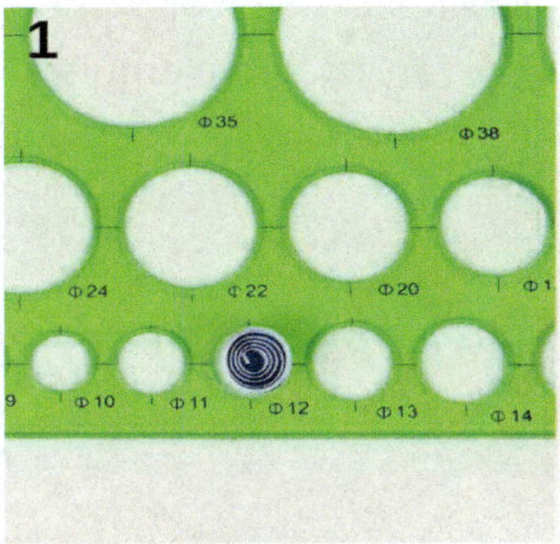

Roll white quilling strip into loose coil and place them into a circular template (Size 12)

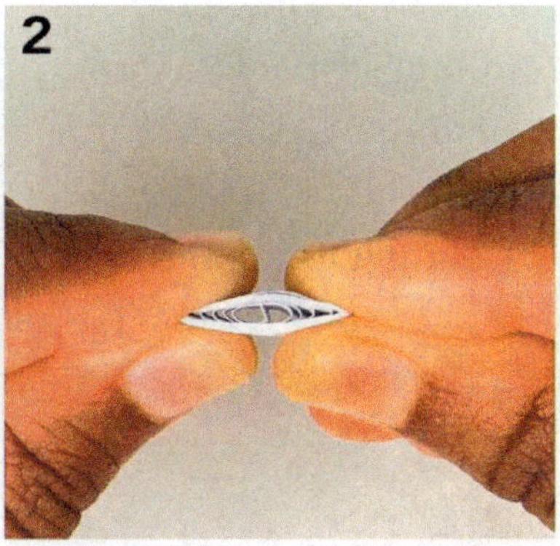

Pinch the coil on opposite sides to create a marquise (eye) shape

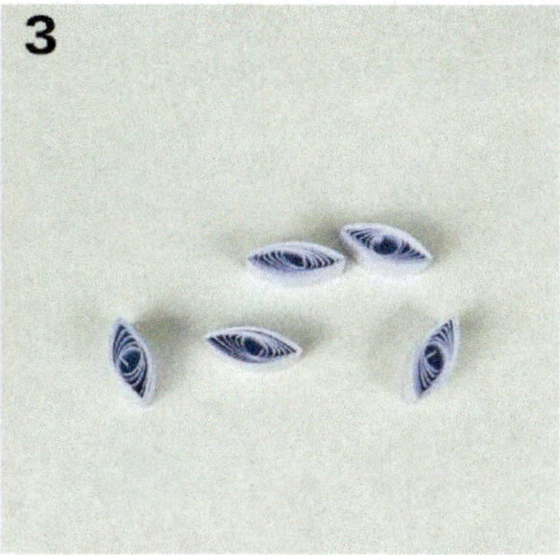

Make 5 marquise shapes for the top cuff of the stocking

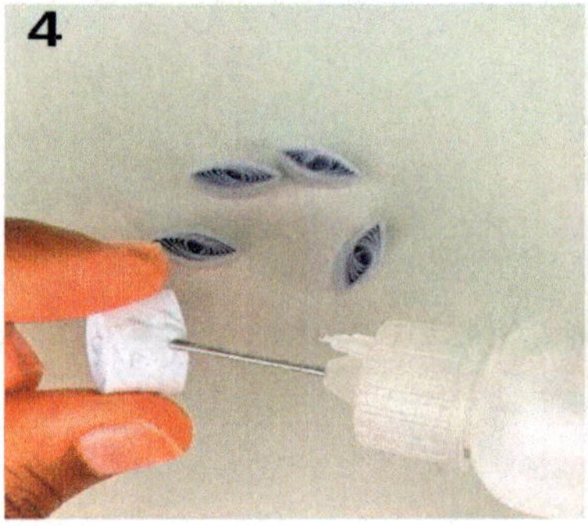

Apply glue to one side of the marquise

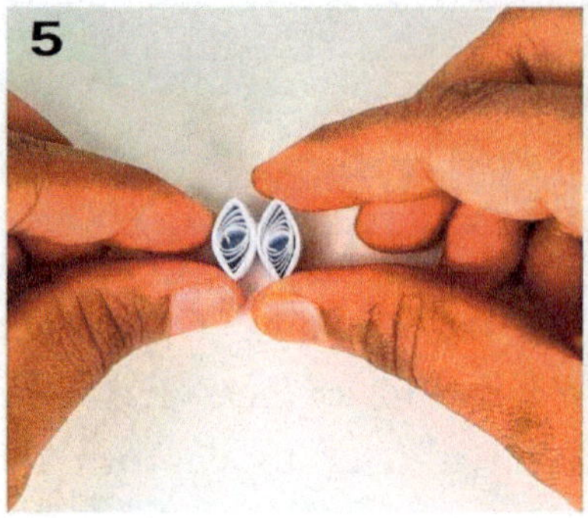

Attach other marquise to the side

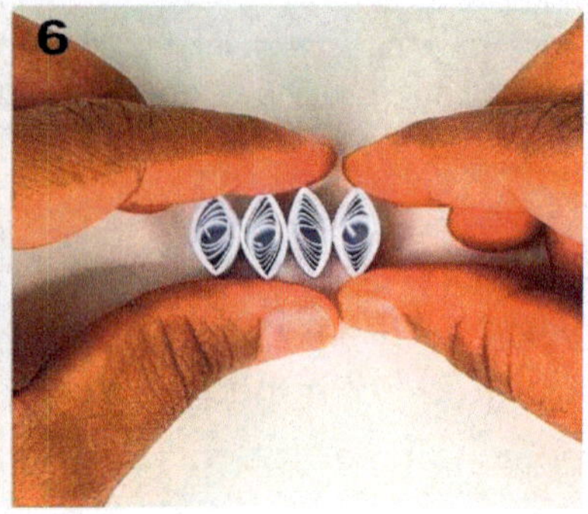

Glue the marquise shapes side by side to form the cuff of the stocking.

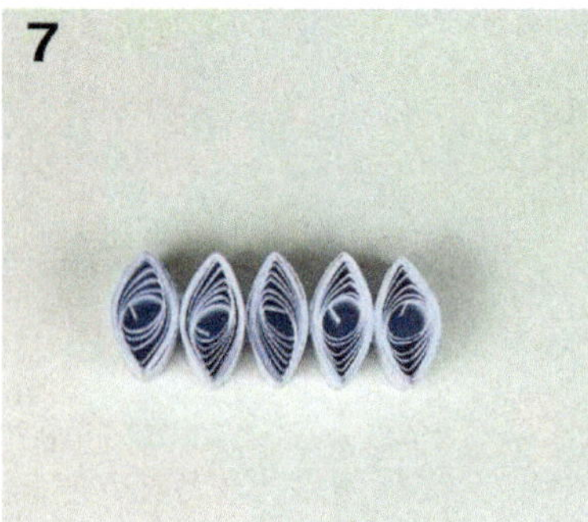

Glue all the 5 marquise shapes side by side

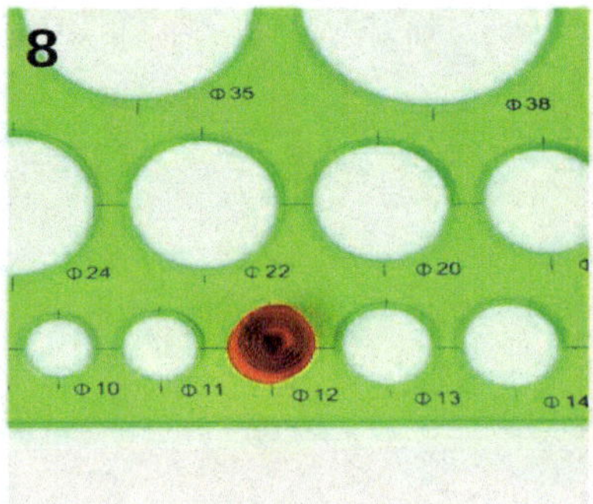

Begin by rolling a red quilling strip into a loose coil and place the coil into a circular template (Size 12) to allow it to expand evenly

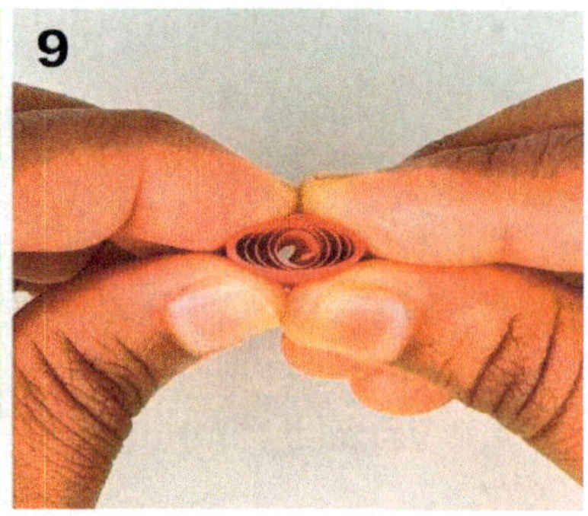

Pinch the coil on opposite sides to create a marquise (eye) shape

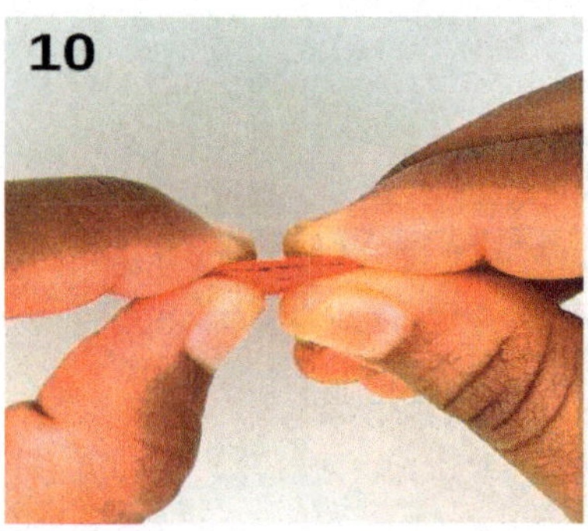

Pinch the marquise on the remaining two sides to create a diamond shape

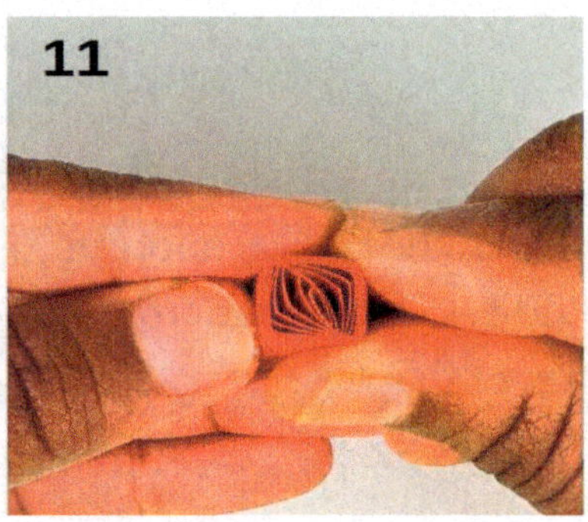

Continue shaping until the coil forms a square shape

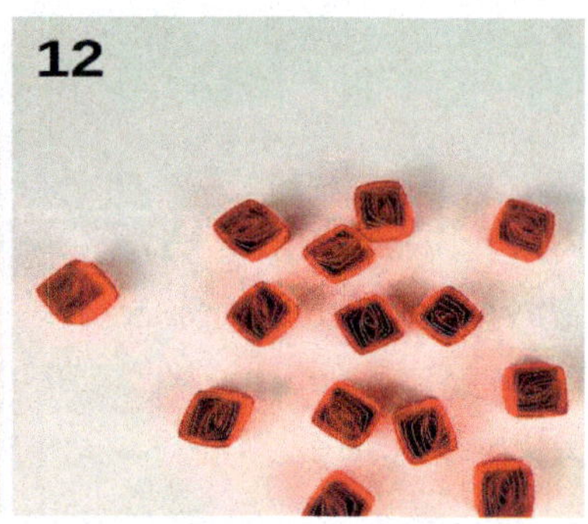

Repeat this process to create several red square shapes (14 Nos). These will form the body of the stocking

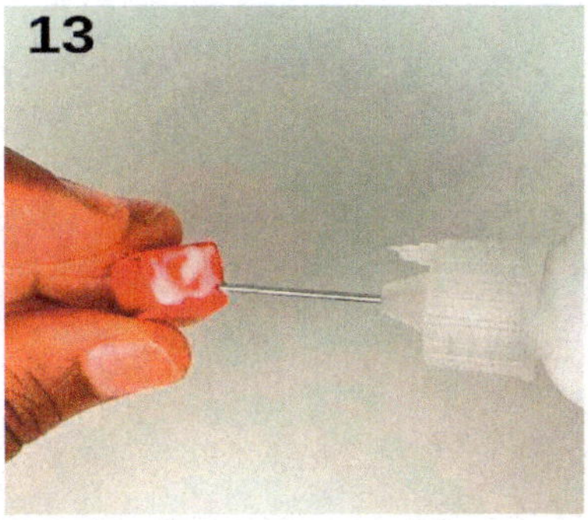

Apply glue to one of the edges of the square

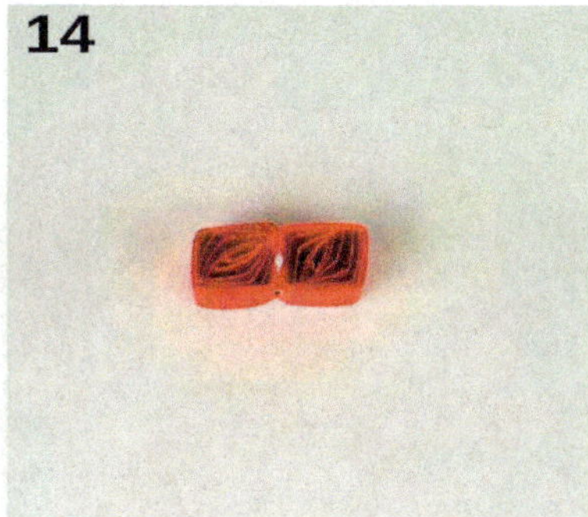

Glue another square together

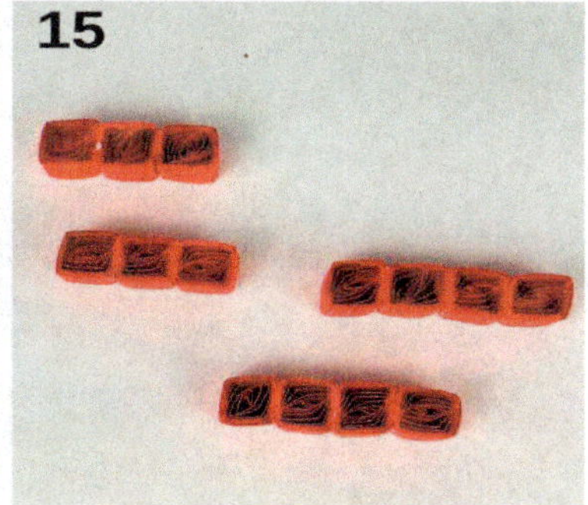

Glue 3and 4 squares in a row. Make 2 of them in each

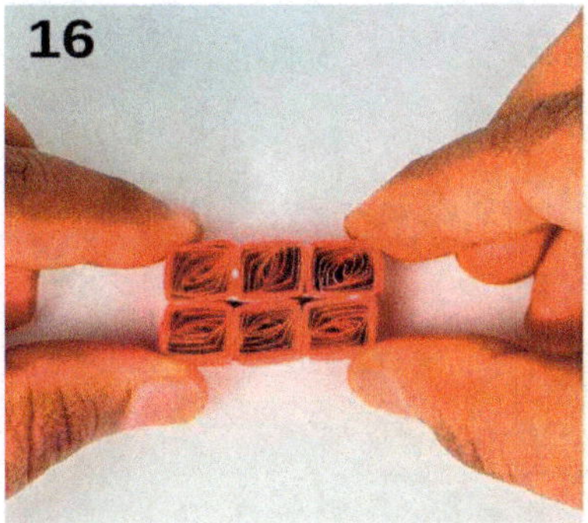

Attach 2 rows of squares together

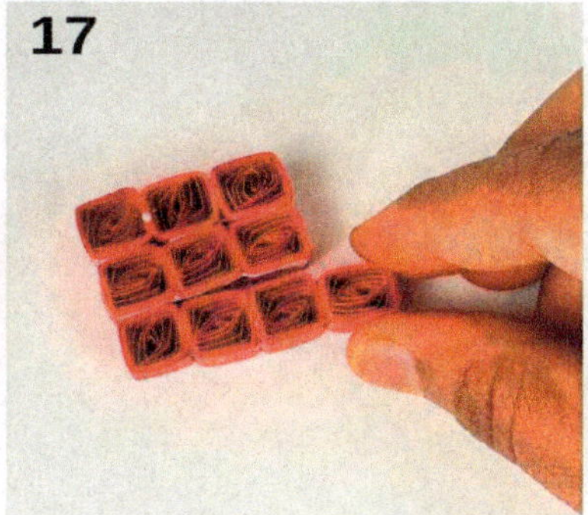

Continue to glue the rows together to create the full stocking shape

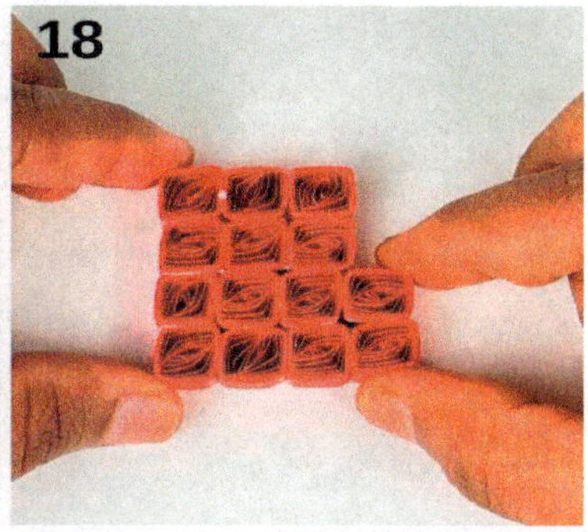

Ensure that all squares are securely glued together, forming a solid stocking structure

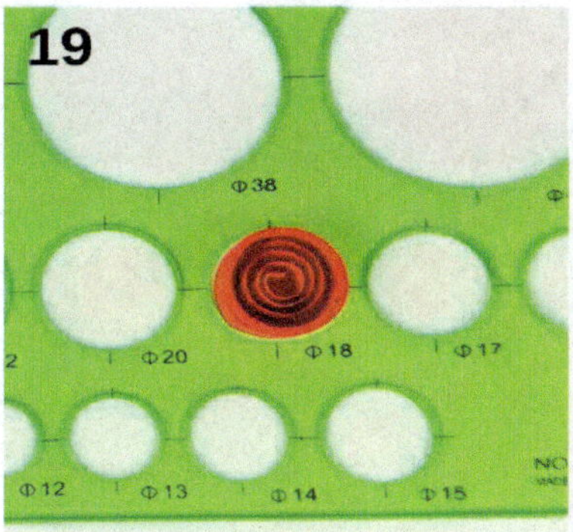

Begin by rolling a red quilling strip into a loose coil and place the coil into a circular template (Size 18) to allow it to expand evenly

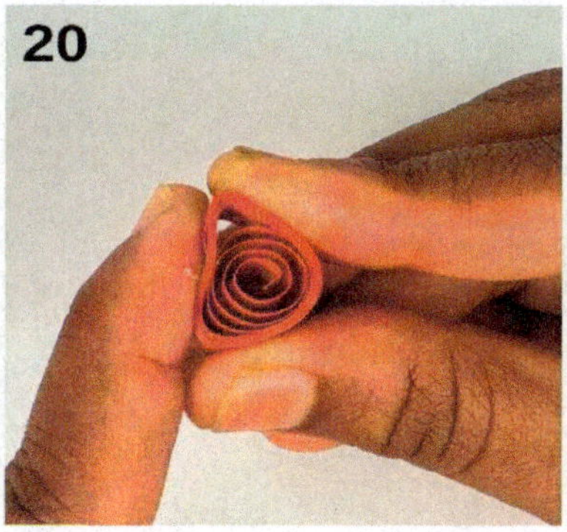

Flatten one side of the coil by pressing it against the index finger

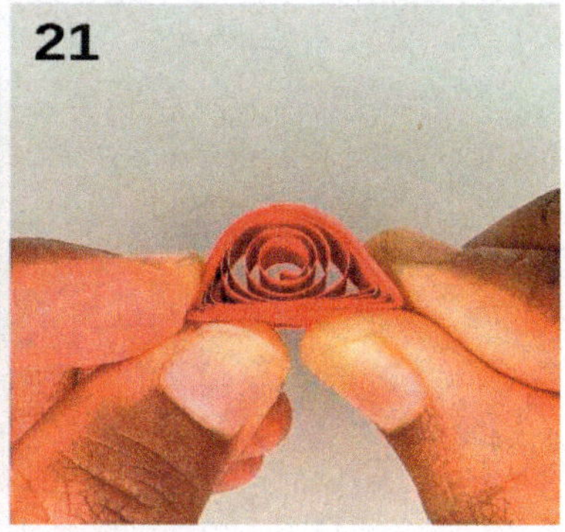

Pinch the two points and make it a semicircle

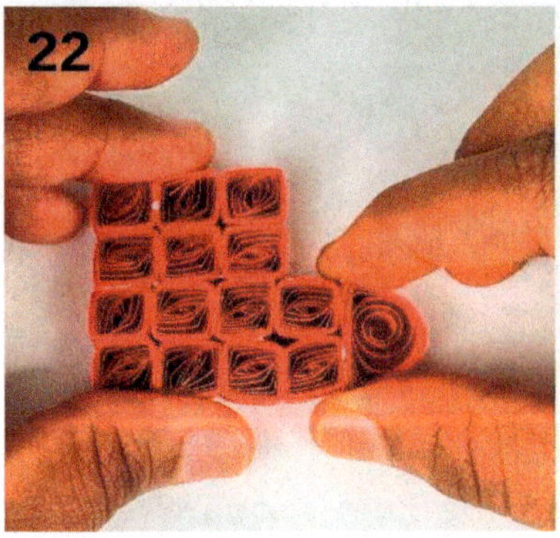

Attach the semicircle to the front of the main body

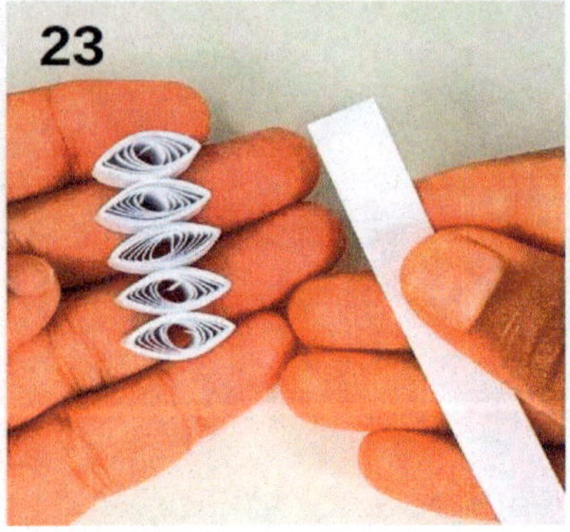

Take a white quilling strip

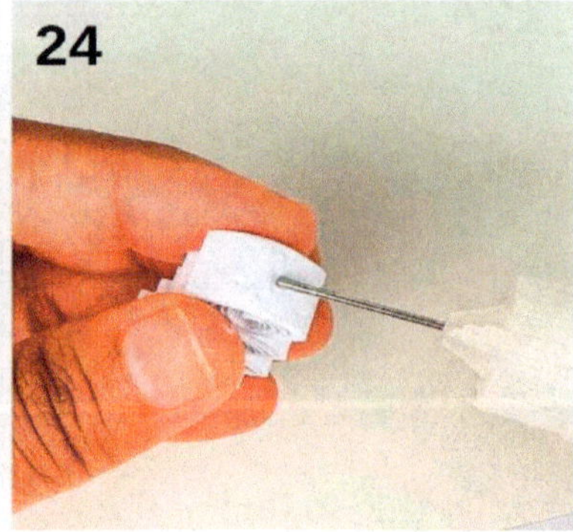

Apply some glue to one side of the eye shape

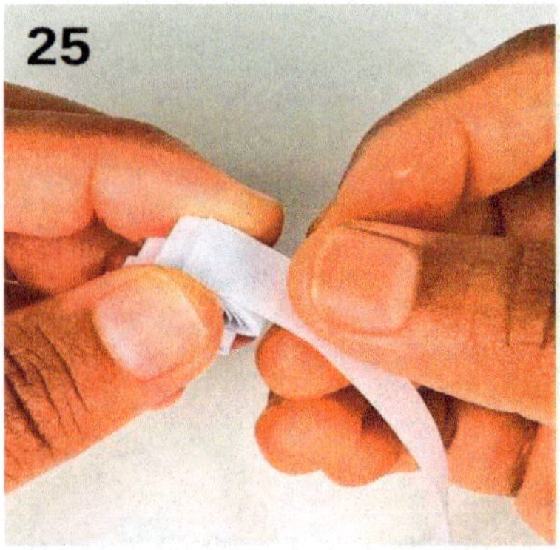

Wrap the quilling strip around the marquise

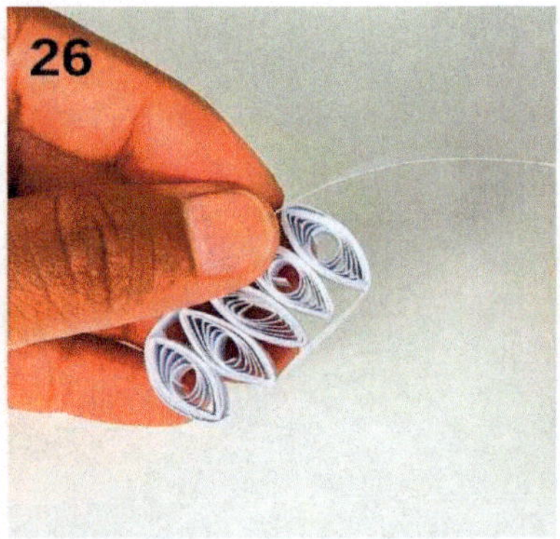

Continue to wrap till the other end of the strip

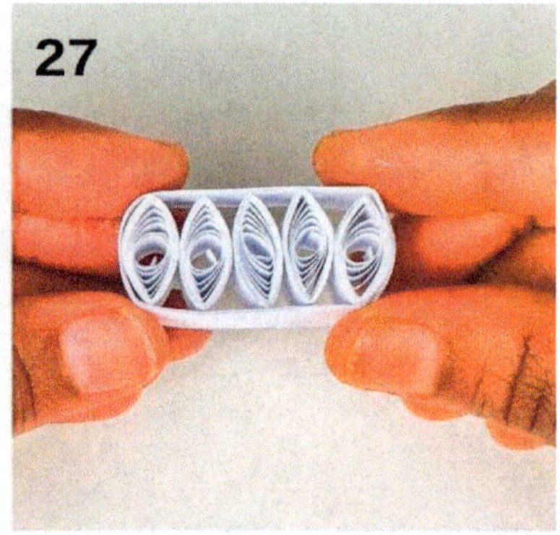

Glue the end and this will be the cuff of the stocking

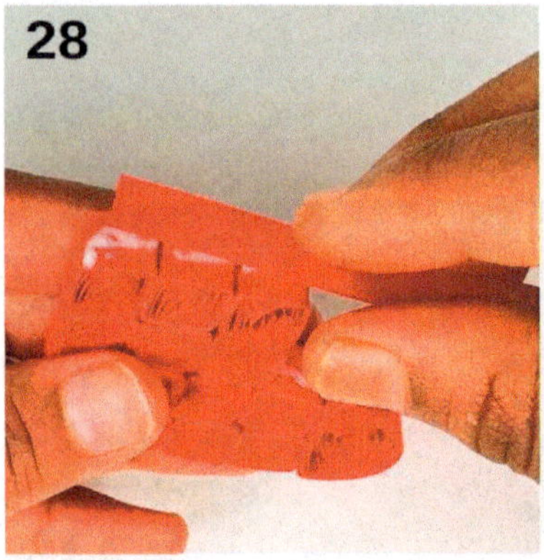

Wrap red colour strip around the body of the stocking

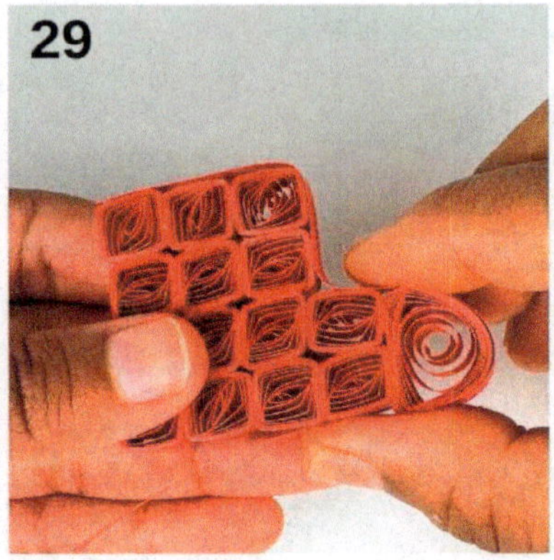

Apply glue and continue to wrap

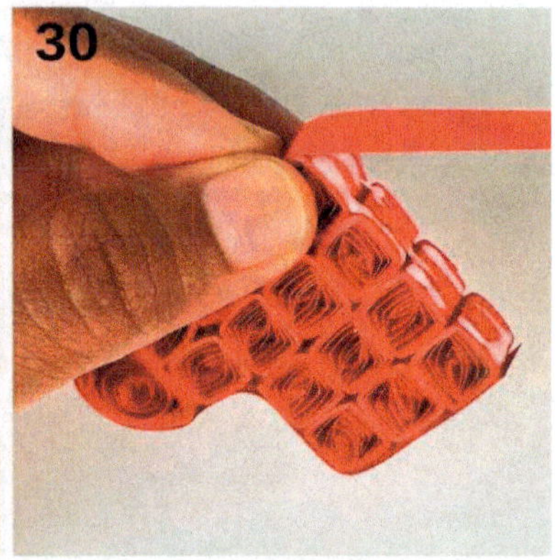

Wrap till the other end of the strip is reached

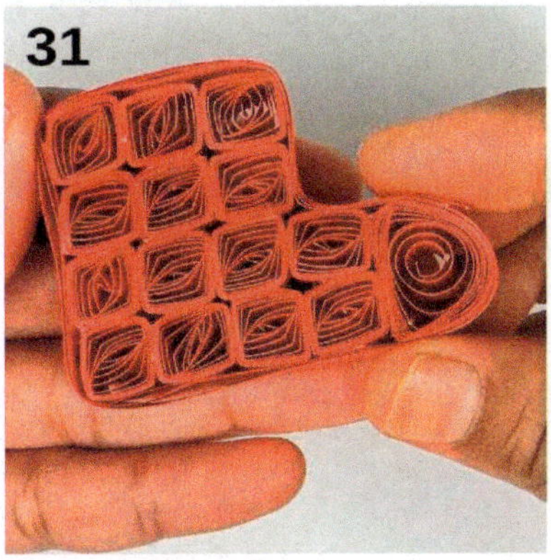

This completes the main body of the stocking

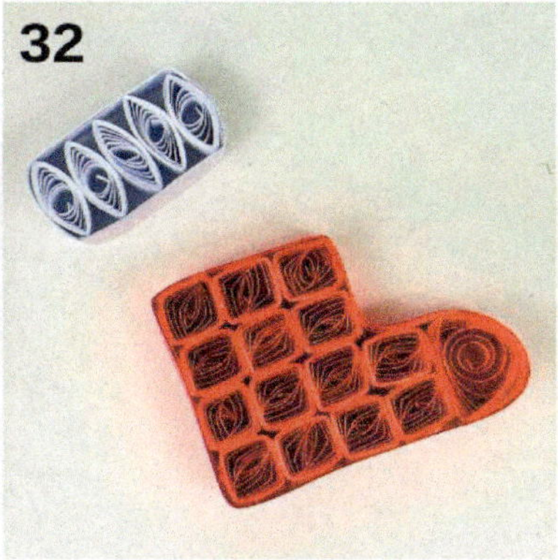

Align and attach the white cuff to the top of the stocking

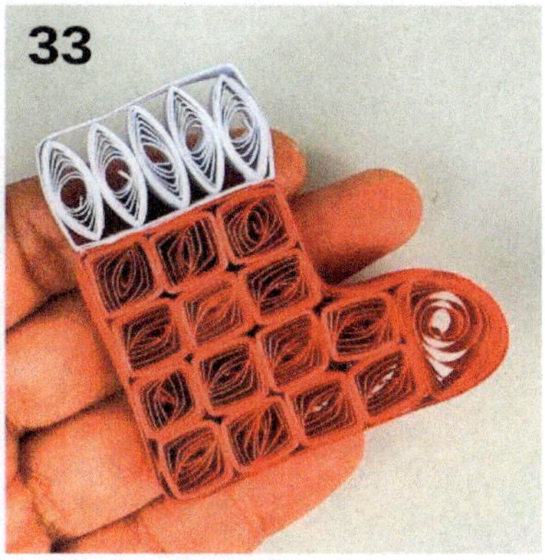

Ensure the cuff is securely attached and aligned properly

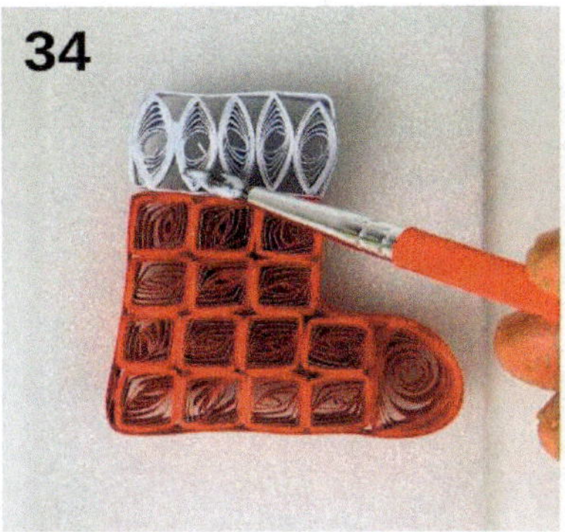

If needed, apply a thin layer of varnish along the front and back of the stocking to reinforce its shape

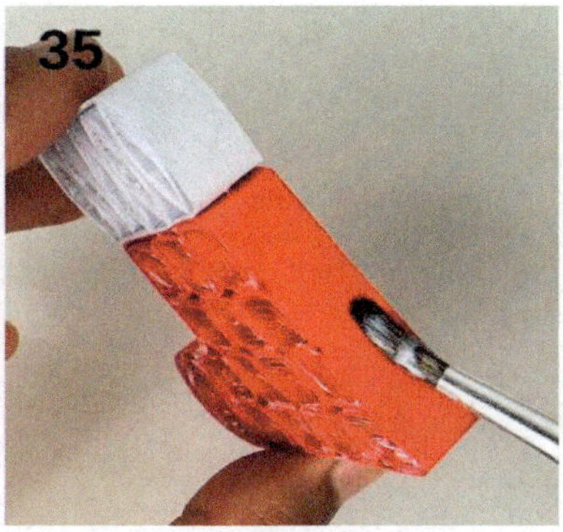

Apply thin layer to the sides of the stocking as well

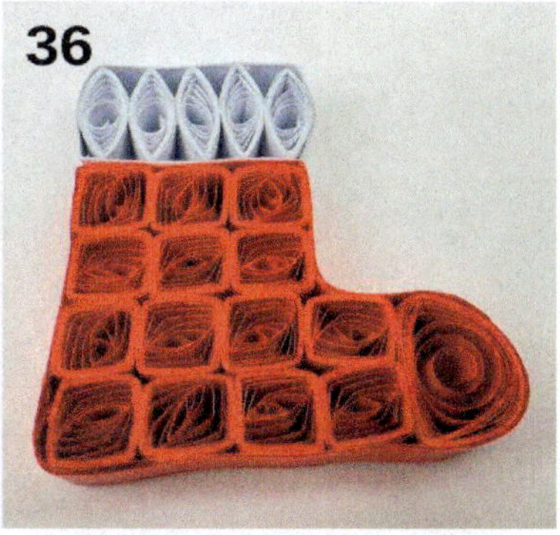

Leave the varnish to dry completely before handling

MODERN AND ABSTRACT DESIGNS

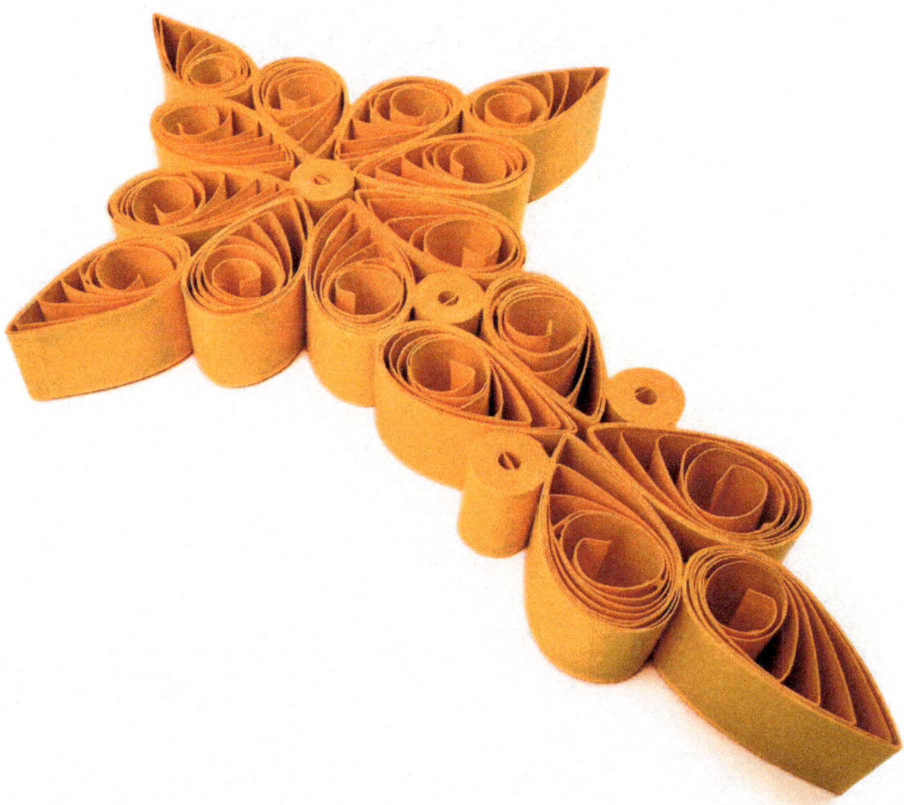

CROSS

Paper quilled cross is a meaningful and intricate craft that uses rolled and shaped paper strips to create a delicate cross design. Perfect for holiday cards, ornaments, or religious decor, this handmade project adds a personal and artistic touch to your Christmas celebrations. It's a beautiful way to honour the spiritual significance of the season with creativity.

Materials Needed:

- Quilling paper strips 10 mm wide in Yellow
- Slotted Quilling tool
- White glue
- Small scissors
- Tweezers
- Quilling board / Circular ruler
- Fine brush
- Varnish (Optional)

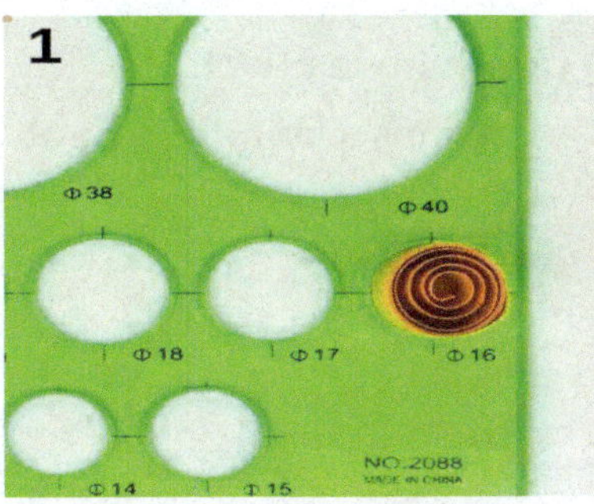

Start by rolling a quilling strip into a loose coil and place the coil into a circular template (Size 16) to allow it to expand evenly, then secure the end with a dab of glue

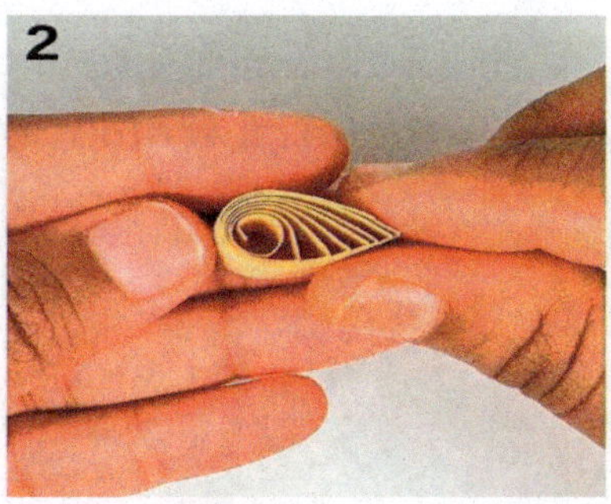

Pinch one side of the loose coil to create a teardrop shape

Repeat this process to create multiple teardrop shapes (16 Nos), which will form the petals

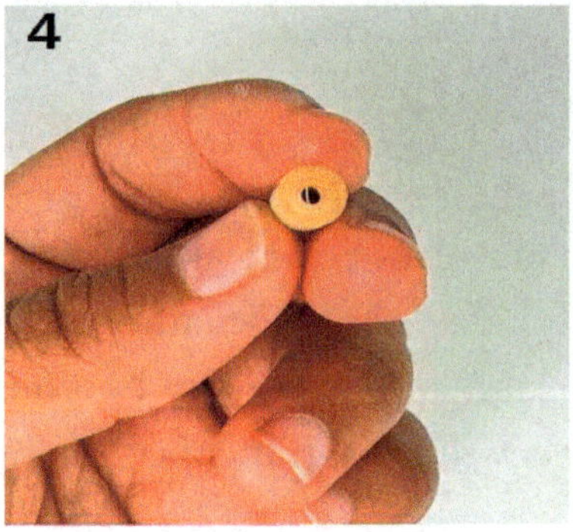

Create a small tight coil using another strip to serve as the centre of the flower

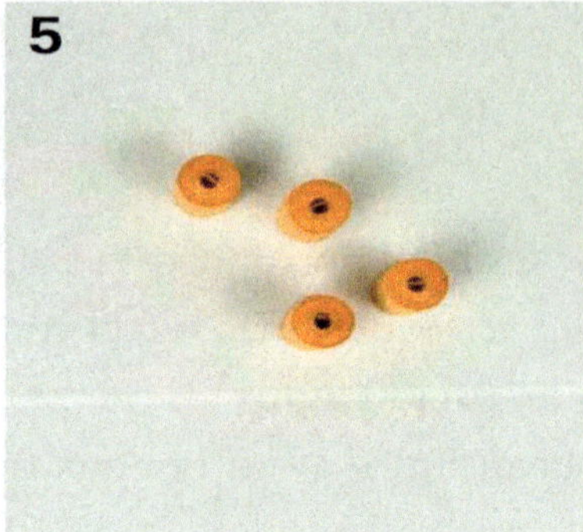

Make 4 similar tight coils

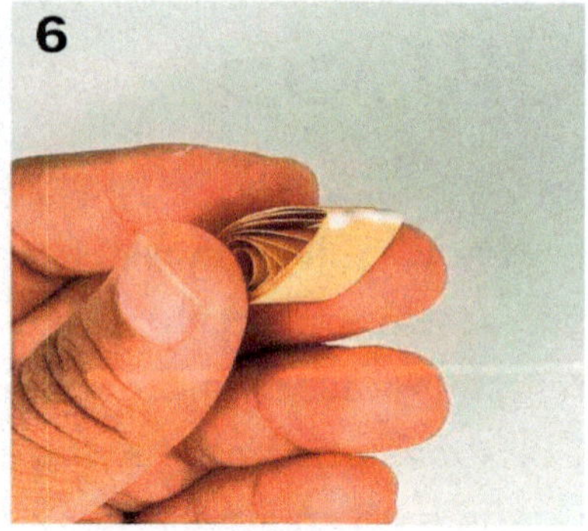

Apply glue to the pointed edge of the teardrop

Attach one teardrop shape to the tight coil

Attach another tear drop next to the first tear drop

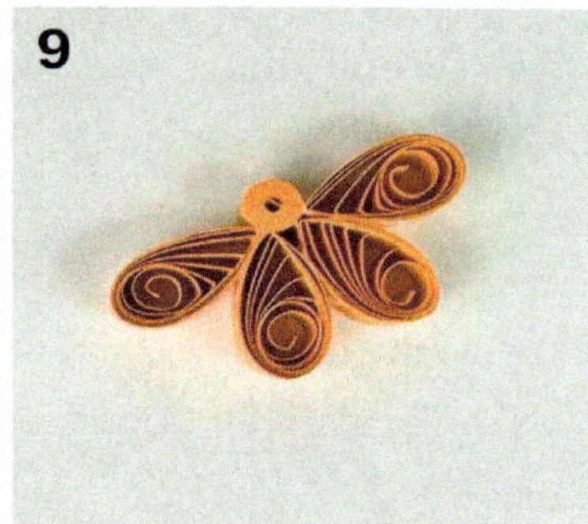

Continue to attach the teardrops around the tight coil

Continue attaching teardrop shapes around the centre coil to form a flower.

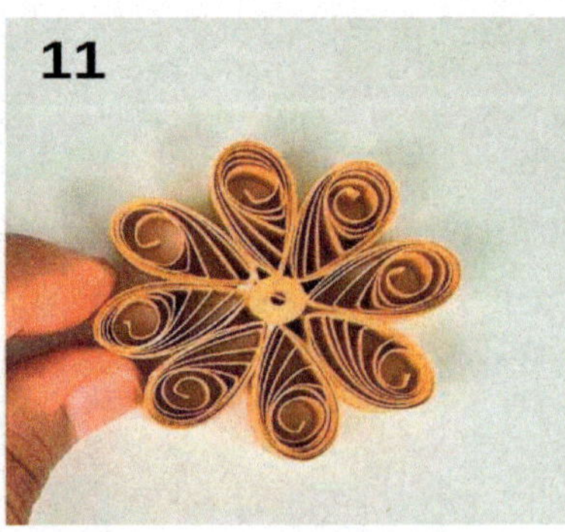

Ensure they are evenly spaced

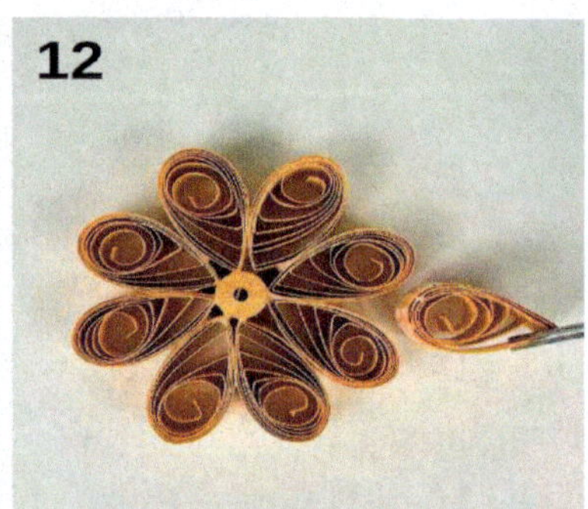

Start forming the cross by adding a teardrop shape to the right side of the central flower

Attach another teardrop on the left side, extending the arms of the cross

Attach a teardrop on the centre of the top side

Attach a tight coil in the bottom centre of the flower

Attach a tear drop shape to the left side of the tight coil

Continue adding teardrop shapes to lengthen the cross's arms, ensuring symmetry

Add additional teardrop shapes to the bottom of the cross to extend its length.

Ensure that the cross is symmetrical and that all pieces are securely glued

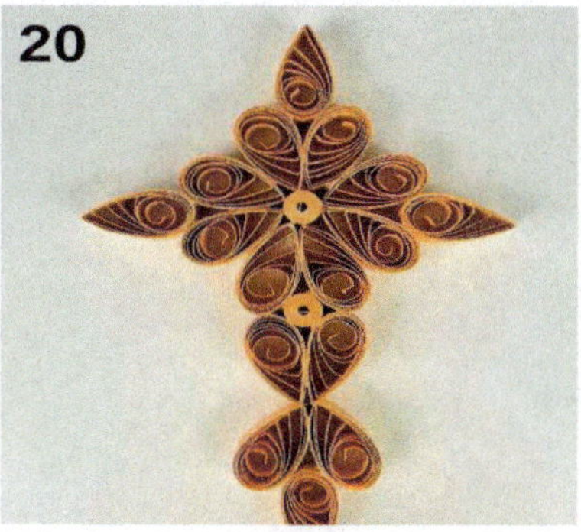

Attach a tear drop shape in the bottom of the cross

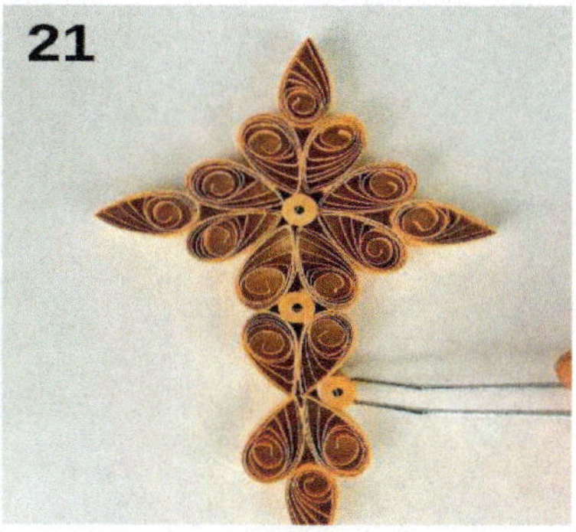

Add tight coils to fill in gaps

Attach a tight coil on the left side and let the glue dry completely

If needed, apply a thin layer of varnish along the front and back of the cross to reinforce its shape

Let it dry completely

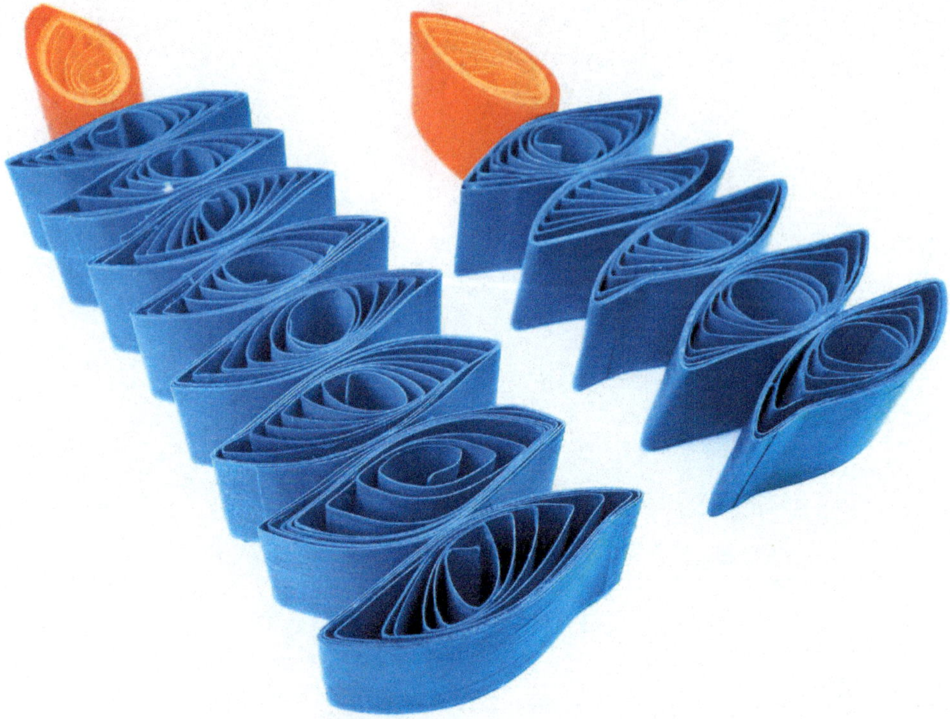

CANDLES

Paper quilled Christmas candle is an elegant craft that uses rolled and shaped paper strips to form a festive candle design, completed with flames. This intricate project is perfect for ornaments, holiday cards, or seasonal displays, adding a warm and handmade touch to your Christmas decor. It's a creative way to bring the glow of the season into your home.

Materials Needed:

- Quilling paper strips 10 mm wide in Blue, Orange and Yellow
- Slotted Quilling tool
- White glue
- Small scissors
- Tweezers
- Quilling board / Circular ruler
- Fine brush
- Varnish (Optional)

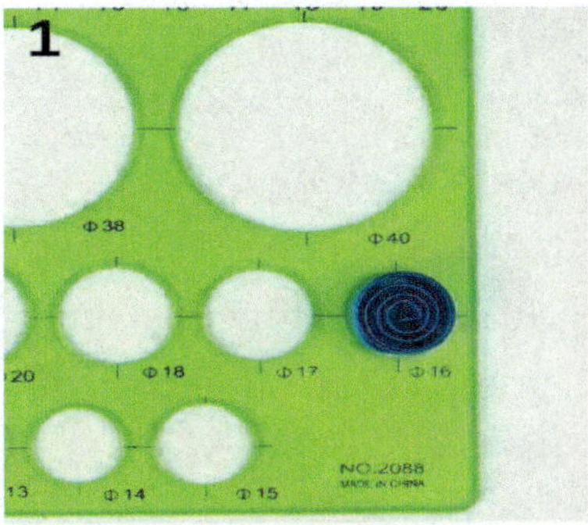

Roll a blue quilling strip into a loose coil and place the coil on a circular template (Size 16) to allow it to expand evenly. Secure the end with the glue

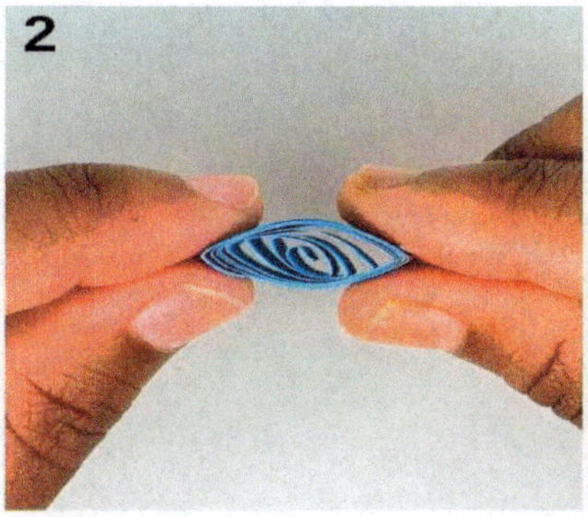

Pinch the coil on the opposite sides to create a marquise (eye) shape

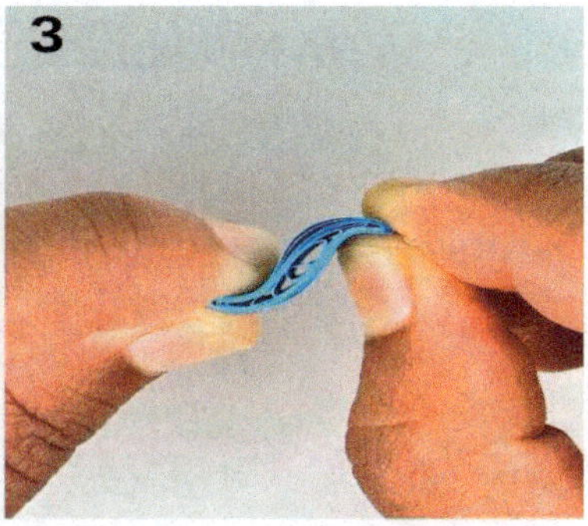

Slightly bend the ends of the marquise in opposite direction

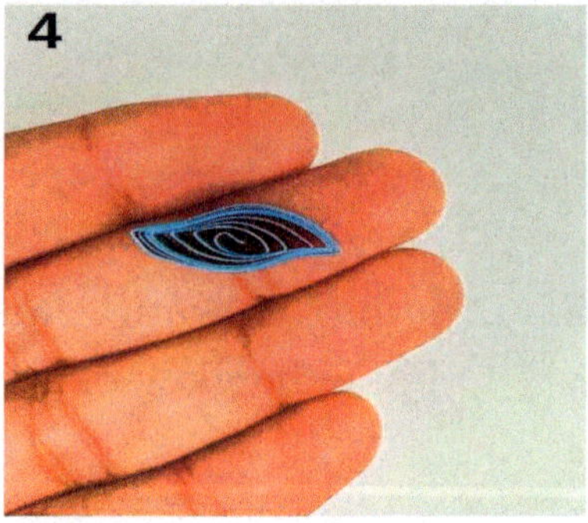

This will result in a curved marquise

Make several curved marquise shapes for the candle body, ensuring they are all consistent in size.

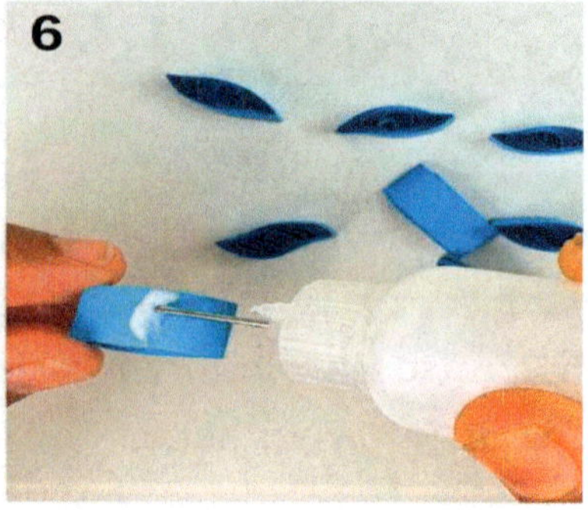

Apply glue to the centre of the curved marquise shapes

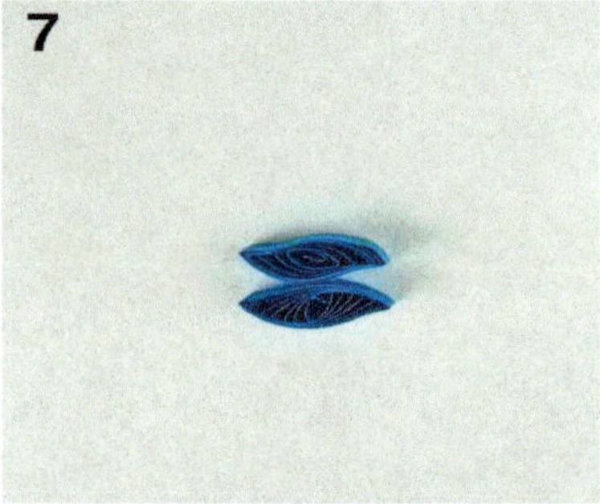

Attach another curved marquise shape on the top

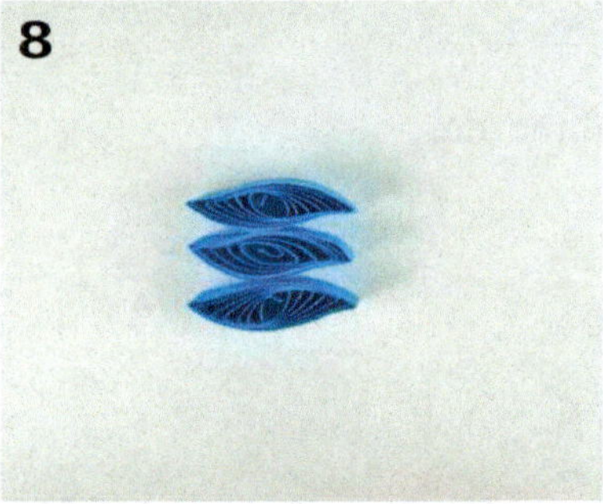

Continue to stack marquise shape

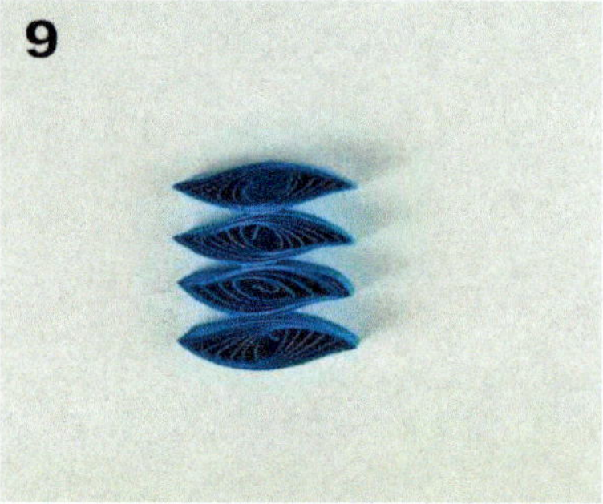

Begin stacking the marquise shapes vertically, gluing them together one on top of the other to form the body of the candle

Continue to stack and glue the marquise shapes

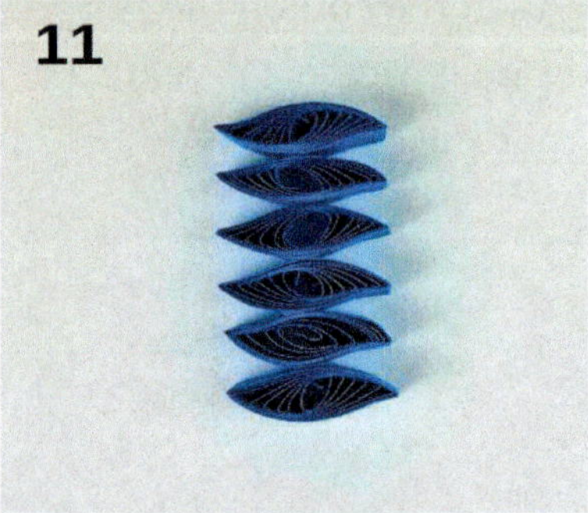

Make sure they are in a straight line

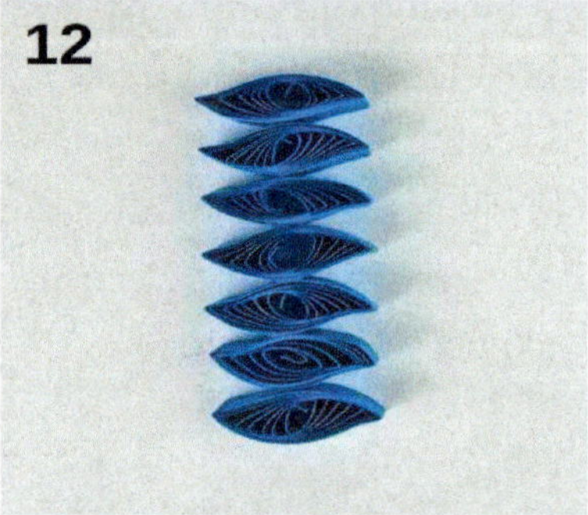

Repeat the process until you reach the desired height for the candle.

13

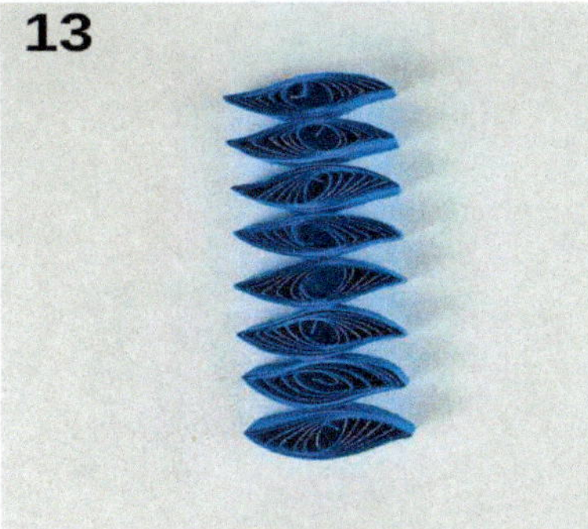

Let the glue dry completely

14

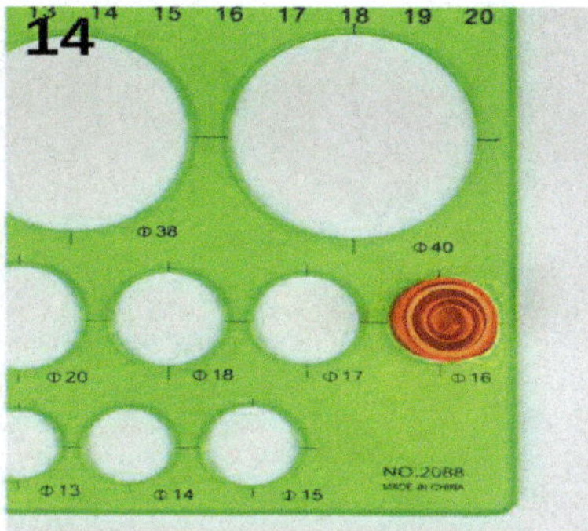

Glue the ends of yellow and orange strips. Start rolling from the yellow strips in to a loose coil and place the coil into a circular template (Size 16) to allow it to expand evenly. Secure the end with the glue

15

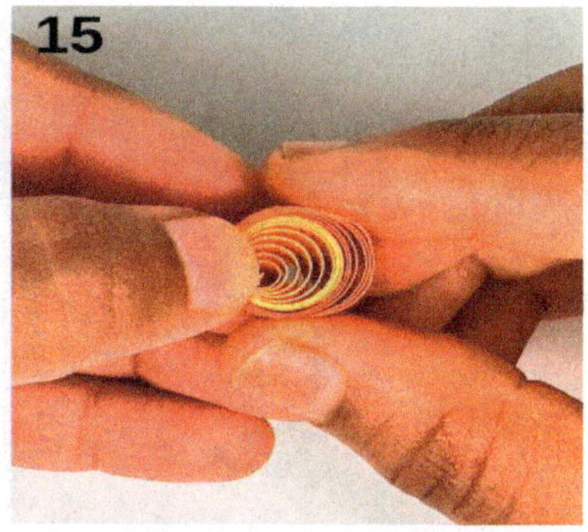

Place the coil between the fingers

16

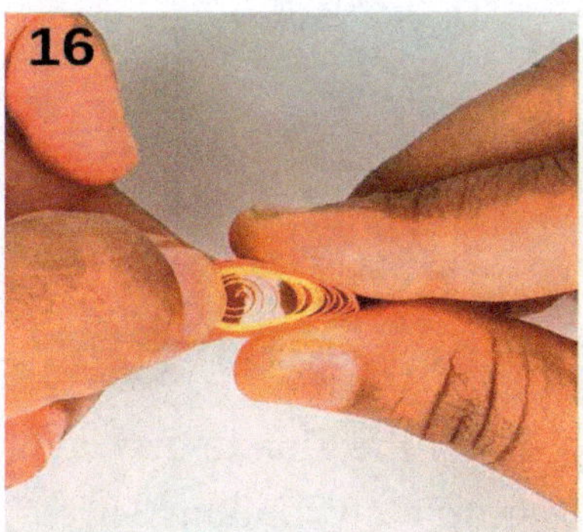

Hold the centre and pinch one end of the coil

17

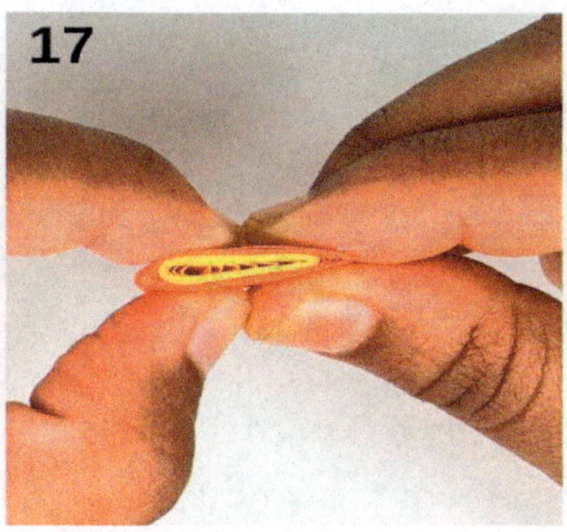

Slightly pinch the other side to form a teardrop shape with a pointed end, resembling a flame

18

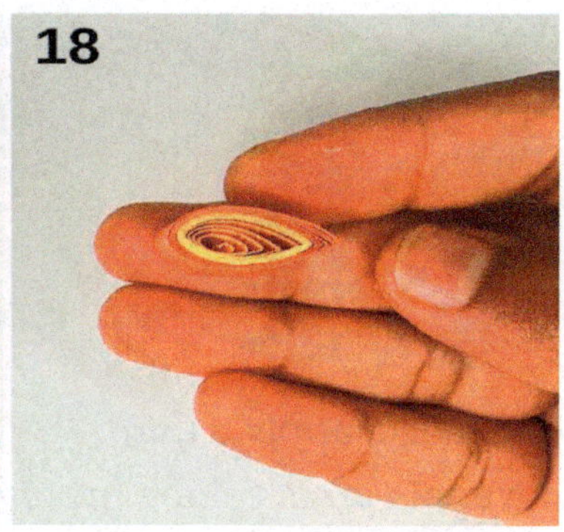

Ensure that the flame is well-formed and consistent in shape

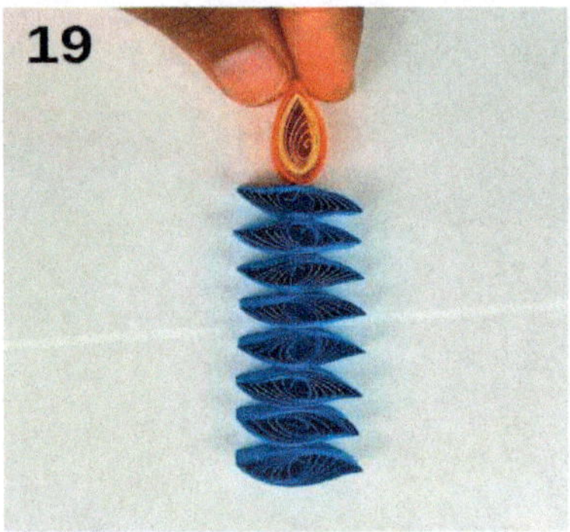

Apply glue to the base of the flame. Attach the flame to the top of the candle body, pressing it gently to secure it

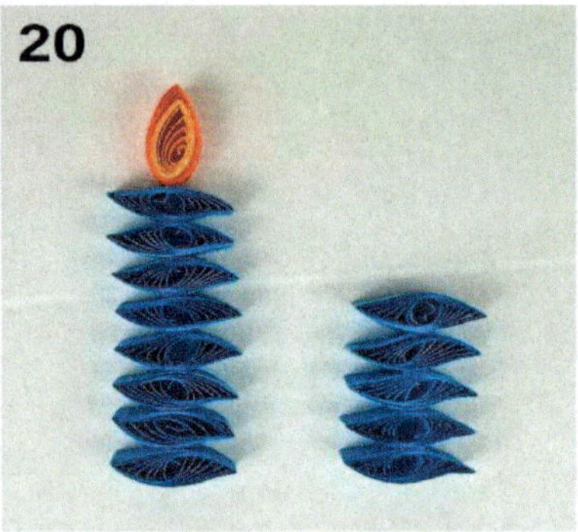

Repeat the process and make a smaller candle

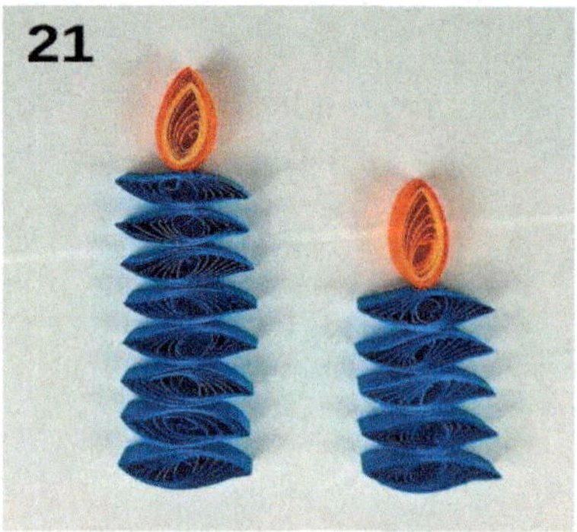

Attach the flame to the top of the small candle body

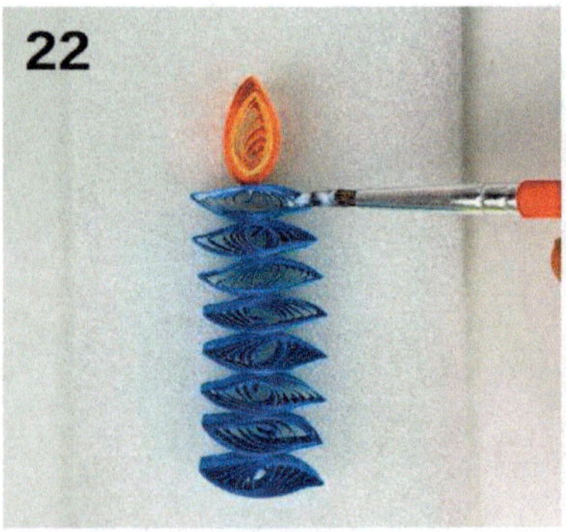

If needed, apply a thin layer of varnish along the front and back of the candles to reinforce its shape

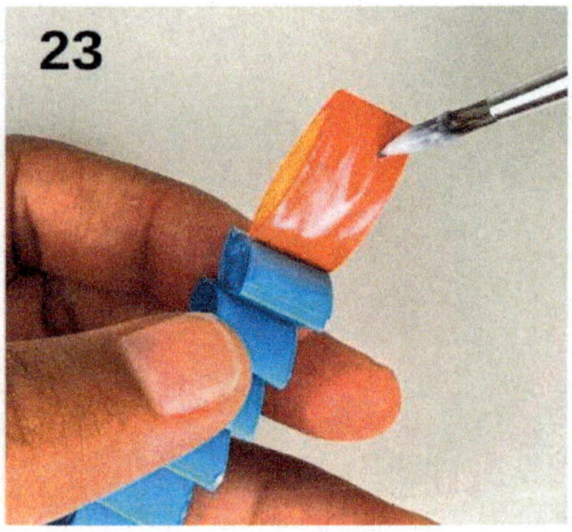

Apply a thin coat to the sides of the candle

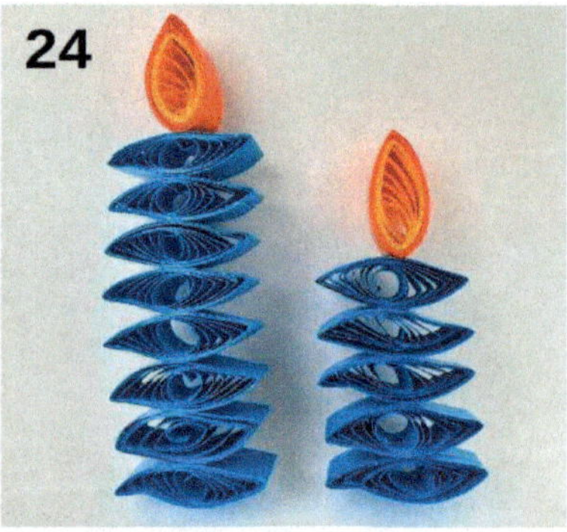

Allow the glue to dry completely, making sure the candle stands upright and the flame is securely attached

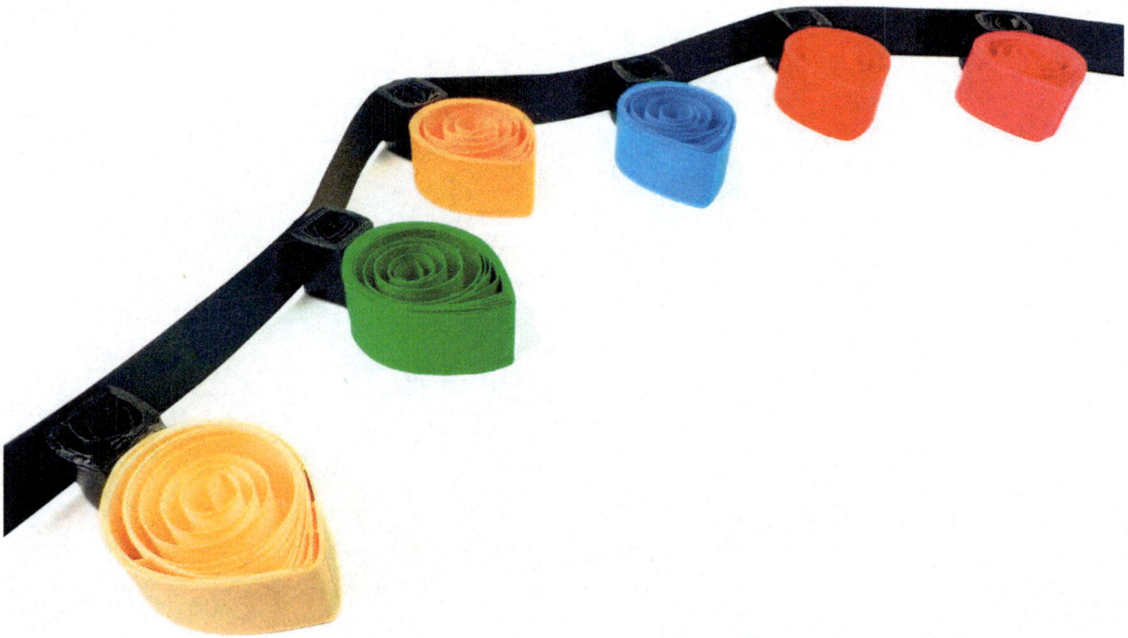

CHRISTMAS LIGHTS

Paper quilled Christmas light string is a festive craft that transforms rolled and shaped paper strips into a delicate design resembling a string of holiday lights. This intricate project adds a colourful, handmade touch to cards, ornaments, or seasonal displays. It's a creative and whimsical way to brighten up your Christmas decor.

Materials Needed:

- Quilling paper strips 10 mm wide in Red, Green, Blue, Yellow, Pink, Cream and Black
- Slotted Quilling tool
- White glue
- Small scissors
- Tweezers
- Quilling board / Circular ruler
- Fine brush
- Varnish (Optional)

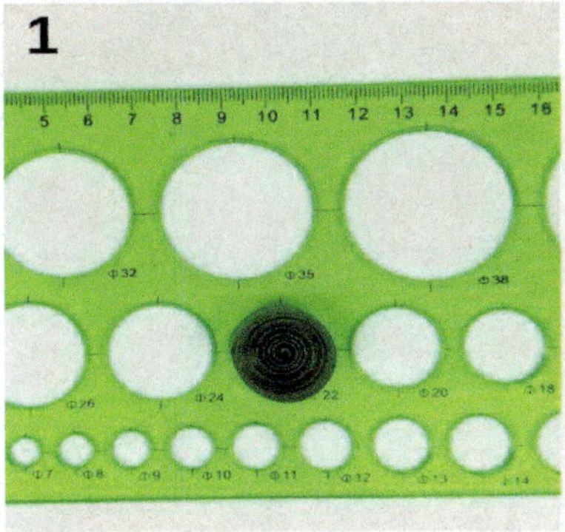

Start by rolling a quilling strip (e.g., green) into a loose coil and place the coil into a circular template (Size 22) to allow it to expand evenly. Secure the end with glue

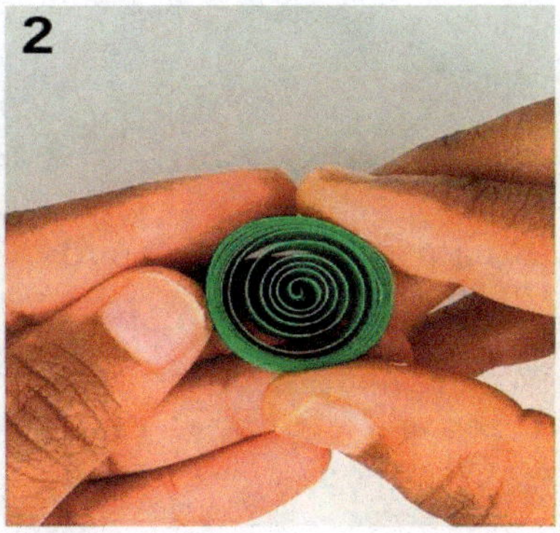

Place the loose coil between the fingers

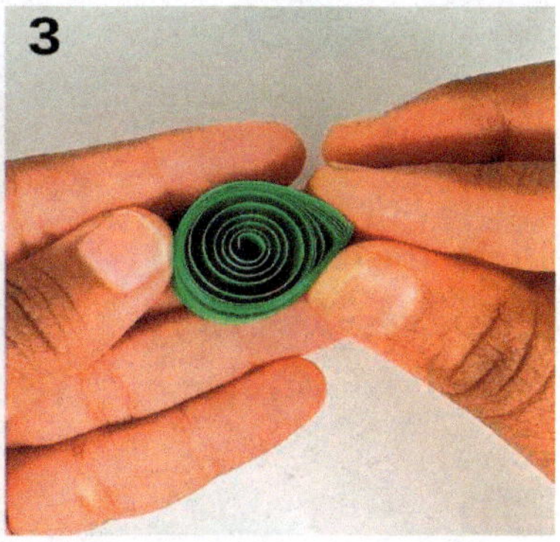

Start by slightly pinching one end of the coil

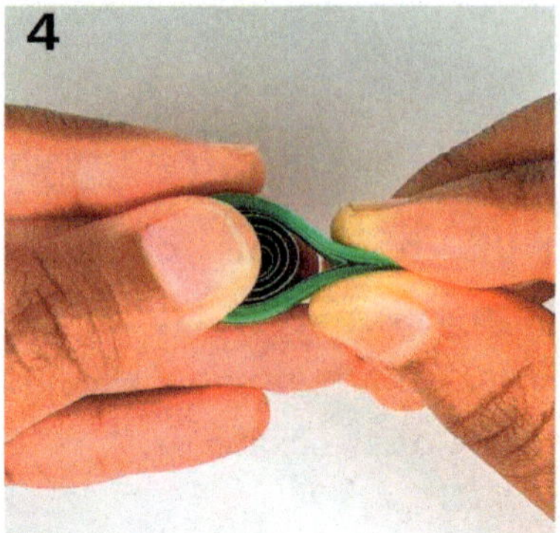

Pinch one side of the coil only at the top to form a teardrop shape, resembling a light bulb

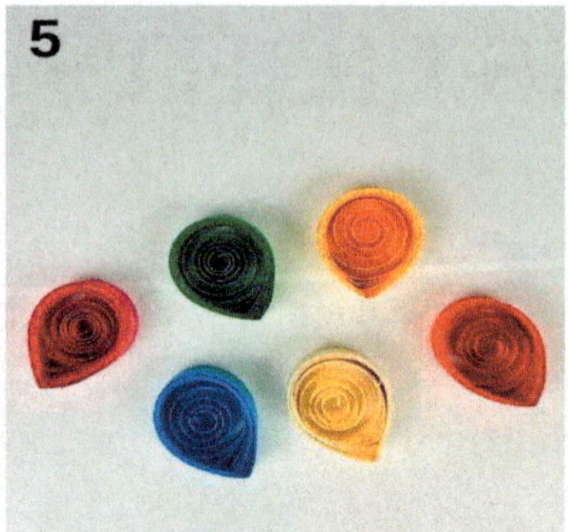

Repeat this process with different coloured quilling strips to create multiple teardrop-shapes

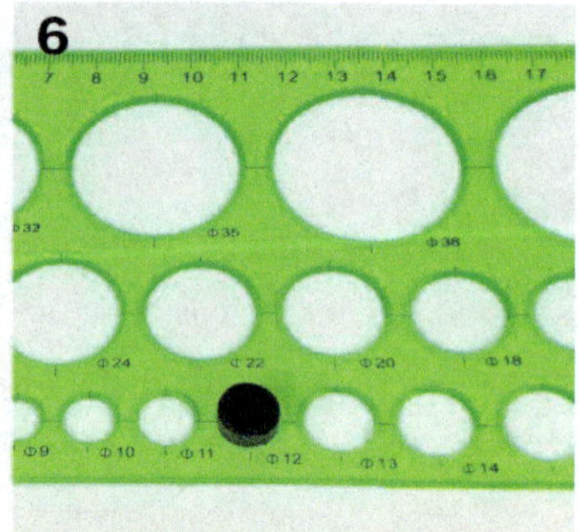

Roll a black quilling strip into a loose coil and place the coil into a circular template (Size 12) to allow it to expand evenly. Secure the end with glue

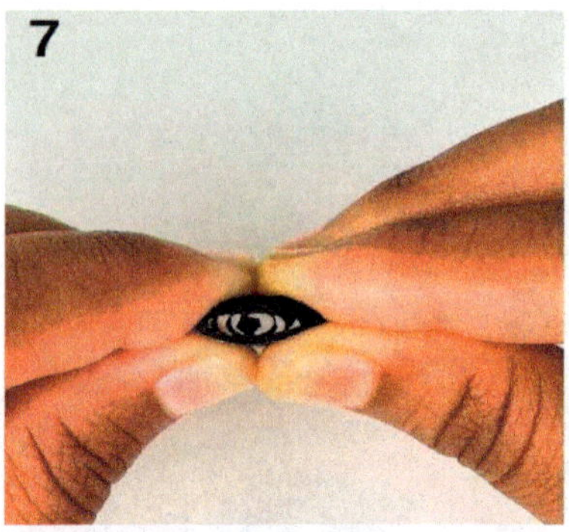

Pinch the coil on two opposite sides to form a marquise (eye) shape

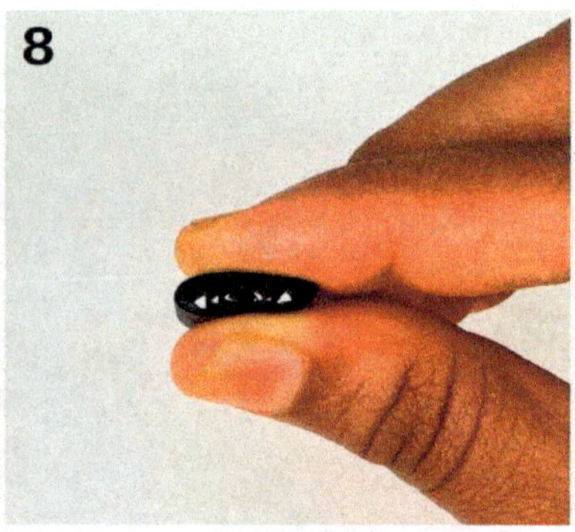

Rotate and pinch the ends again to create a small square shape

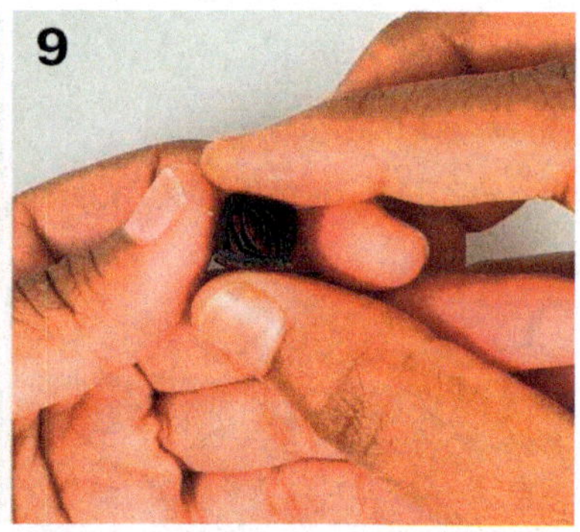

This will be the light bulb base

Repeat this process to create enough bases for all your light bulbs

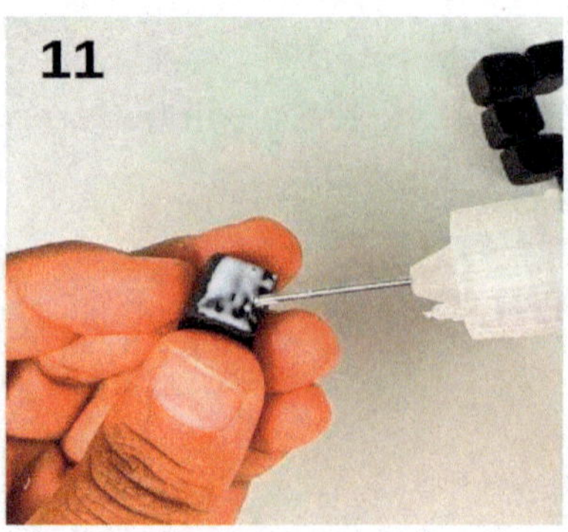

Apply glue to one side of the square

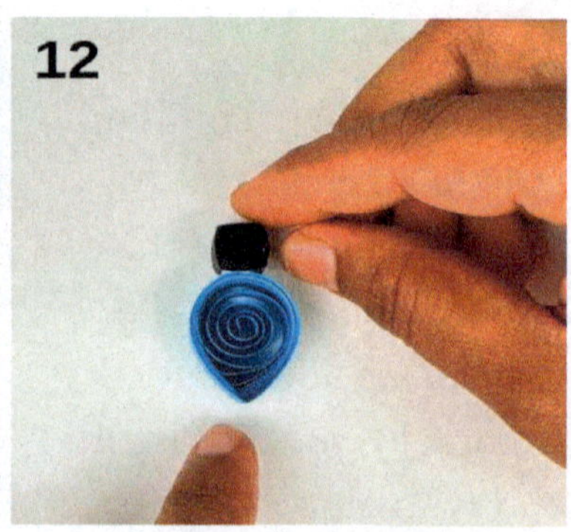

Attach it to the rounded end of the teardrop shape (light bulb)

Attach the black square bases to the coloured light bulb shapes, ensuring they are centred and secure

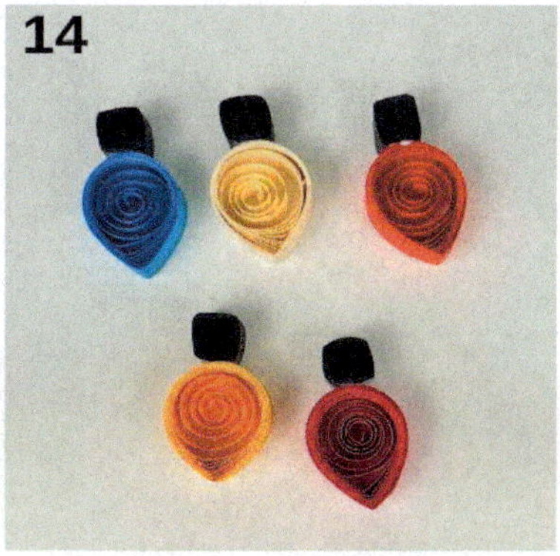

Repeat the process and attach the bulb bases to the bulbs

Allow the glue to dry completely before moving on to the next step

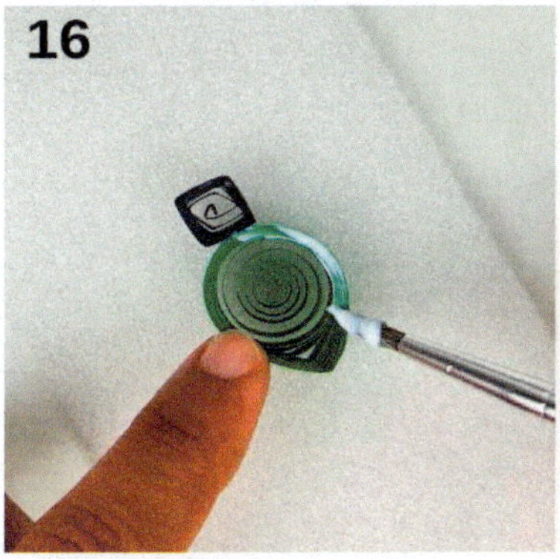

Apply a thin layer of varnish to the front and back of the lights

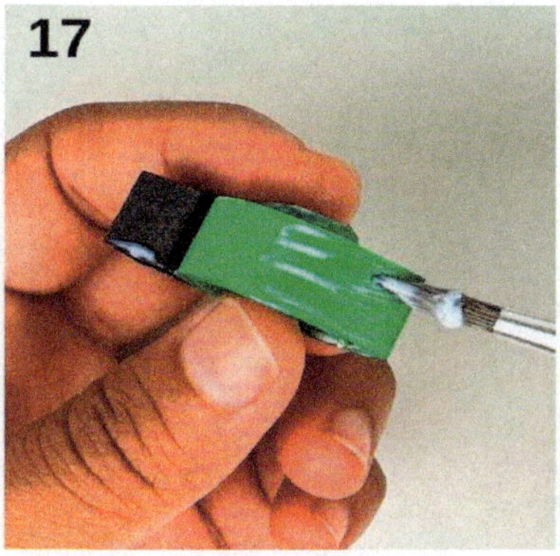

Apply a thin coat to the sides of all the light bulbs

Take two black paper strips

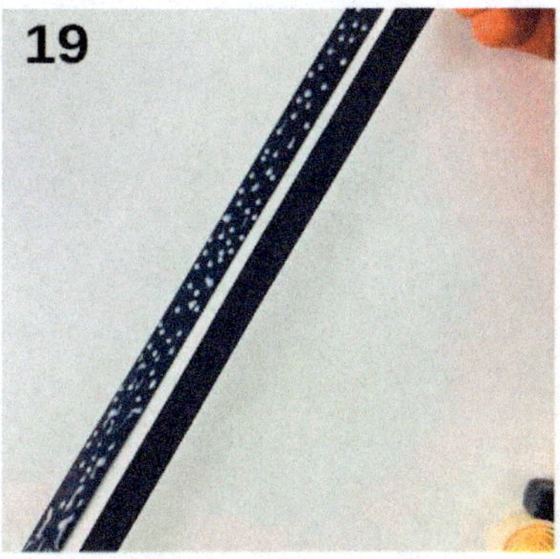

Apply glue to one of the black strips and place the other on the top of it and secure

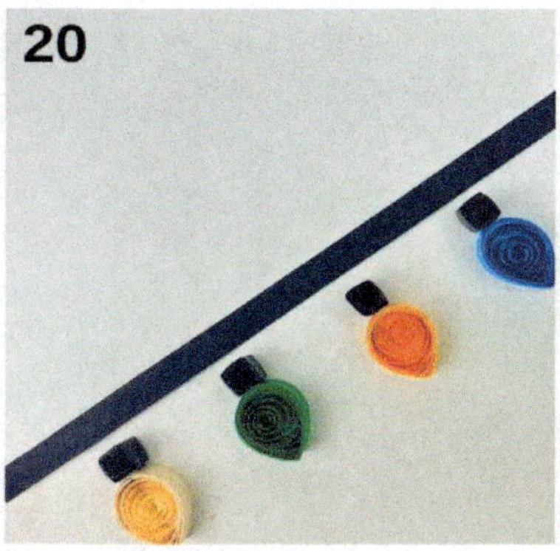

Lay the strip flat on your working surface

Apply glue to the back of the black base of each light bulb

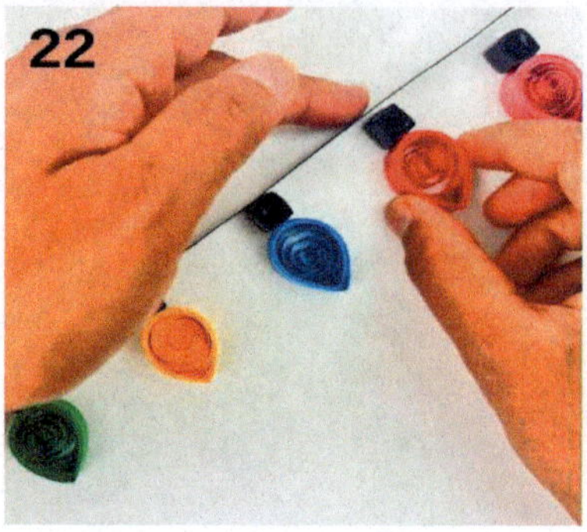

Attach the bulbs to the black strip, evenly spacing them out along the length of the strip

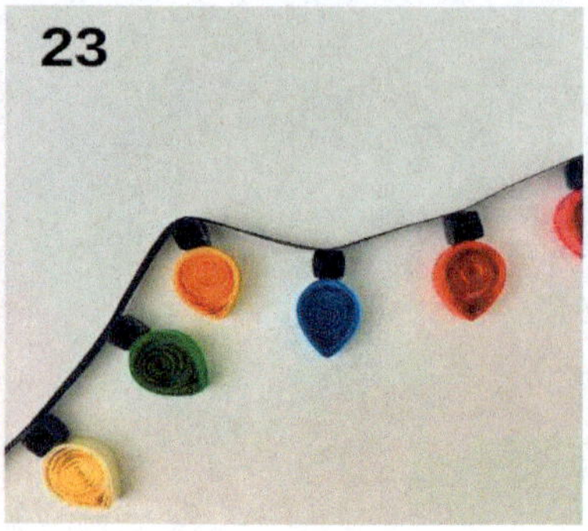

Press down gently to ensure the bulbs stick to the string securely

Allow the entire piece to dry, and then it's ready to display

CHRISTMAS BAUBLE

Paper quilled Christmas bauble is a delightful craft that uses rolled and shaped paper strips to create an intricate, festive ornament. Perfect for decorating trees, cards, or holiday displays, this handmade bauble adds a personal and artistic touch to your seasonal decor. It's a creative way to bring elegance and charm to your Christmas celebrations.

Materials Needed:

- Quilling paper strips 10 mm wide in different shades of blue and white
- Slotted Quilling tool
- White glue
- Small scissors
- Tweezers
- Quilling board / Circular ruler
- Fine brush
- String or thread for hanging the bauble
- Varnish (Optional)

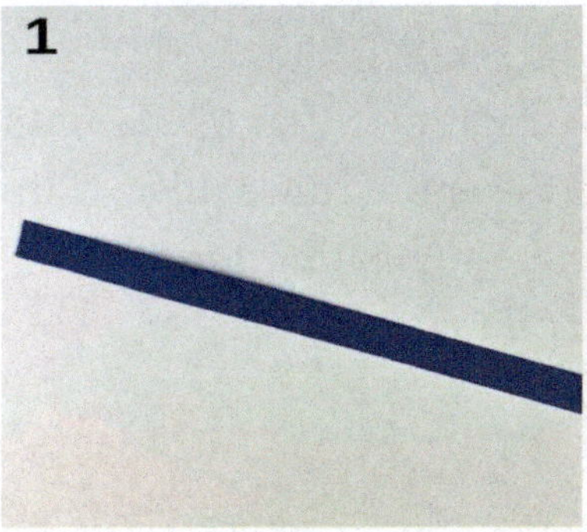

Take a blue colour 10 mm wide paper strip

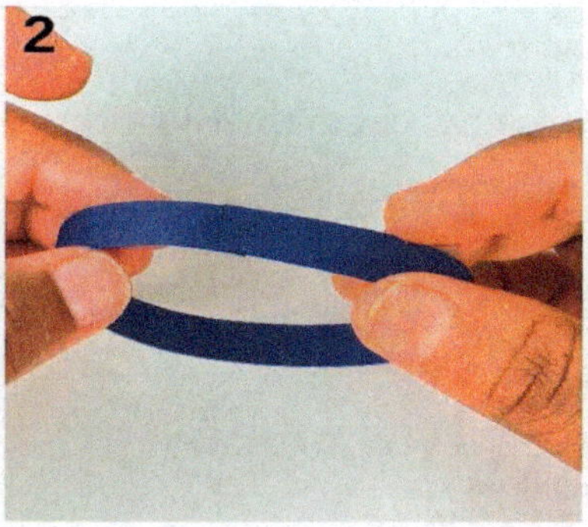

Glue the ends together to form a loop, as shown. This will be the outer rim of your bauble

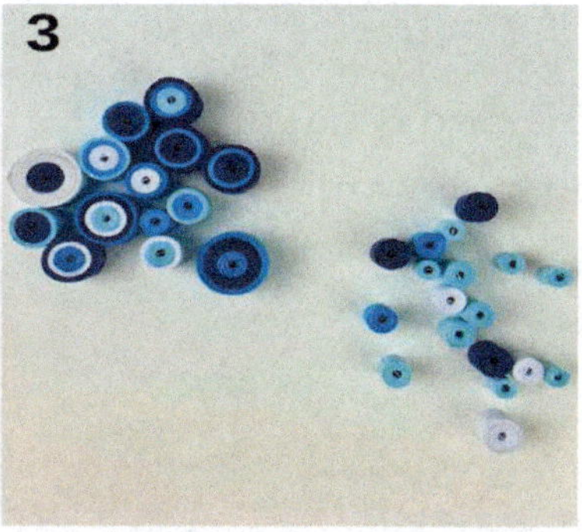

Roll tight coils of quilling paper in combination of different shades of blue and white and also make tight coils in single colour. Secure the end of each coil with a dab of glue.

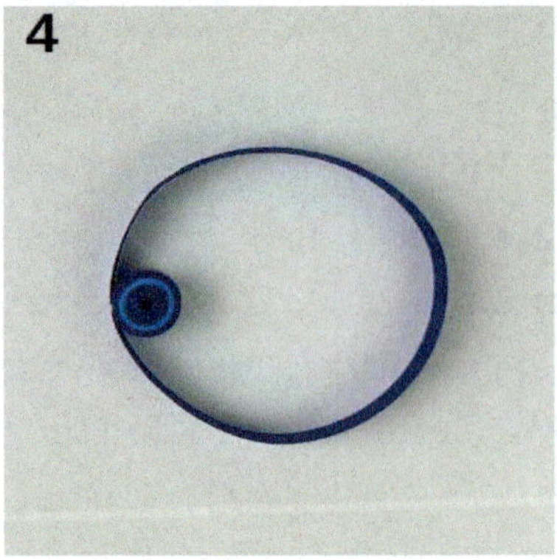

Begin placing and gluing the coils inside the rim

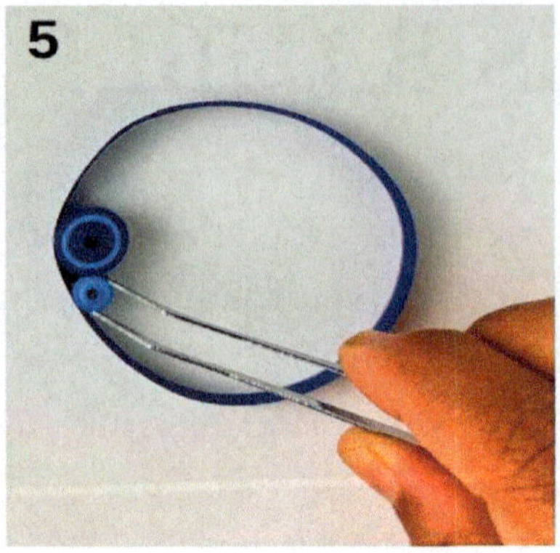

Apply glue to the sides of the coil and attach to the adjacent coil

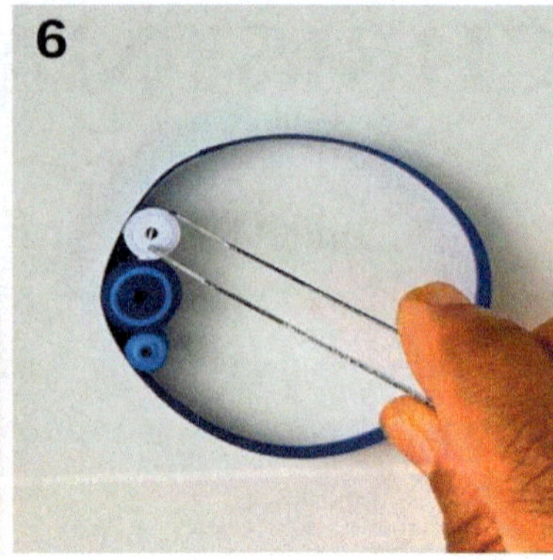

Make sure the coils fit snugly together

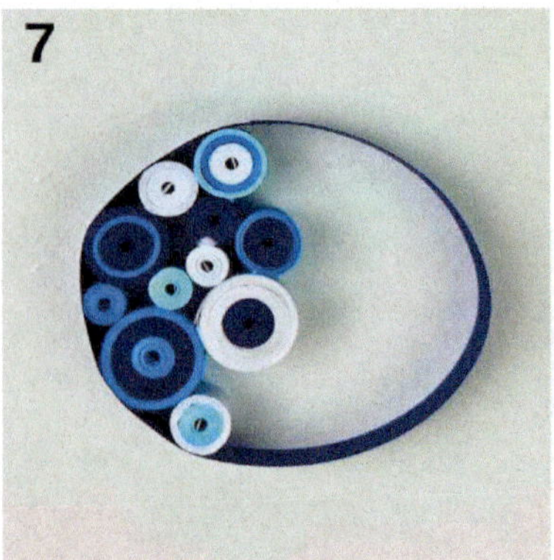

Start from the edge and move towards the centre

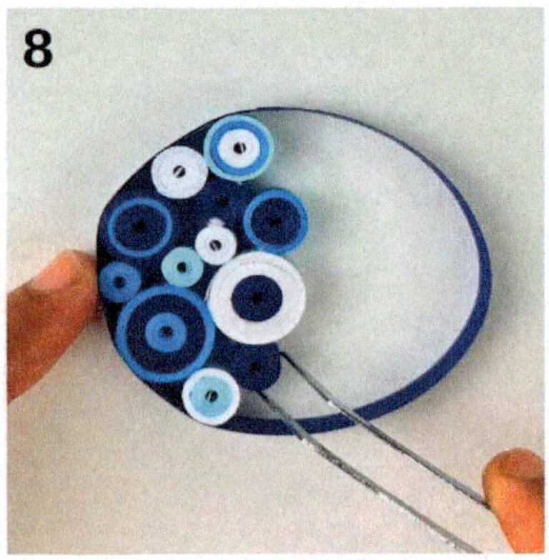

Use tweezers to adjust the placement

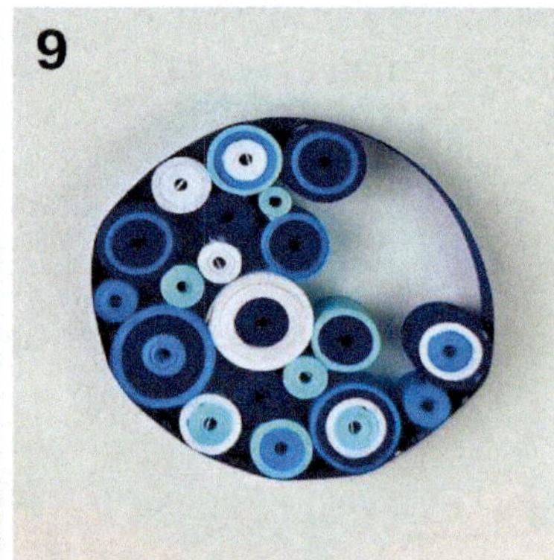

Continue adding coils until the entire rim is filled with them, creating a mosaic effect

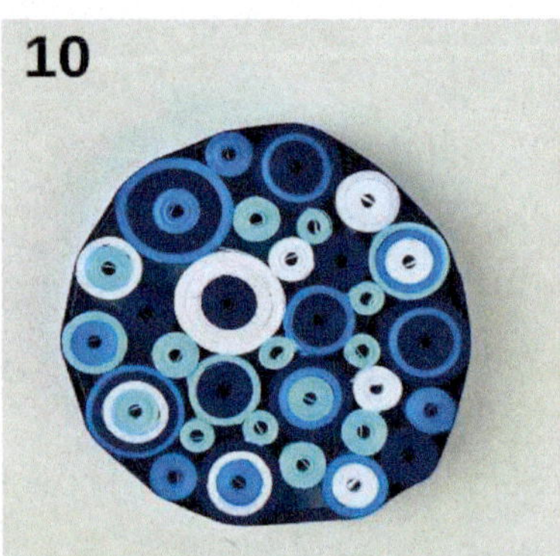

Let the glue dry completely

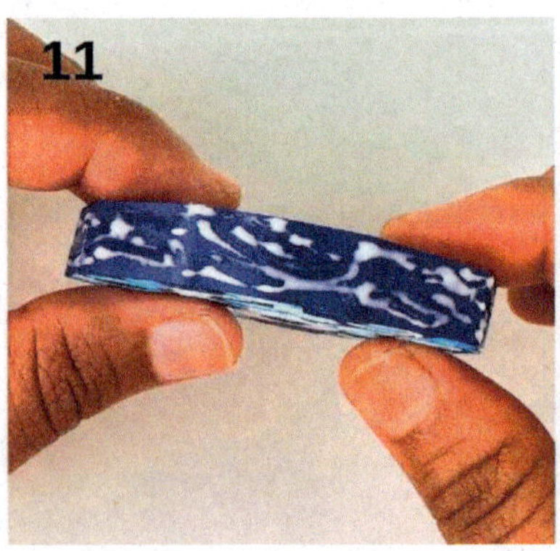

Apply glue to the outer rim of the bauble

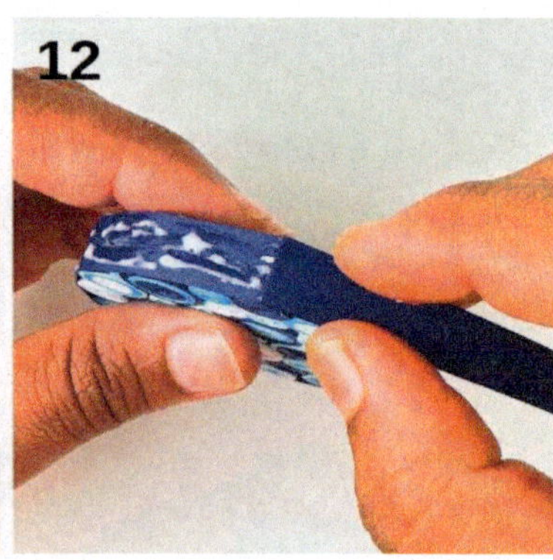

Attach a blue colour strip and wrap it around

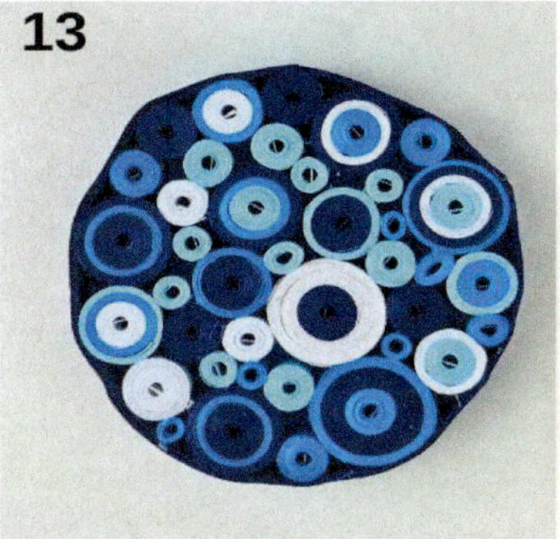

Base of the bauble is ready

For the top of the bauble, create a larger tight coil using a blue strip of paper

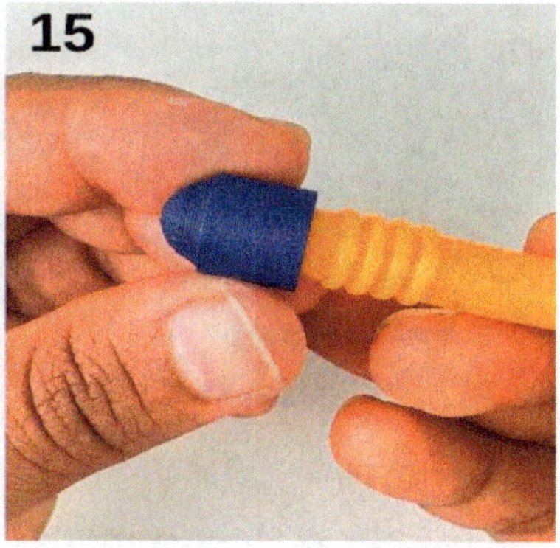

Use a quilling tool or any round object to shape the coil into a dome. This will be the cap for the bauble

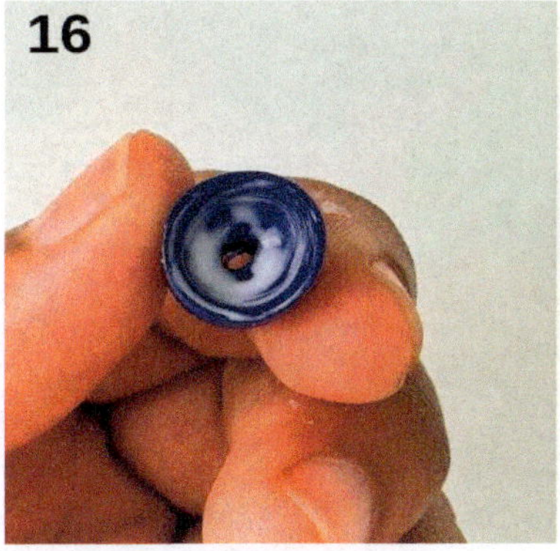

Spread glue to the inner side of the dome to retain its shape

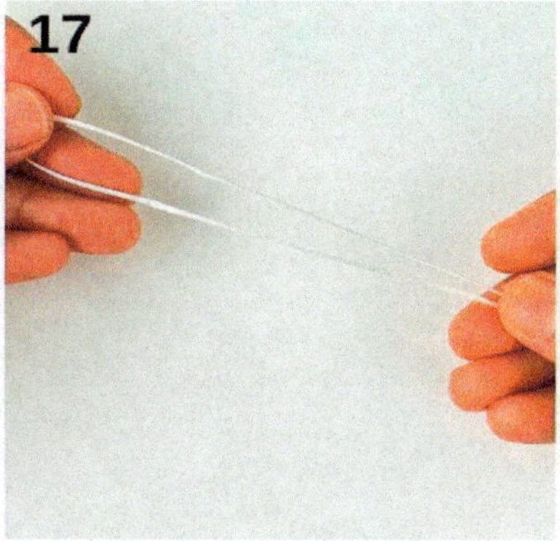

Use a string or thin satin ribbon of required length

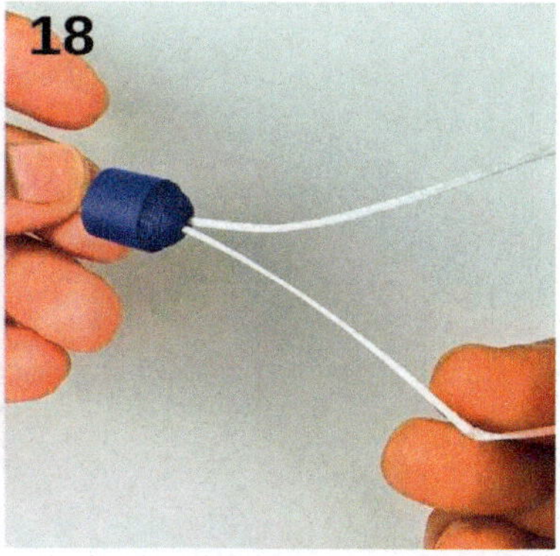

Insert the string through the centre of the cap

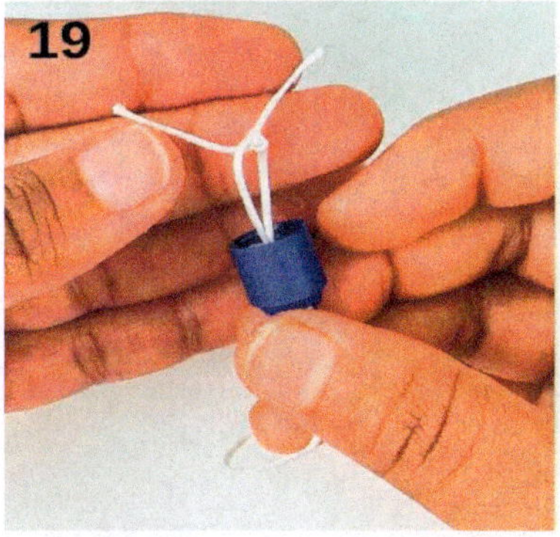

Tye a knot at the end to secure it

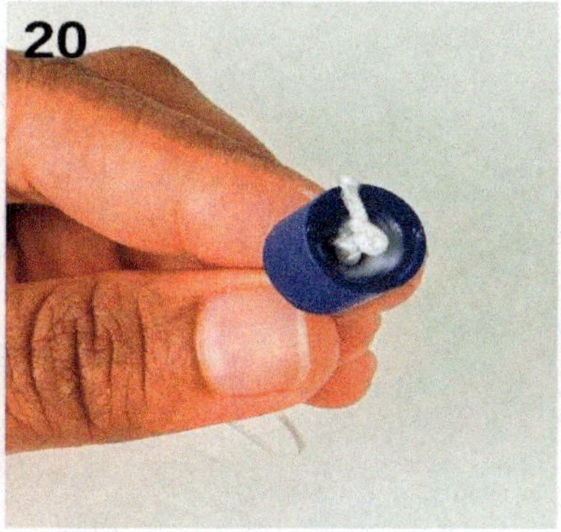

Cut the excess string and let the glue dry completely

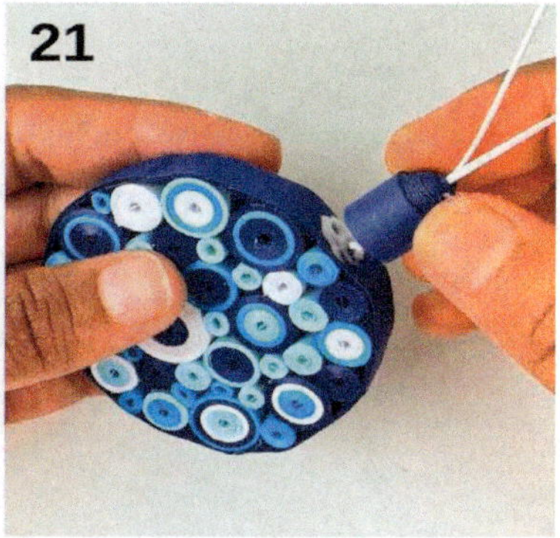

Apply little glue in the outer rim

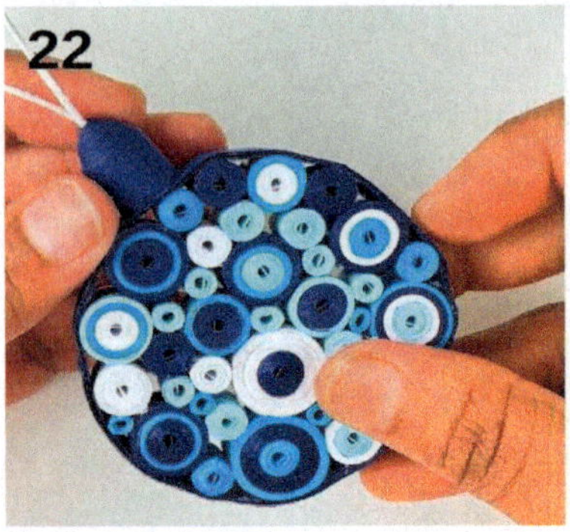

Glue the cap to the top of the bauble, making sure the string hangs freely from the top for easy hanging

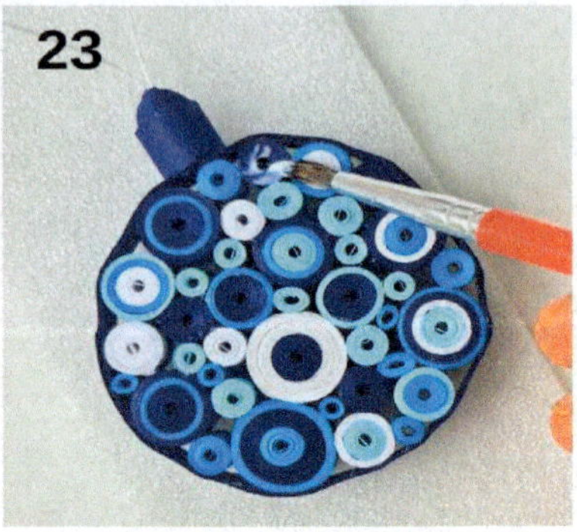

If needed, apply a thin layer of varnish along the front and back of the bauble to reinforce its shape

Allow the bauble to dry completely. Once everything is dry, your paper quilled bauble is ready to be hung on the Christmas tree!

POINSETTIA

Paper quilled poinsettia is a beautiful and intricate craft that uses rolled and shaped paper strips to recreate the iconic holiday flower. This handmade project is perfect for adding a festive touch to cards, ornaments, or seasonal decor. It's a creative way to bring the vibrant beauty of poinsettias into your Christmas celebrations.

Materials Needed:

- Quilling paper strips 10 mm wide in Red and Green
- Slotted Quilling tool
- White glue
- Small scissors
- Tweezers
- Quilling board / Circular ruler
- Fine brush
- Varnish (Optional)

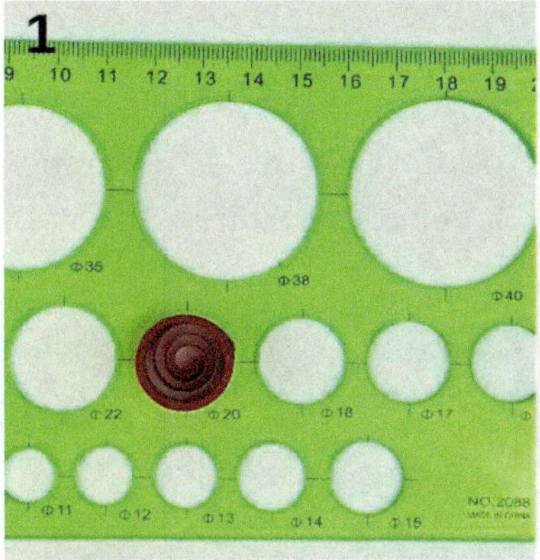

Glue the end of 2 red quilling strips and rolls into a loose coil and place the coil into a circular template (Size 20) to allow it to expand evenly. Secure the end with glue

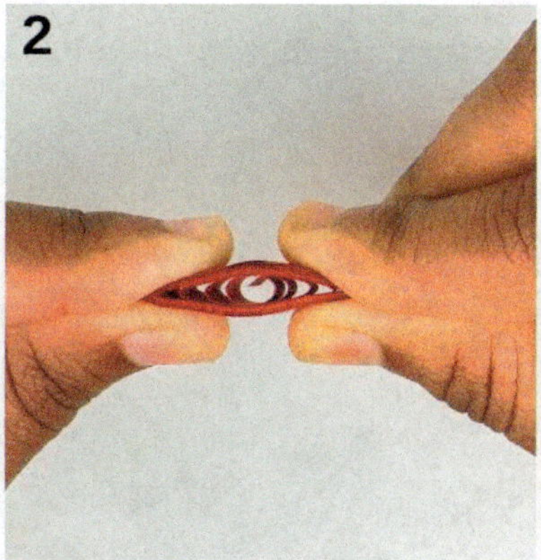

Pinch both ends to form a marquise shape

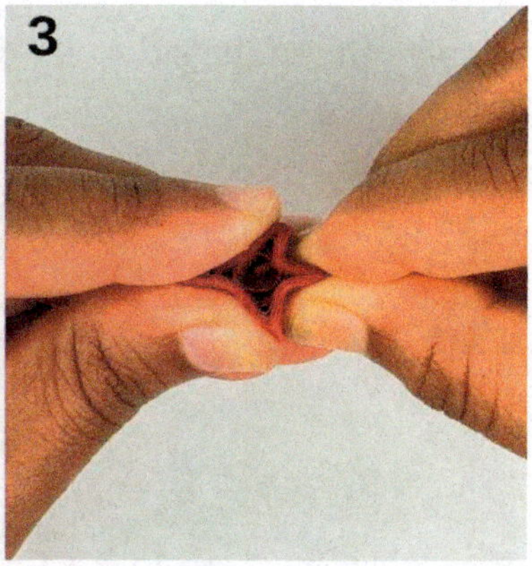

Gently press each marquise shape and pinch at 2 points, giving it a petal-like appearance

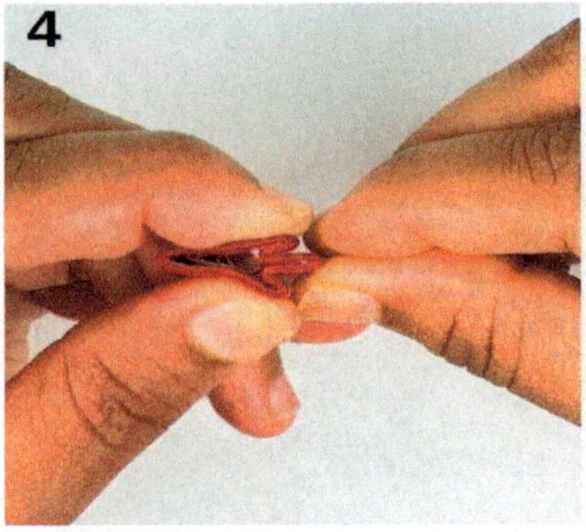

Repeat the pinching to create a petal shape with multiple folds

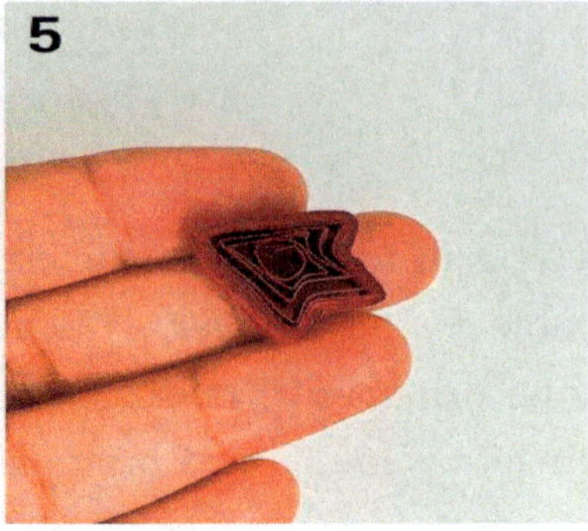

This will be the petal of the flower

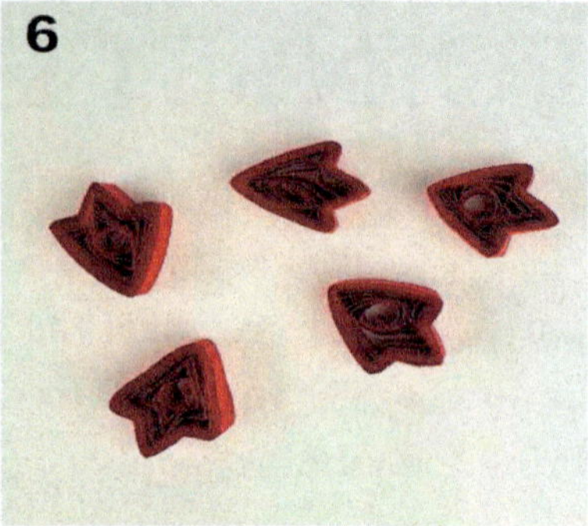

Repeat this process to create five red petals

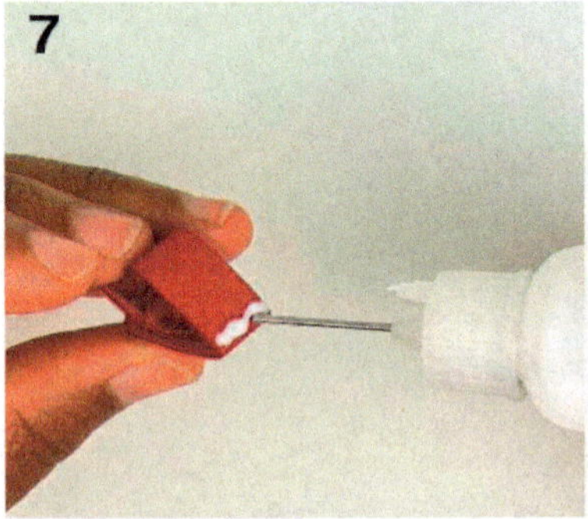

Apply glue to the sides of the red petal

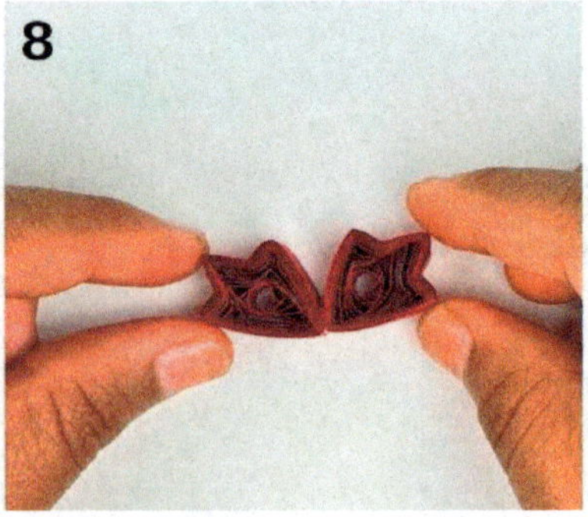

Attach another petal to it

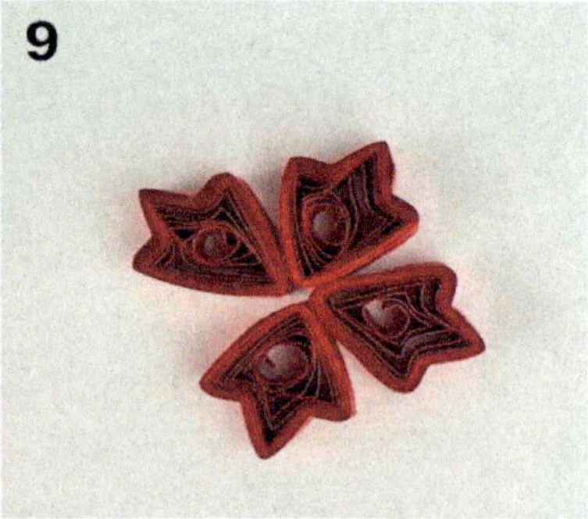

Repeat the process and arrange them in a circular pattern, forming the first layer of the poinsettia

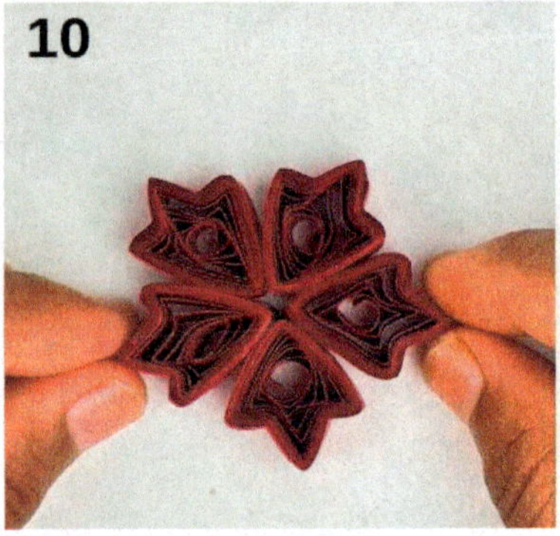

Continue gluing all the petals together to form the base of the flower

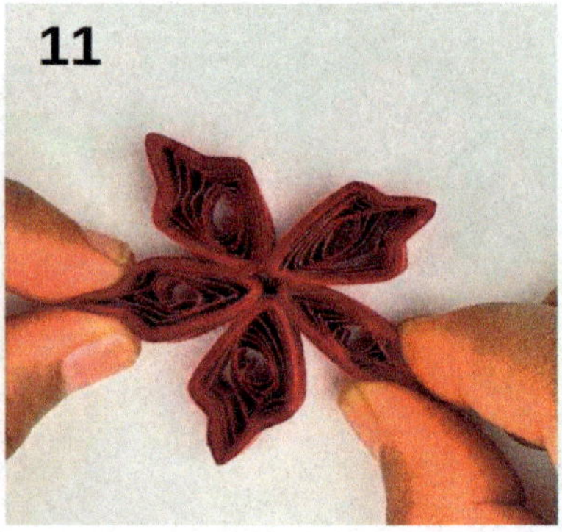

Press each petal as shown to create space for the leaves

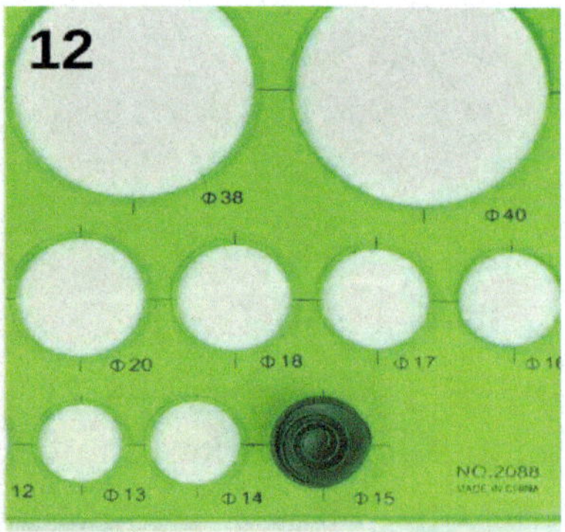

Roll 1 green colour strip into a loose coil and place the coil into a circular template (Size 15) to allow it to expand evenly. Secure the end with glue

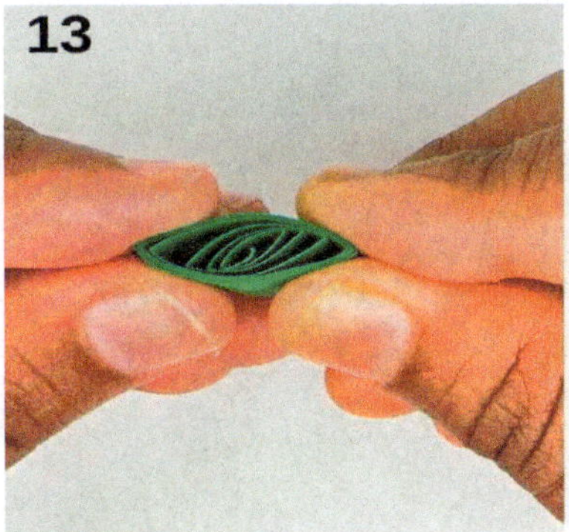

Pinch both ends to form a pointed oval or marquise shape

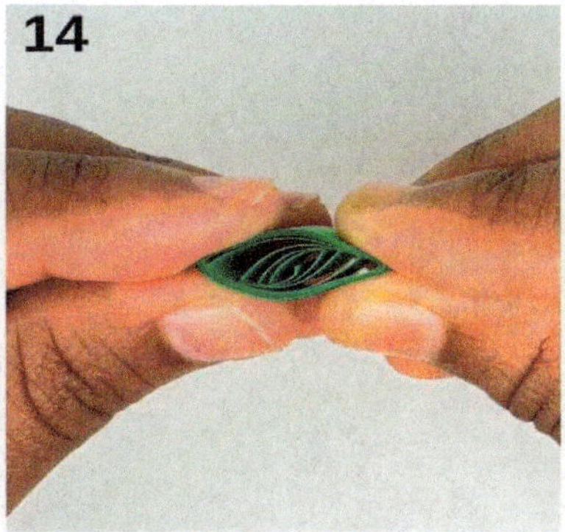

Repeat the same process as for the red petals

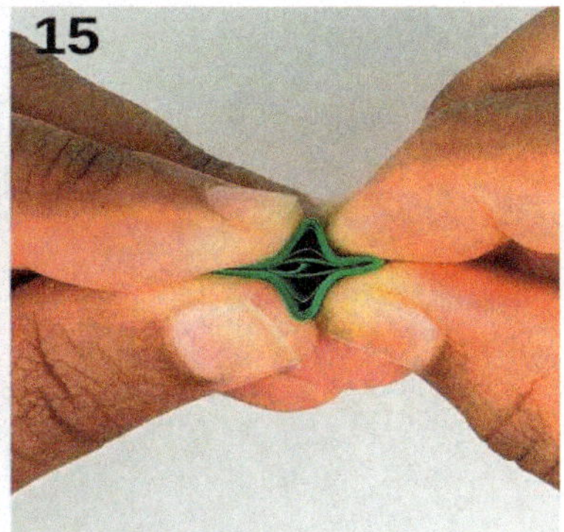

Gently press each marquise shape and pinch at 2 points, giving it a petal-like appearance

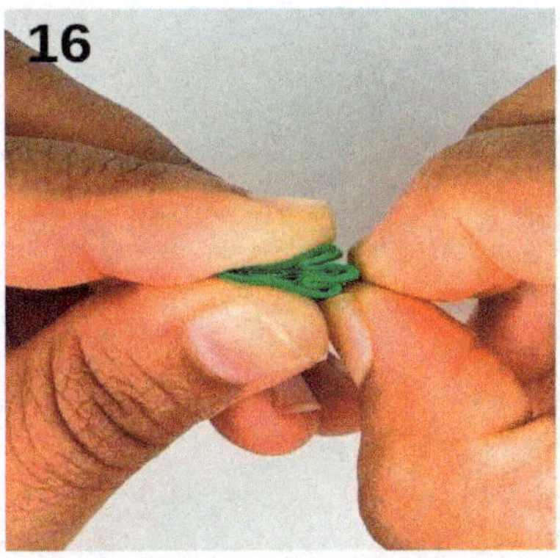

Repeat the pinching to create a petal shape with multiple folds

Create five green leaves in total

Apply glue to the green leaves and arrange them in between the red petals

Glue the leaves around the flower petals to form a complete Poinsettia

Ensure all the petals and leaves are well aligned and glued securely

Leave it to dry completely

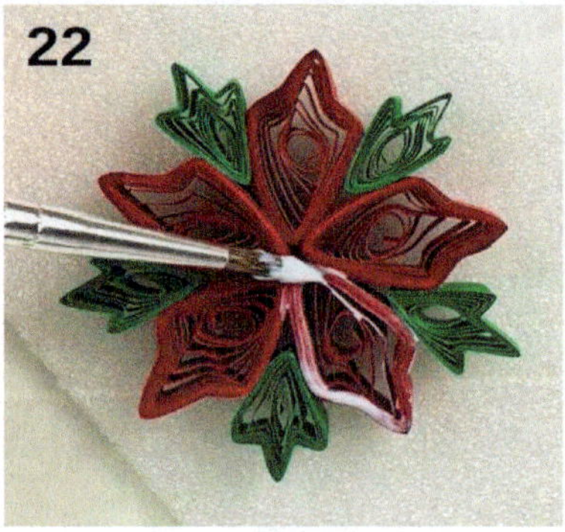

If needed, apply a thin layer of varnish along the front and back of the poinsettia to reinforce its shape

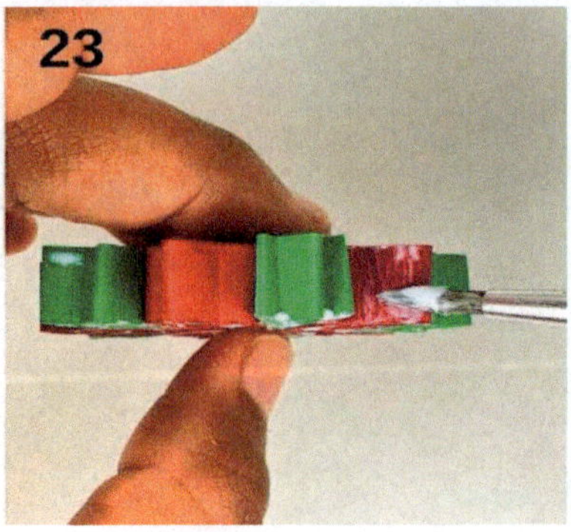

Apply a coat of varnish to the sides too

Once the poinsettia is fully assembled and dried, you can use it as a decoration for cards, ornaments, or other holiday crafts

FESTIVE CHARACTERS

REINDEER

Paper quilled reindeer is a charming and intricate craft that uses rolled and shaped paper strips to form a festive reindeer design. This handmade project adds a playful and creative touch to holiday cards, ornaments, or seasonal decor. It's a delightful way to capture the magic of Christmas in a unique, artistic way.

Materials Needed:

- Quilling paper strips 10 mm wide in 2 shades of Brown and Beige
- Quilling paper strips 3 mm wide in Black, Cream and Red
- Slotted Quilling tool
- White glue
- Small scissors
- Tweezers
- Quilling board / Circular ruler
- Fine brush
- Varnish (Optional)

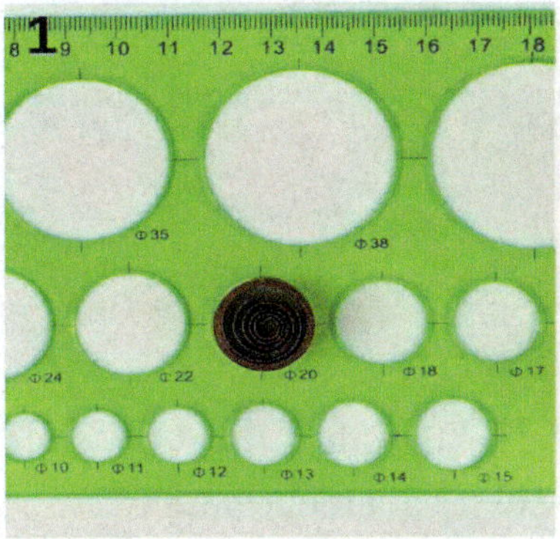

Attach the end of 2 light brown strips and roll into a coil and place the coil into a circular template (Size 20) to allow it to expand evenly. Secure the end with glue

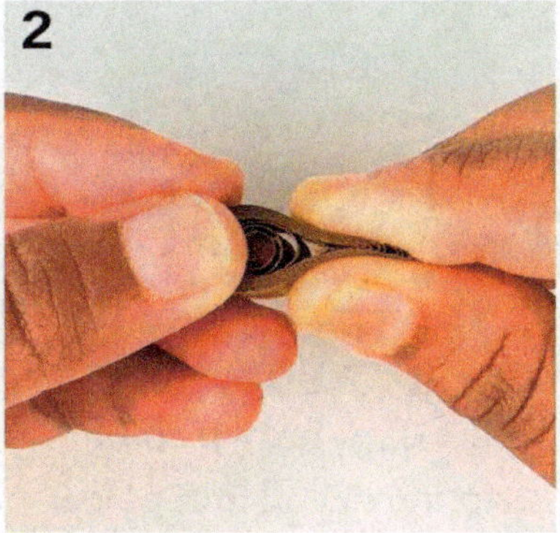

Shape it into a teardrop by pinching one side.

Repeat the above process to create another teardrop shape. Curve the ends of both the teardrops as shown in the next picture

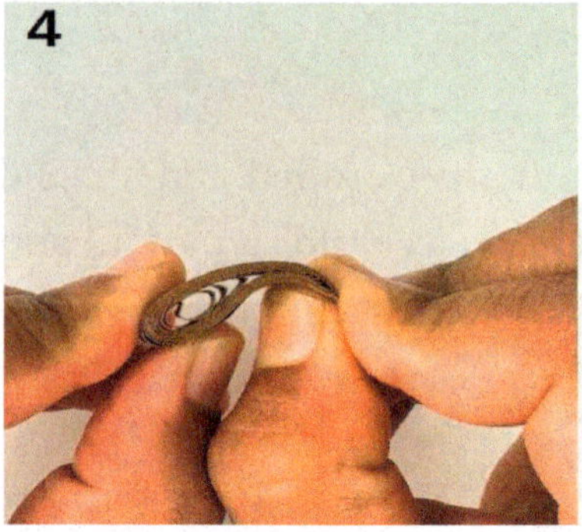

Gently curve the pointed end of the tear drop

Glue the ends of 7 light brown strips and roll into a coil and slightly loosen them. Attach the curved teardrop shape on top right of a larger brown coil

This will be reindeer's head

Attach another teardrop shape on top left of a larger brown coil

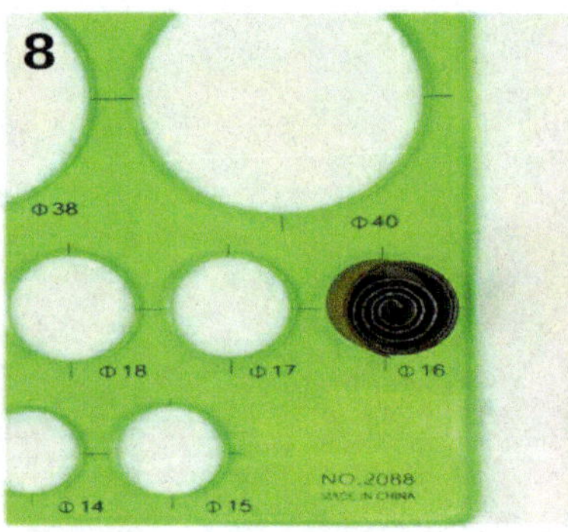

Roll 1 dark brown colour strip into a coil and place the coil into a circular template (Size 16) to allow it to expand evenly. Secure the end with glue

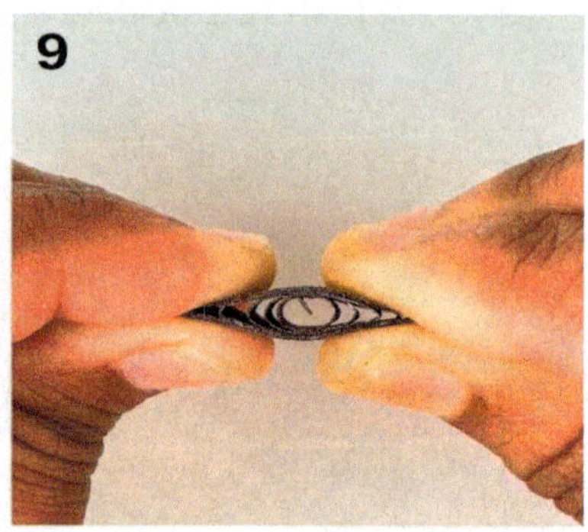

Pinch both ends of the coil to form an eye shape (marquise)

Repeat this step to create another identical marquise shape. This will be for antlers

Attach one to the top left of the head

Attach another on the top right of the head

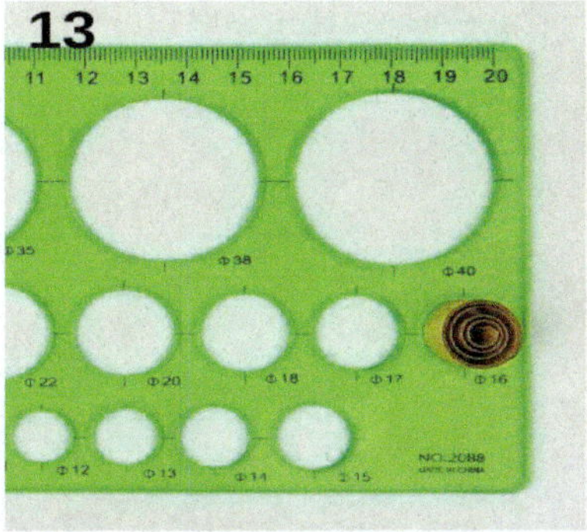

Roll 1 beige colour strip into a coil and place the coil into a circular template (Size 16) to allow it to expand evenly. Secure the end with glue

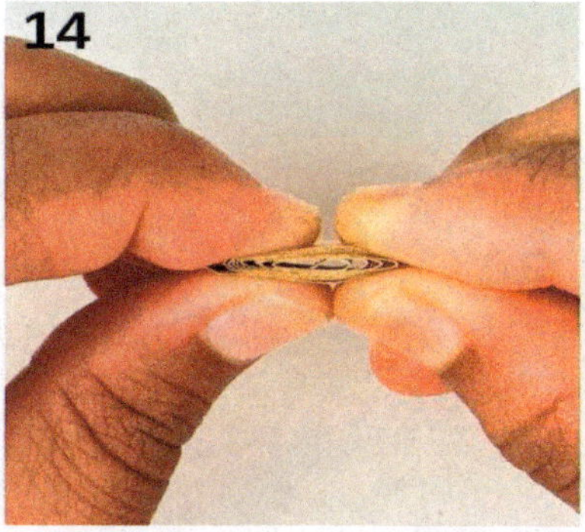

Pinch both ends of the coil to form an eye shape (marquise)

Repeat this step to create another identical marquise shape. These will be the reindeer's ears

Attach one ear to the right side of the reindeer's head

Attach the other ear to the left side of the reindeer's head

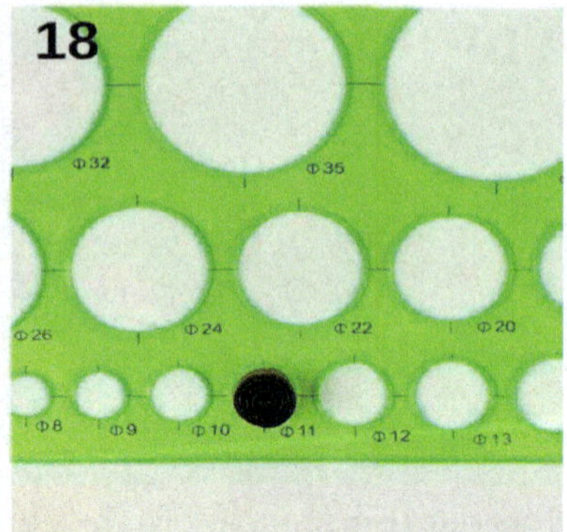

Roll ½ cut dark brown colour strip into a coil and place the coil into a circular template (Size 11) to allow it to expand evenly. Secure the end with glue

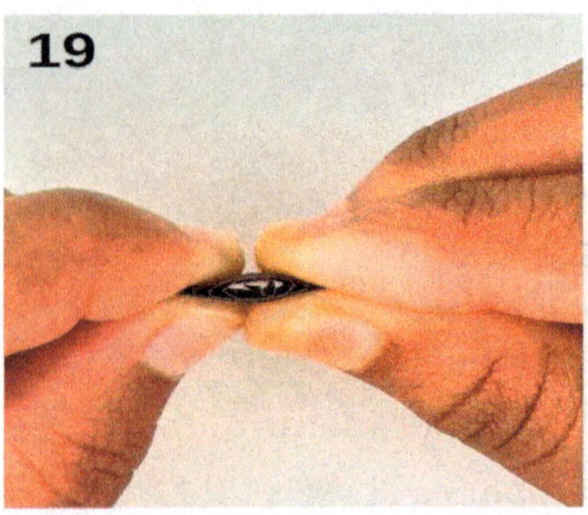

Pinch both ends of the coil to form an eye shape (marquise)

These are used for giving additional details to the antlers

Repeat the previous step to create multiple eye-shaped segments for the antlers (you'll need a total of 6 pieces, three for each antler)

Attach these marquise shapes at an angle on the top of the main antler

Glue three of these eye shapes on each side above the head to form the antlers.

The shapes should fan out like branches from a tree

Repeat the process and glue all the marquise shape

Make sure all antler segments are evenly spaced and securely glued

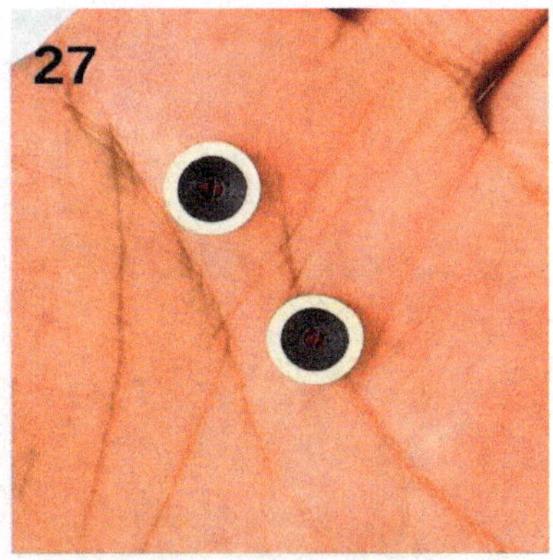

Glue the ends of 3mm single cream and black colour strip and roll into a tight coil starting from the black colour strip and secure the end with glue. This will be the eyes of the reindeer. Make 2 eyes in similar size.

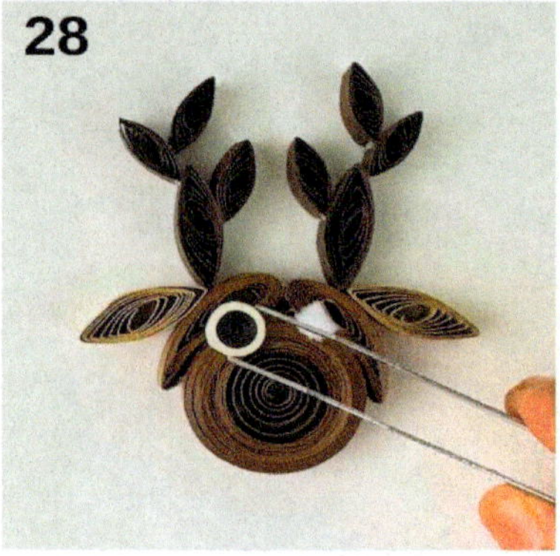

Place a small amount of glue on the back of the eye and attach it to the reindeer's face just below the ears

Attach the other eye as shown

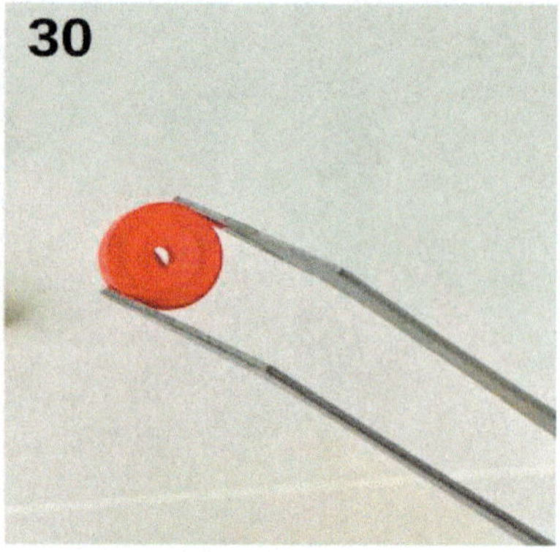

Create a red tight coil for the nose with 3mm red colour strip

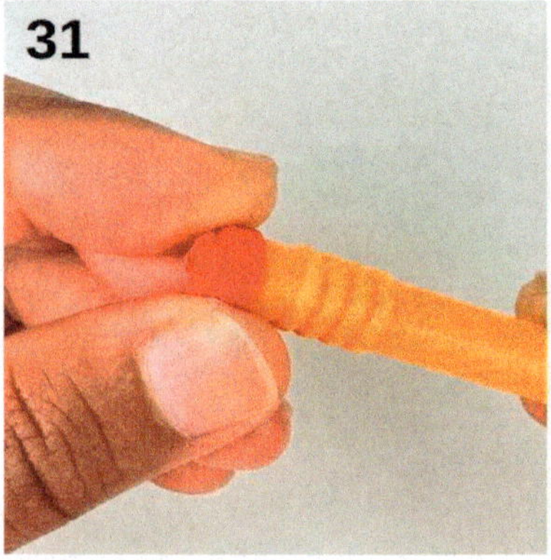

Slightly shape them into a dome by pressing the centre gently

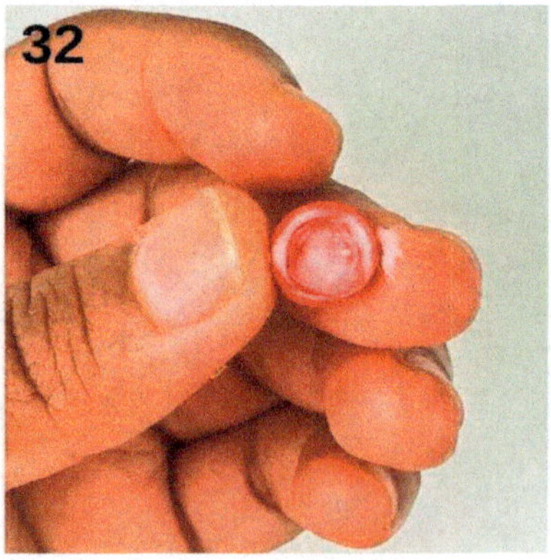

Spread glue to the inner side of the dome to retain its shape

Glue the red nose in the centre of the face, below the eyes

If needed, apply a thin layer of varnish along the front and back of the reindeer to reinforce its shape

Once dry, your paper quilled reindeer is ready to be used as a holiday decoration

SNOWMAN

Paper quilled snowman is a fun and festive craft that uses rolled and shaped paper strips to create an adorable snowman design. This handmade project is perfect for holiday cards, ornaments, or winter-themed decor, adding a creative and personal touch to your seasonal decorations. It's a whimsical way to celebrate the joy of the winter season.

Materials Needed:

- Quilling paper strips 10 mm wide in White, Black and Brown
- Quilling paper strips 3 mm wide in Orange, Red and Black
- Slotted Quilling tool
- White glue
- Small scissors
- Tweezers
- Quilling board / Circular ruler
- Fine brush
- Varnish (Optional)

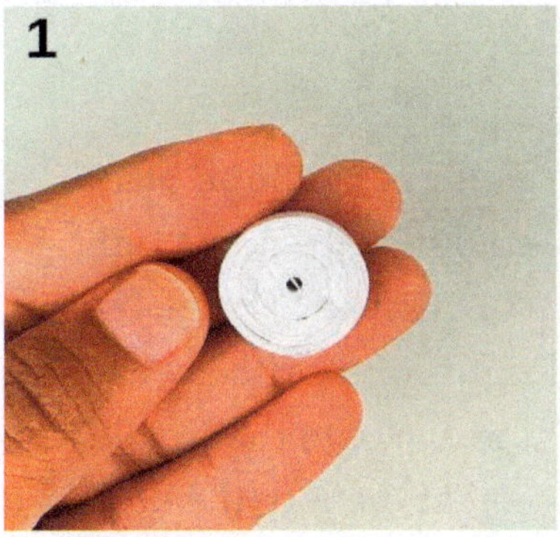

Glue 5 white quilling strips and start rolling into a tight coil. This will be the head of the snowman

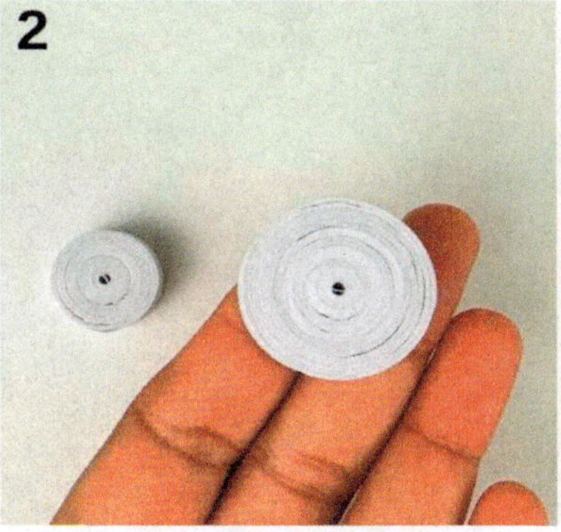

Glue 11 white quilling strips and start rolling into a tight coil. This will be the body of the snowman

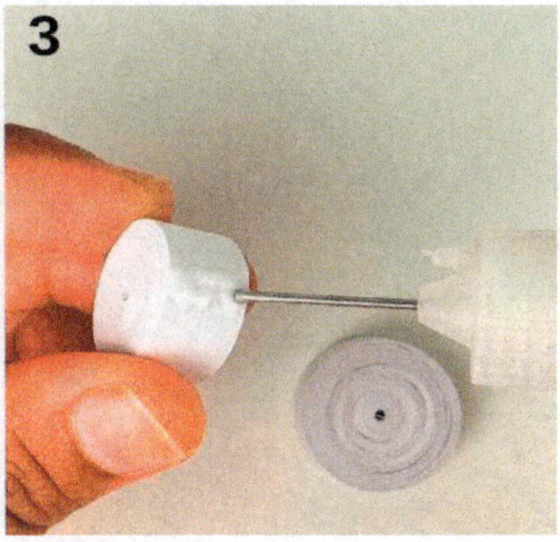

Apply glue to the smaller coil

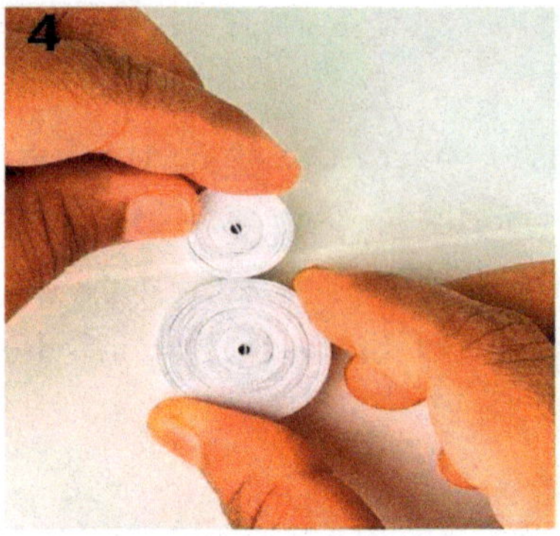

Place it on top of the larger coil to create the snowman's body and head

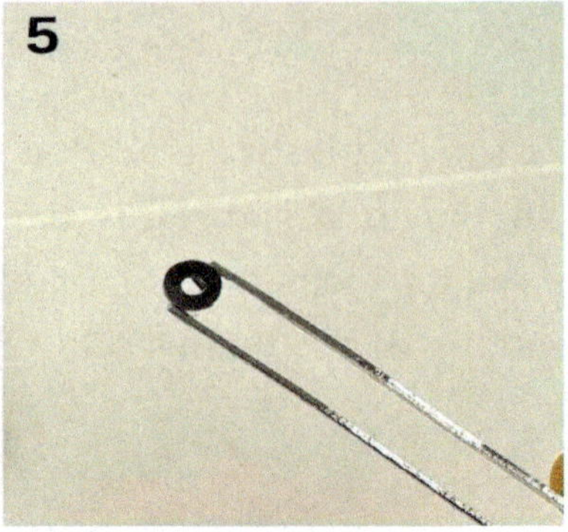

Roll ½ cut 3 mm black colour strip into tight coil to create buttons

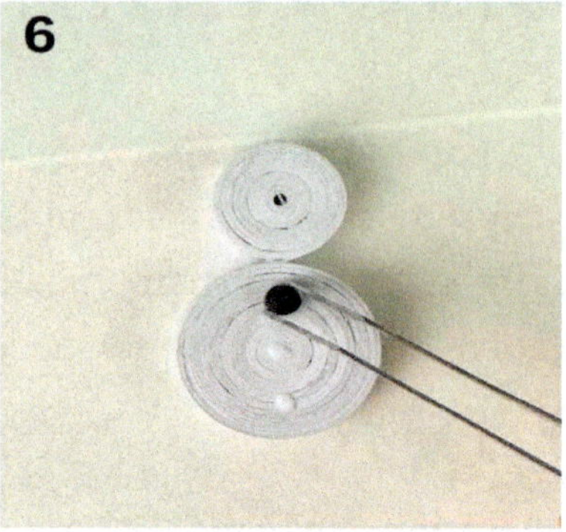

Glue the black coil on the larger body coil

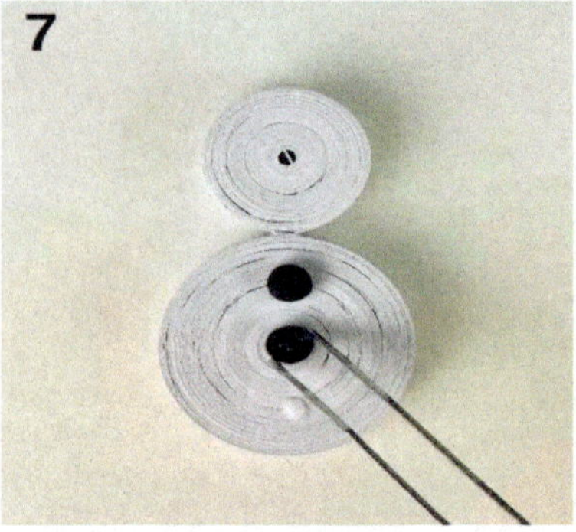

Glue the second button below the first button

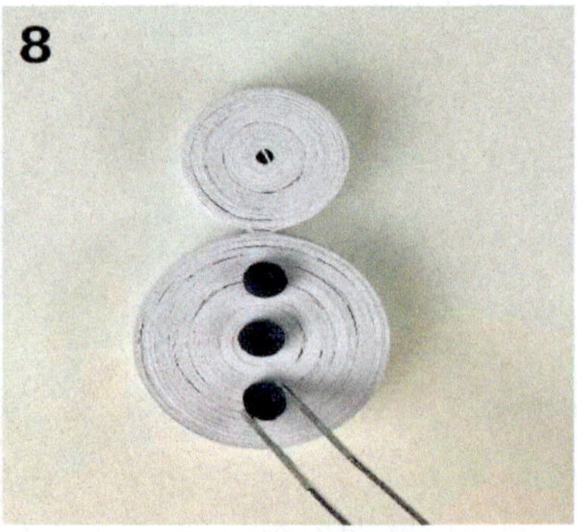

Glue three black coils vertically onto the larger body coil for the buttons

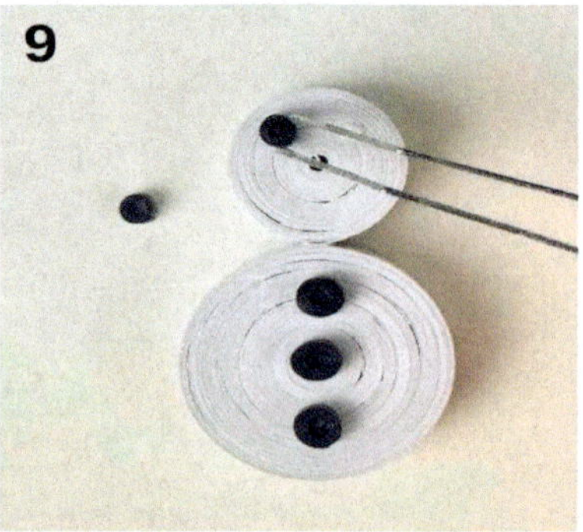

Roll 1/4 cut 3mm black colour strips into a tight coil. Create two small black tight coils for the eyes. Glue the eye onto the smaller coil at the top (the head)

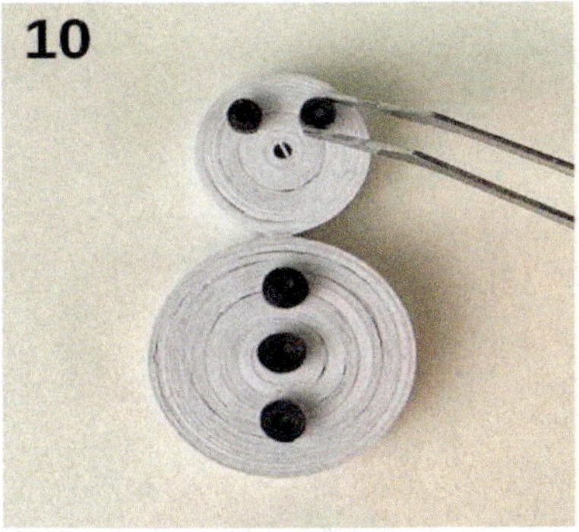

Glue the other eye too

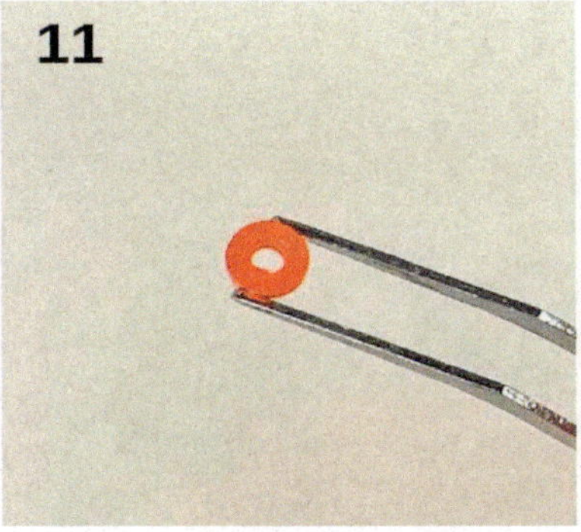

Roll a ½ cut3mm orange strip into a tight coil

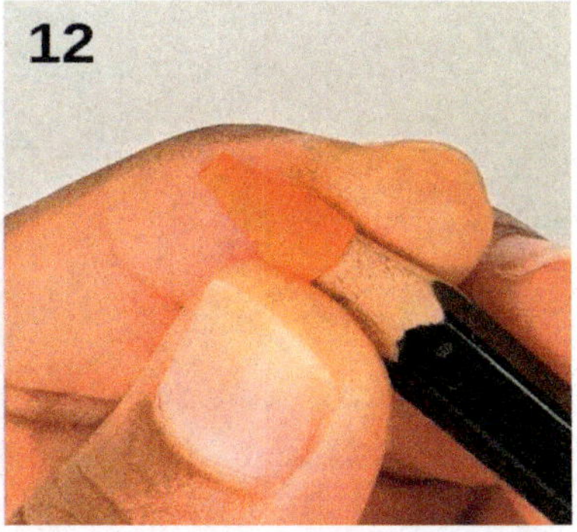

Insert a pencil tip and shape it slightly to resemble a carrot by pressing one end into a cone shape

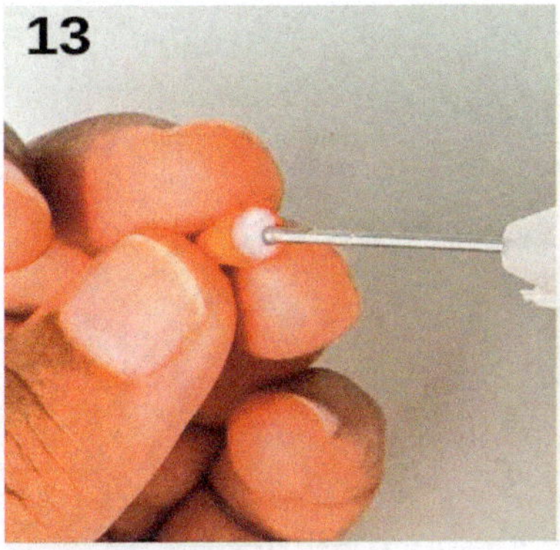

Spread the glue to the inner side of the carrot

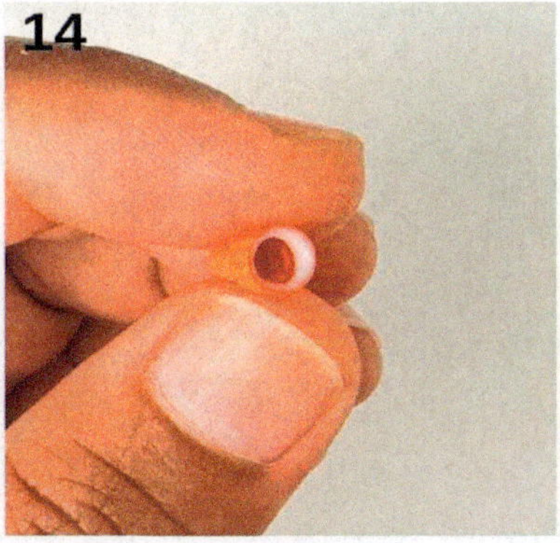

Let it dry so that it can retain the shape

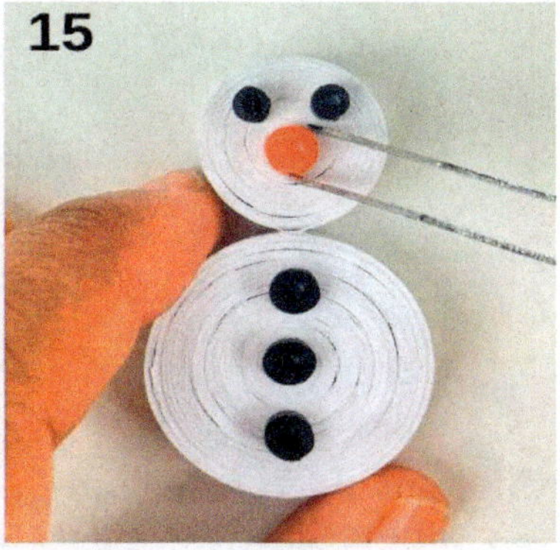

Glue the orange nose in the centre of the face, just below the eyes

Glue the ends of 12 (3mm) black strips and roll it into a tight coil

Glue the ends of 6 (10 mm) black strips and roll it into a tight coil

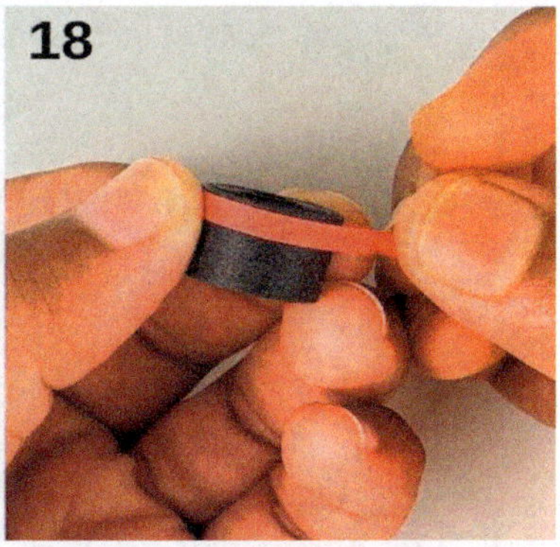

Add a small 3mm red strip around the hat's brim to give it a festive look

Let it dry well

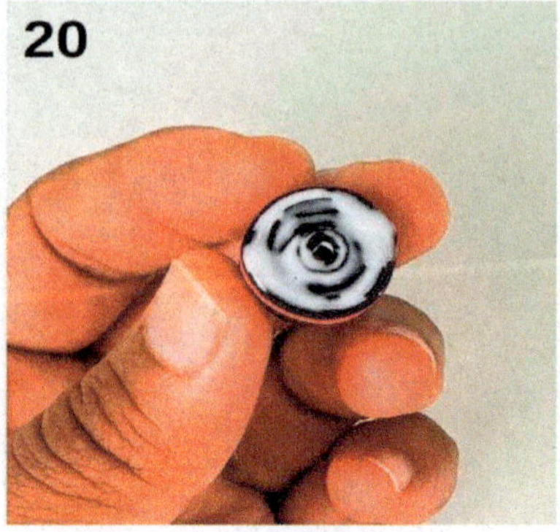

Apply glue to the bottom of the black coil

Place it on top of the larger black tight coil and leave it to dry

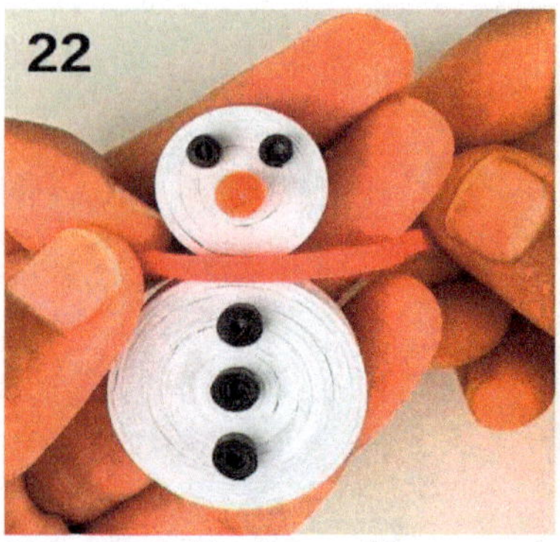

Cut a small piece of 3mm red quilling strip for the scarf and glue it around the space between the head and the body

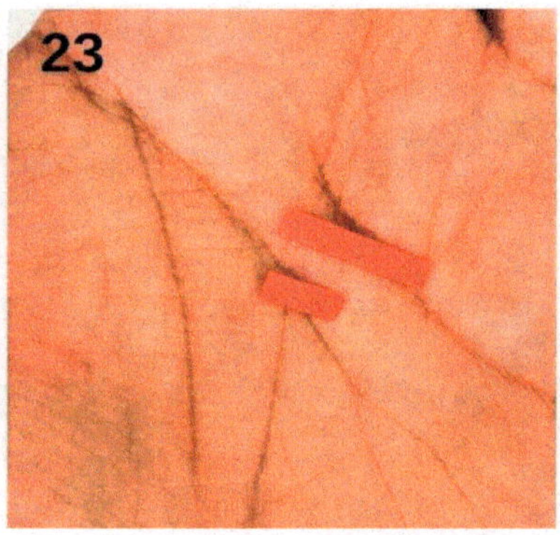

Cut 2 small 3mm red strips (approximately 1.2 cm and 0.6 cm)

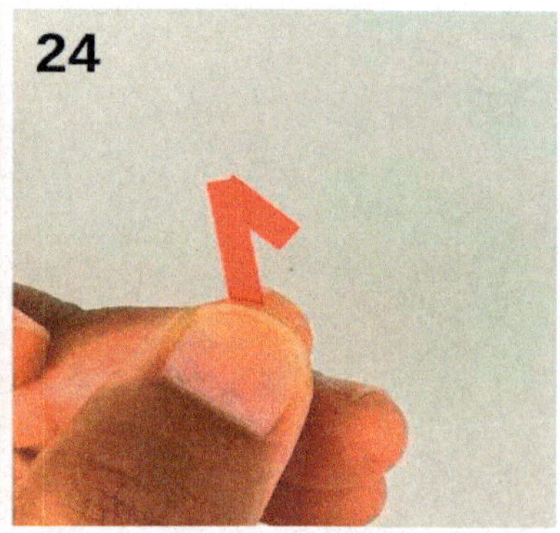

Shape it into an "L" or "V" shape to represent the way a scarf would hang

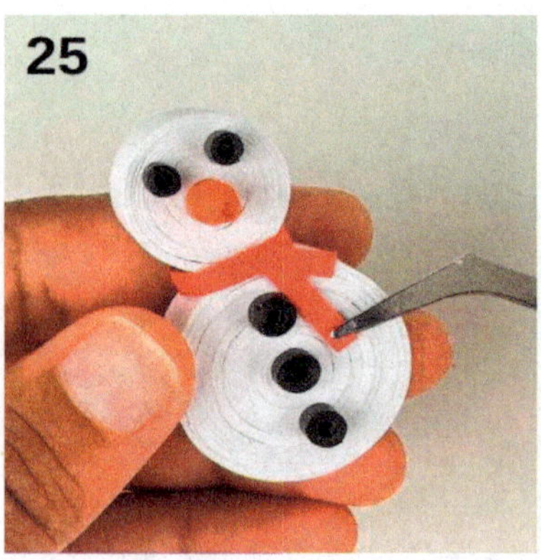

Glue the shape on the front of the scarf on the snowman's neck area

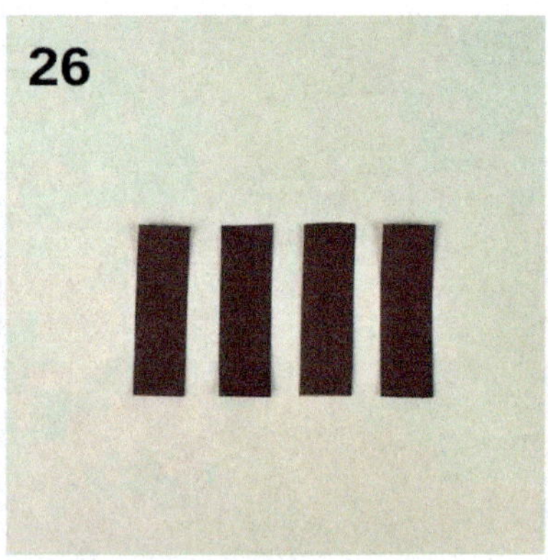

Cut four small strips of brown quilling paper for the arms

Glue two pieces together to create a thicker arm

Glue all the 4 small strips one over the other

Bend slightly to create a more natural arm shape

Cut it into two lengths (2cm and 0.7cm)

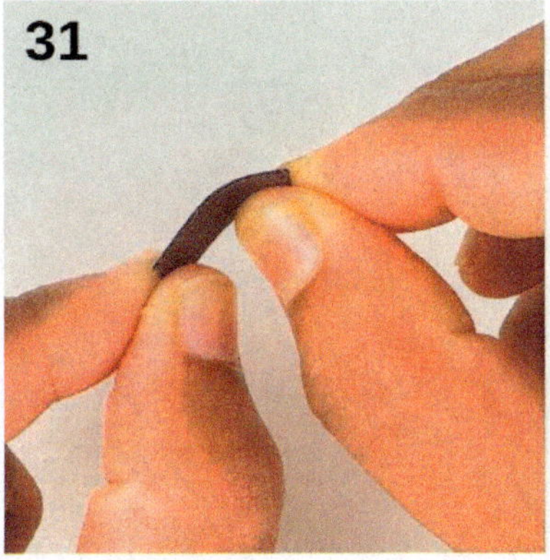

Bend slightly

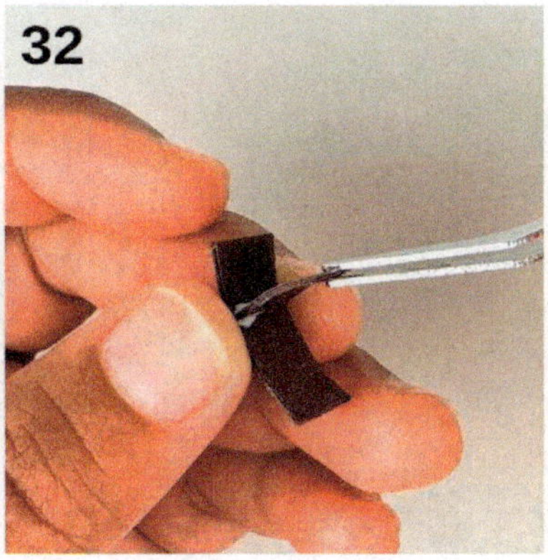

Glue the large piece and the small piece as shown

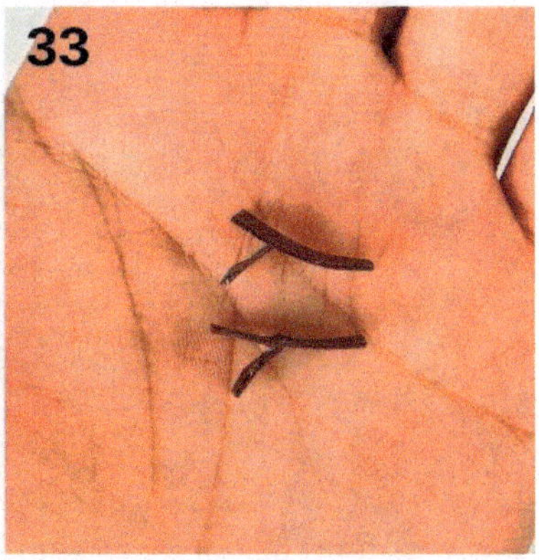

Repeat this for the second arm

Glue the arms to the sides of the snowman's body, angling them as desired

Adjust the arms and scarf as needed to ensure they look natural

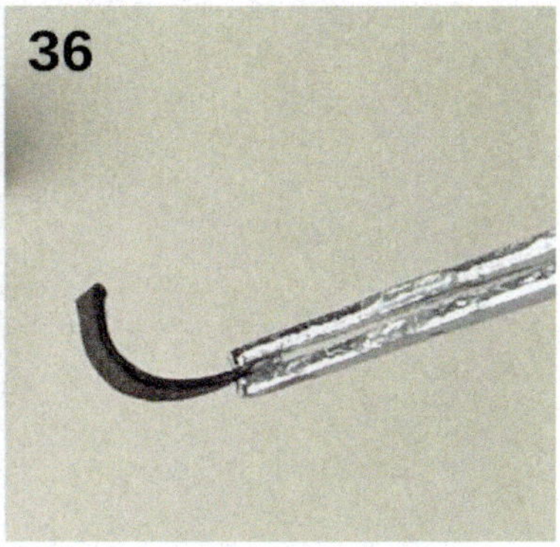

Bend a small 3mm black colour strip

Attach it below the nose as shown

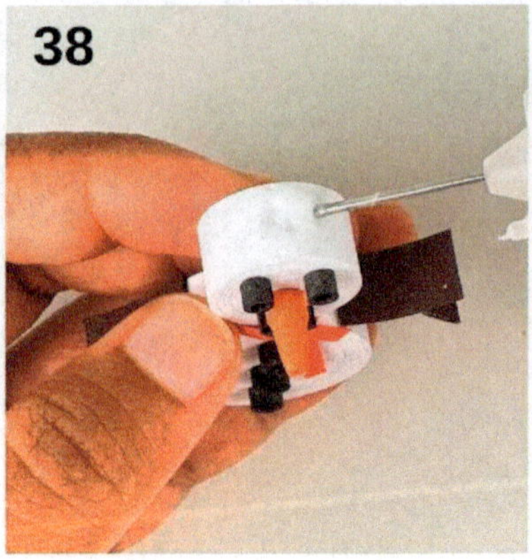

Apply glue to the top of the head

Attach the hat securely

Ensure all parts are glued and aligned properly

If needed, apply a thin layer of varnish along the front and back of the snowman to reinforce its shape

Allow it to dry completely before handling

PENGUIN

Paper quilled penguin is a playful and intricate craft that uses rolled and shaped paper strips to form a charming penguin design. This handmade project is ideal for holiday cards, ornaments, or winter decorations, adding a fun and creative touch to your seasonal decor. It's a delightful way to bring some winter cheer with a whimsical, personal flair.

Materials Needed:

- Quilling paper strips 10 mm wide in White, Black, Yellow, Cream and Red
- Quilling paper strips 3 mm wide in Black and Yellow
- Slotted Quilling tool
- White glue
- Small scissors
- Tweezers
- Quilling board / Circular ruler
- Fine brush
- Varnish (Optional)

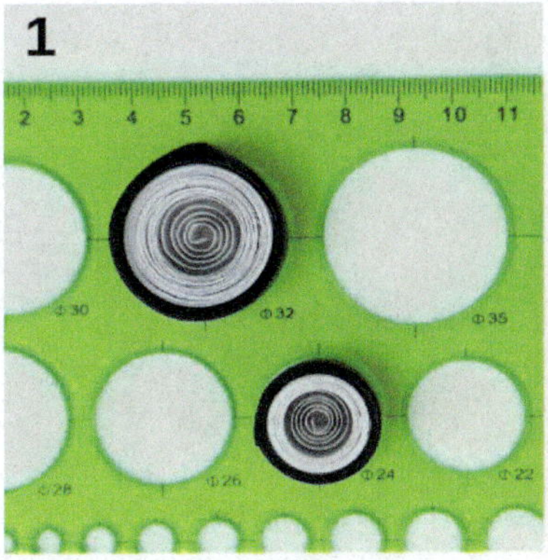

For head glue 4 white & 3 black strips and roll into a coil, place it into a circular template (Size 24). For the body glue 7 white strips & 4 black strips and roll into a coil, place it into a circular template (Size 32) to allow it to expand. Secure the ends with the glue

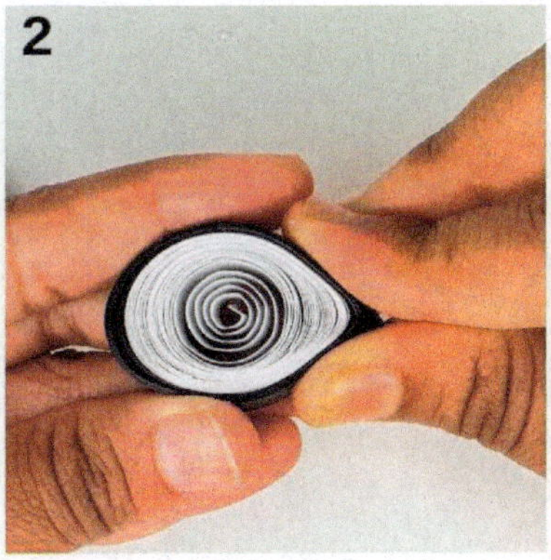

Pinch one end of the larger coil to form a teardrop shape

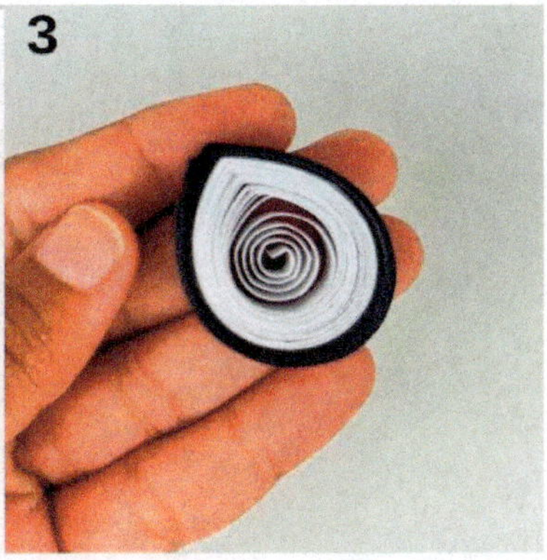

This will be the body of the penguin

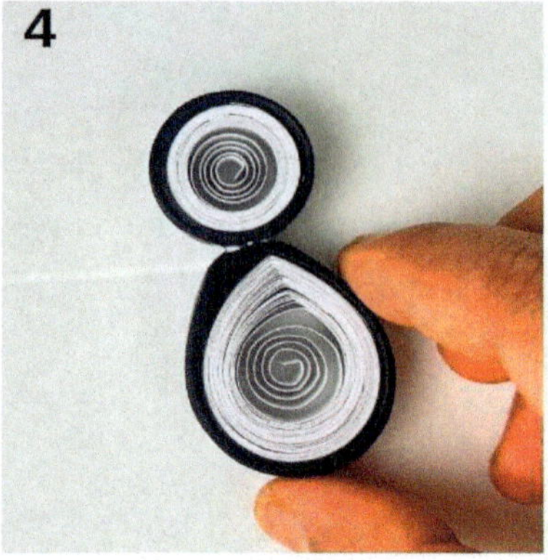

Glue the head coil onto the body coil as shown in the images

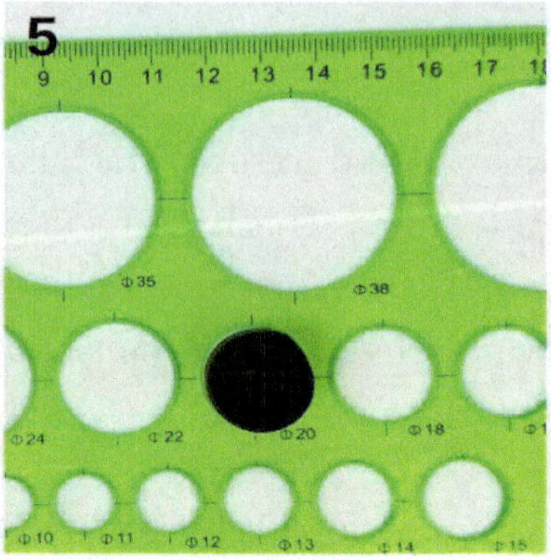

Glue the ends of three black strips and roll into a coil and place the coil into a circular template (Size 20) to allow it to expand evenly. Secure the ends with the glue

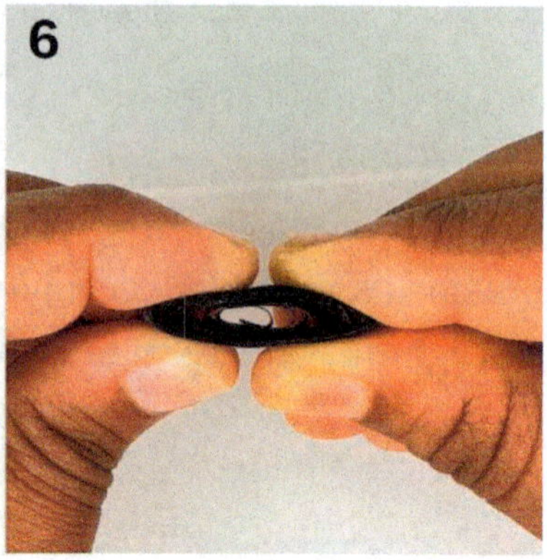

Pinch the coil at opposite ends to create a marquise

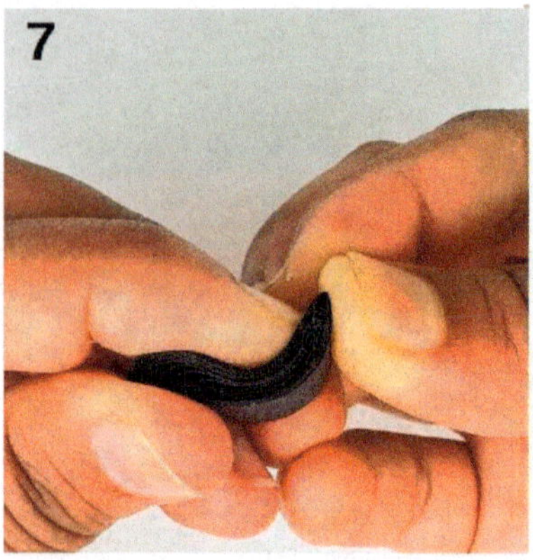

Shape them into crescents by pinching both ends slightly

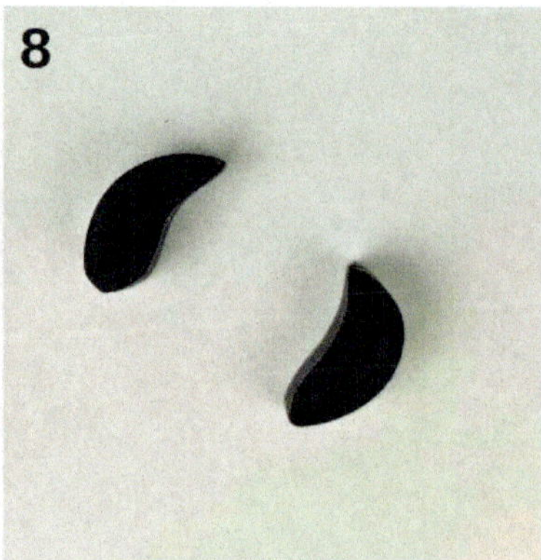

Create two similar shapes. These will be used as the penguin's wings

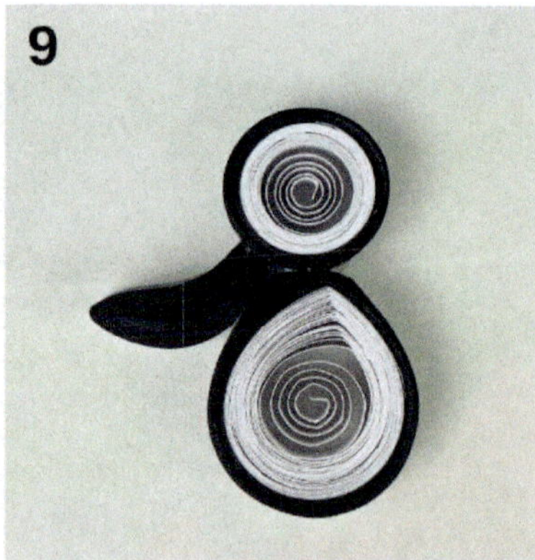

Glue the crescent-shaped wing on one side of the penguin's body.

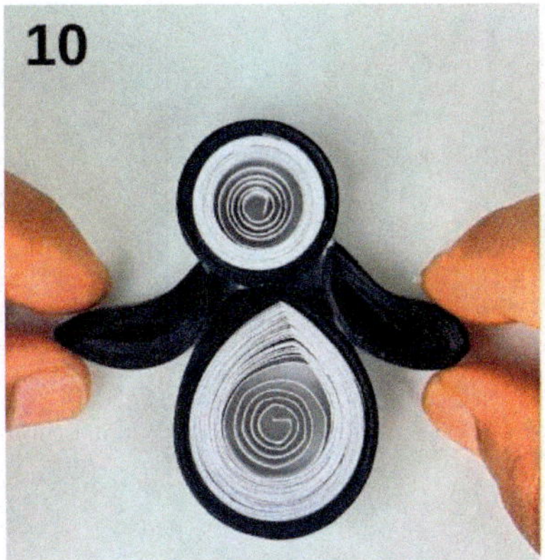

Glue the wing on the other side of the penguin's body.

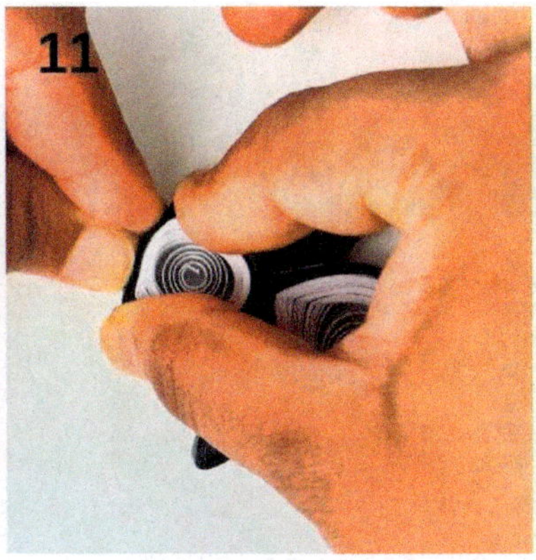

Flatten the head of the penguin slightly

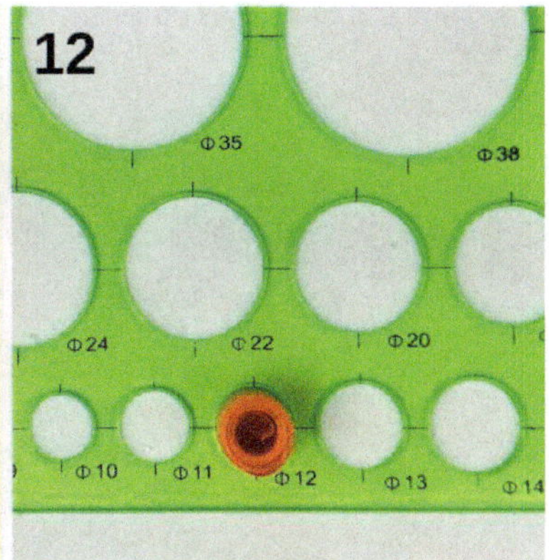

Glue the ends of two yellow strips and roll into a coil and place the coil into a circular template (Size 12) to allow it to expand evenly. Secure the ends with the glue

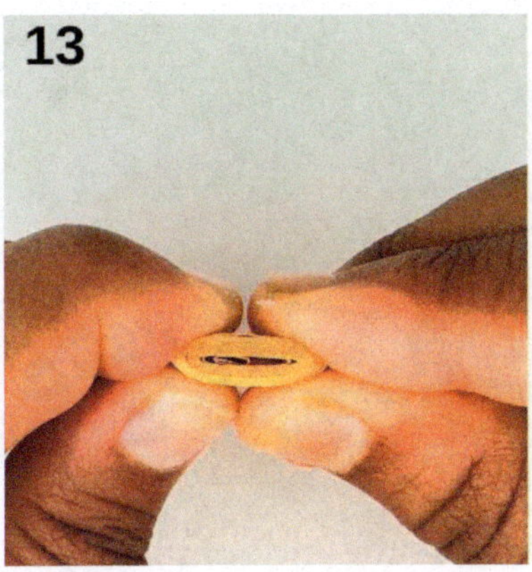

Shape them into small oval by pinching both the sides

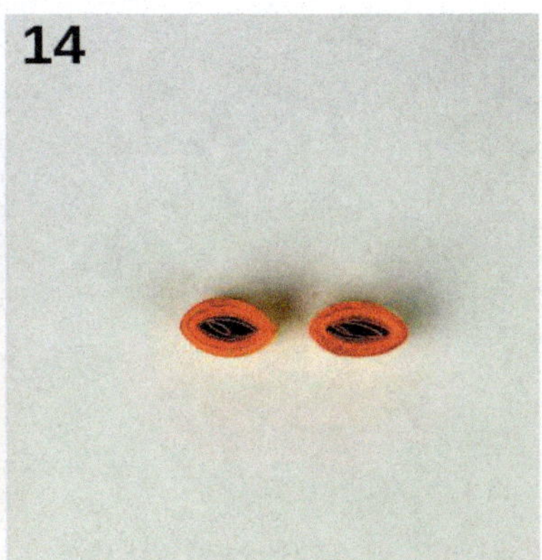

Make 2 of them. These will serve as the penguin's feet

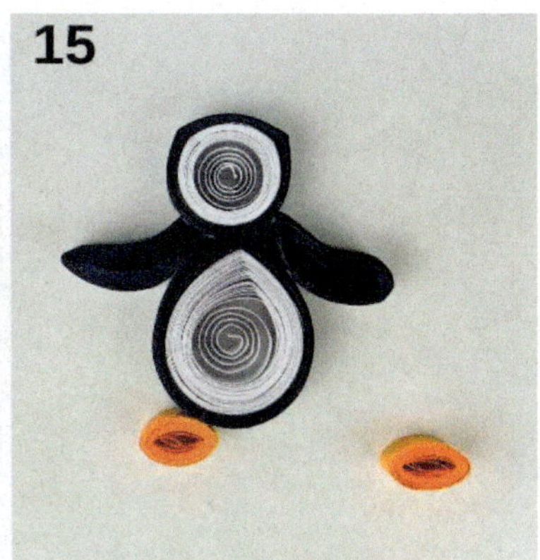

Glue the feet at the bottom of the body coil

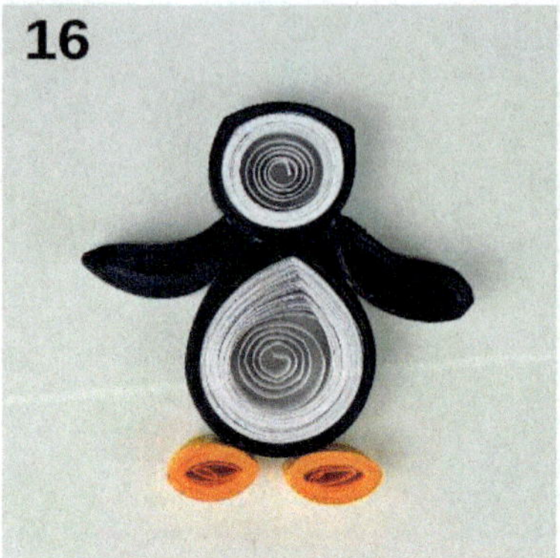

Let it dry well

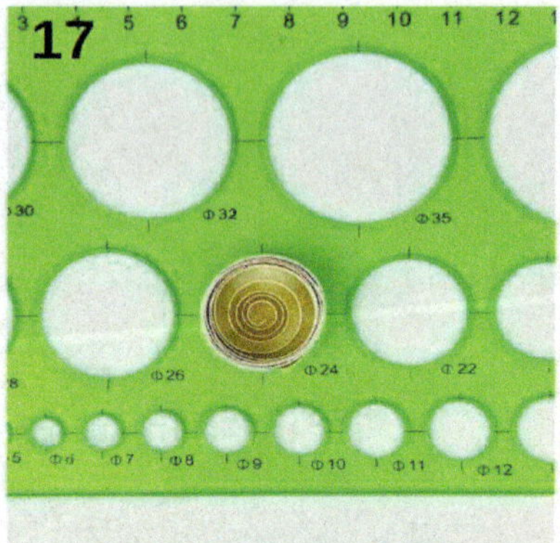

Glue the ends of three cream colour strips and roll into a coil and place the coil into a circular template (Size 24) to allow it to expand evenly. Secure the ends with the glue

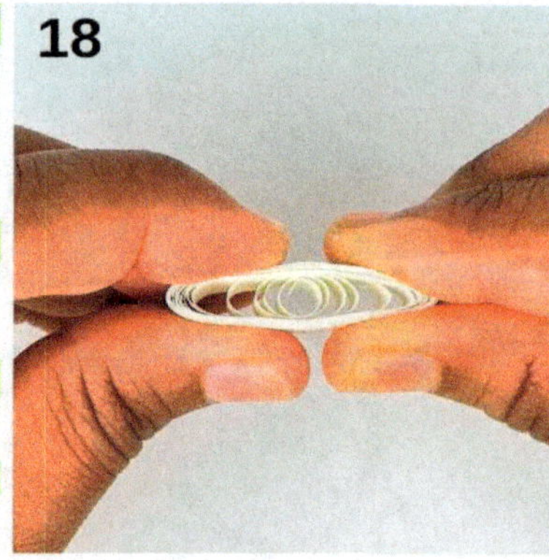

Roll a cream-coloured strip into a tight coil and shape it into an oval by pinching both ends.

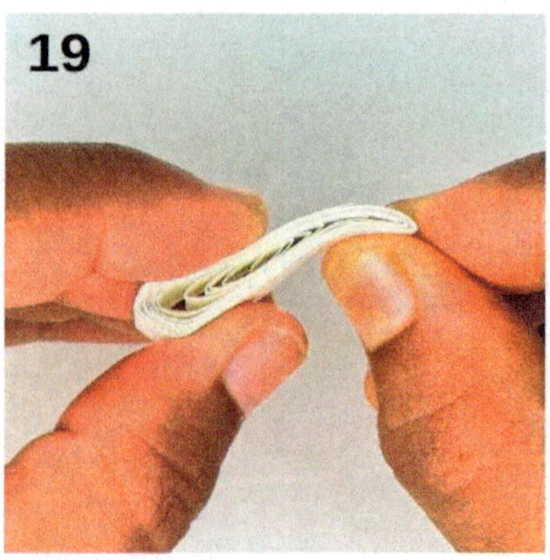

Slightly make a curve at one end. This will be the base of the Santa hat

Attach it to the top of the head

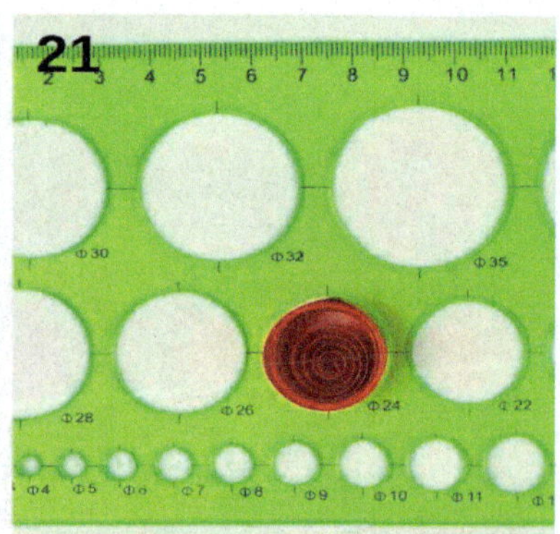

Glue the ends of three red colour strips and roll into a coil and place the coil into a circular template (Size 24) to allow it to expand evenly. Secure the ends with the glue

Press it against the index finger and flatten it

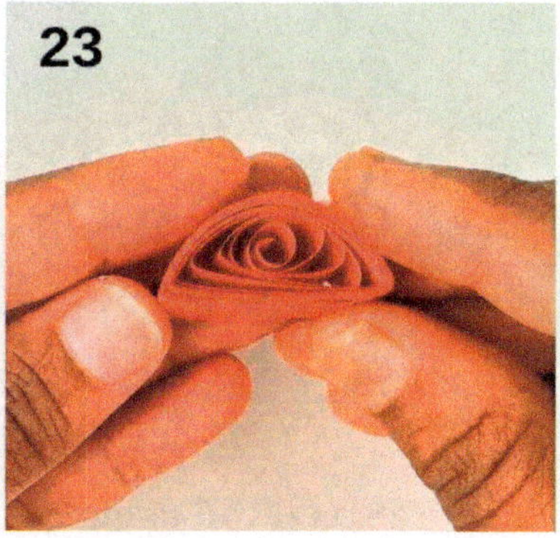

Pinch at two points to create a semicircle

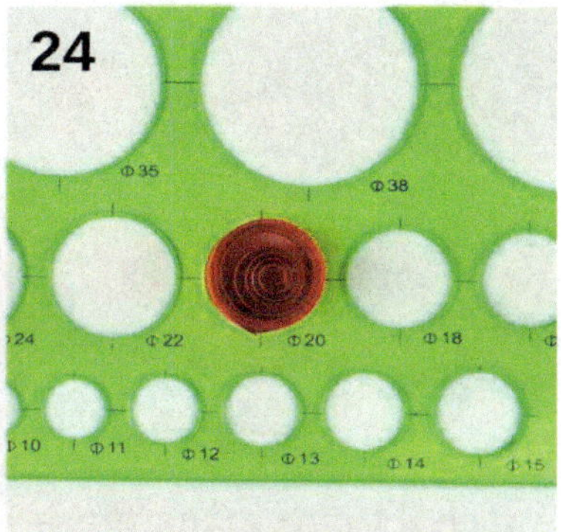

Glue the ends of two red colour strips and roll into a coil and place the coil into a circular template (Size 20) to allow it to expand evenly. Secure the ends with the glue

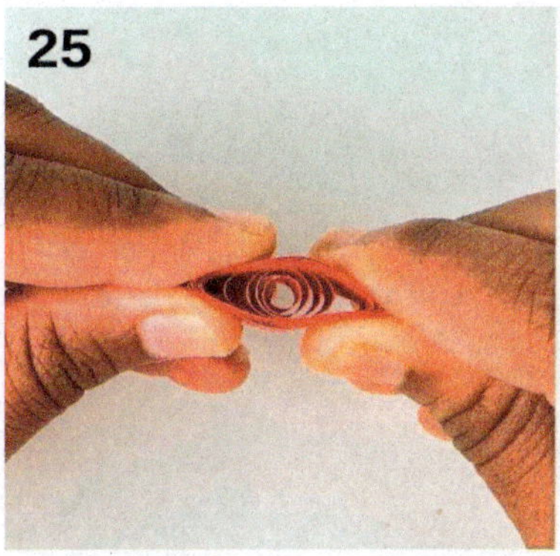

Pinch at opposite ends to create a marquise shape

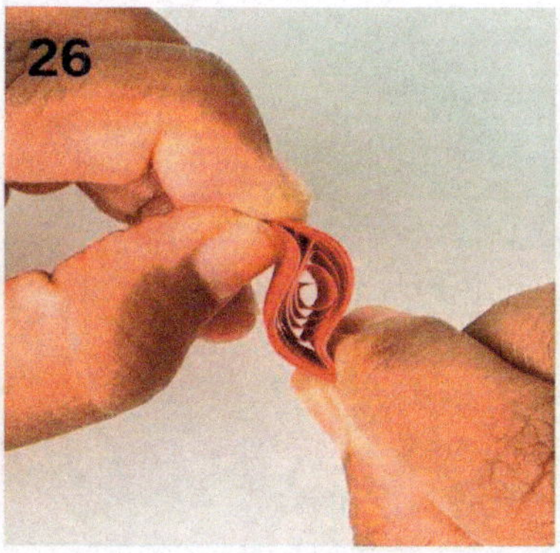

Bend the ends in opposite direction

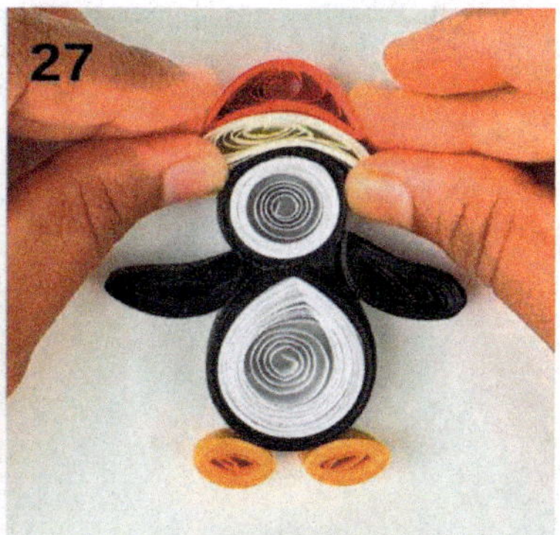

Slightly curve the red semicircle and attach it on top of the cream base. This forms the top part of the Santa hat

Attach the curves marquise on the side of the semicircle

Create a small coil using a cream strip for the pom-pom of the hat and glue it to the end of the hat

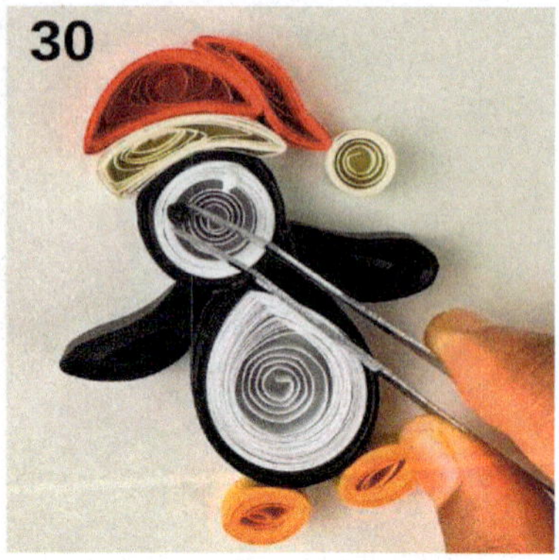

Roll ¼ cut 3mm black strips into tight coils. Make two of them for the eyes. Glue the eye onto the penguin's face

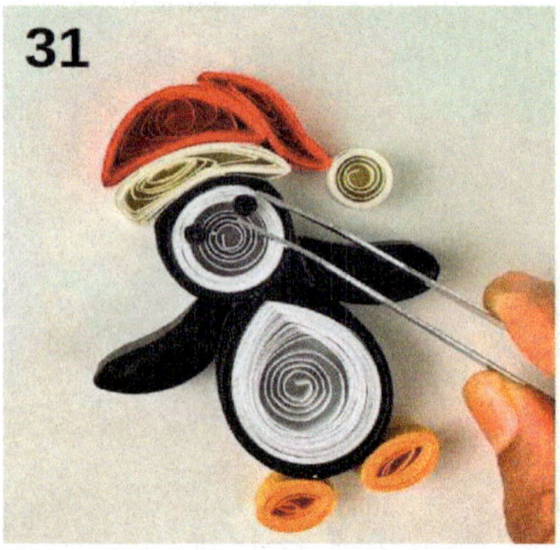

Glue the other eye on the face

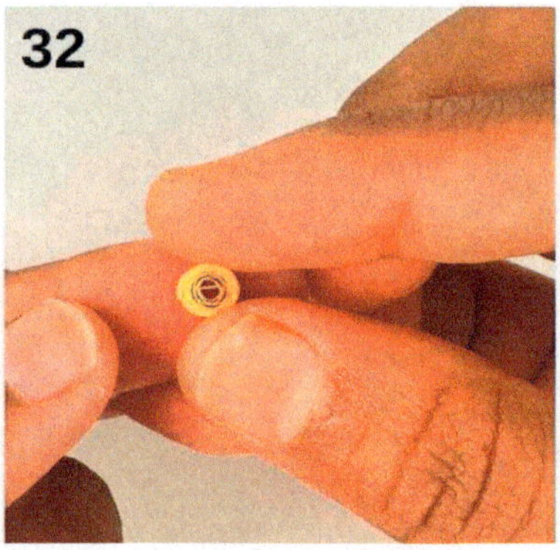

Roll a ½ cut 3mm yellow quilling strip into a tight coil

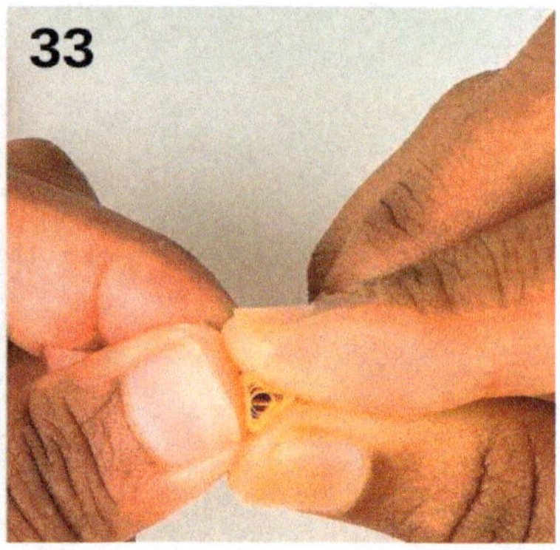

Shape it into a tiny triangle for the beak.

Attach the beak just below the eyes

If needed, apply a thin layer of varnish along the front and back of the Penguin to reinforce its shape

Allow the glue to dry completely before handling your penguin

GINGERBREAD MAN

Quilled gingerbread man is a fun and festive craft project that brings holiday spirit to life. This intricate decoration captures the whimsical charm of the classic holiday cookie, adding a unique, textured touch to seasonal decor. Perfect for ornaments or greeting cards, the quilled gingerbread man is both creative and timeless

Materials Needed:

- Quilling paper strips 10 mm wide in Brown
- Quilling paper strips 3 mm wide in Red, Green and Black
- Slotted Quilling tool
- White glue
- Small scissors
- Tweezers
- Quilling board / Circular ruler
- Fine brush
- Varnish (Optional)

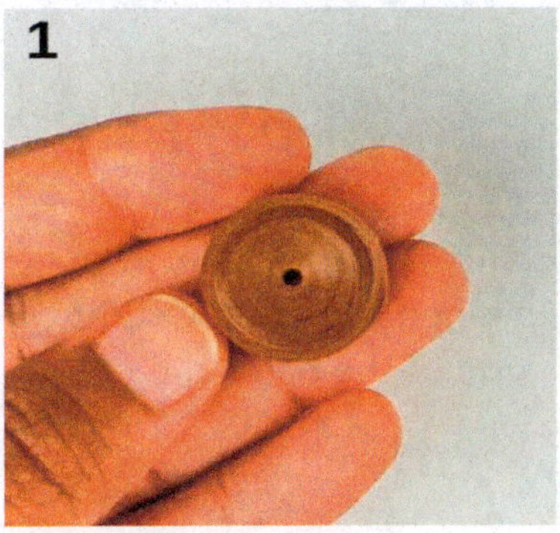

Glue the ends of 6 brown quilling strips and roll into a tight coil to create the head

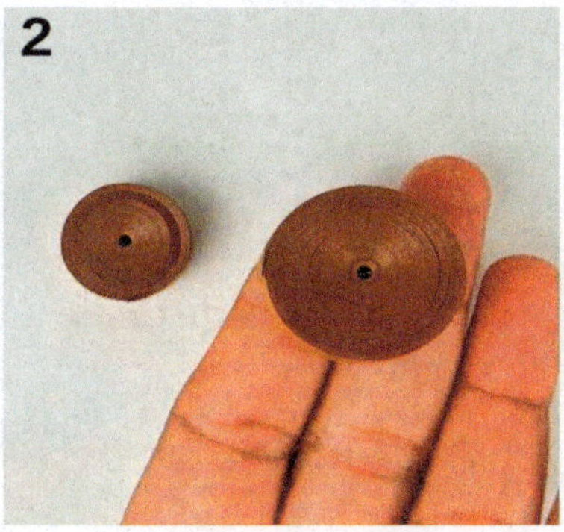

Glue the ends of 12 brown quilling strips and roll into a tight coil to create the body

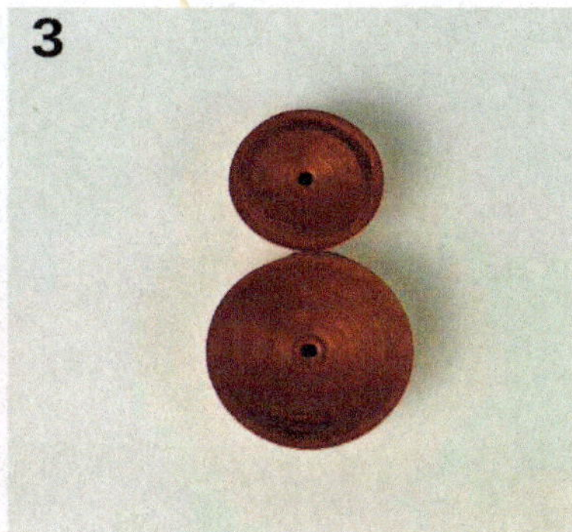

Apply glue to the smaller coil and place it on top of the larger coil to assemble the head and body

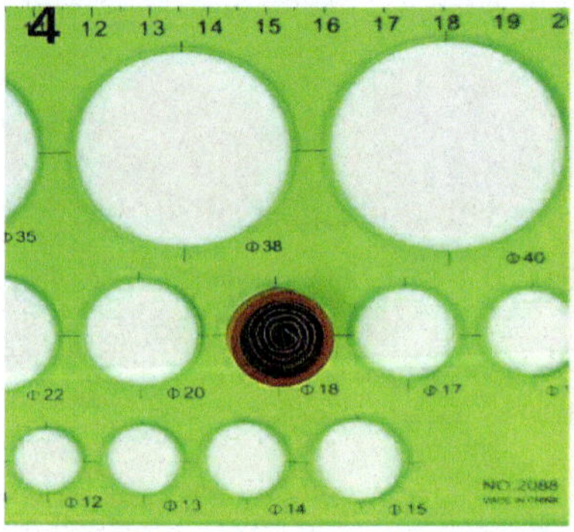

Roll 1 brown strip into a coil and place the coil into a circular template (Size 18) to allow it to expand evenly. Secure the ends with the glue

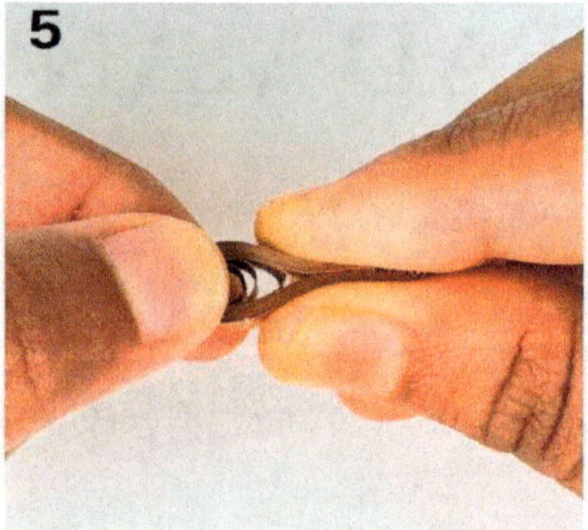

Shape them into teardrops by pinching one side

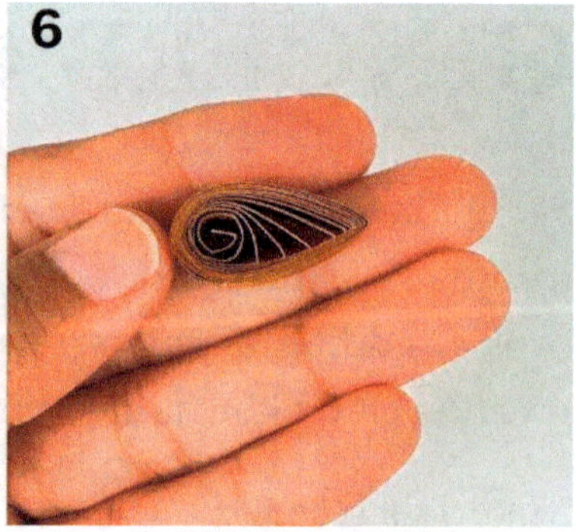

These will serve as the gingerbread man's arms

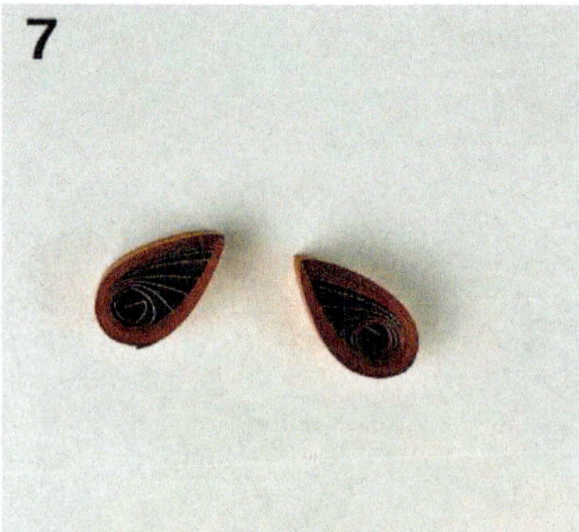

Make 2 similar shapes

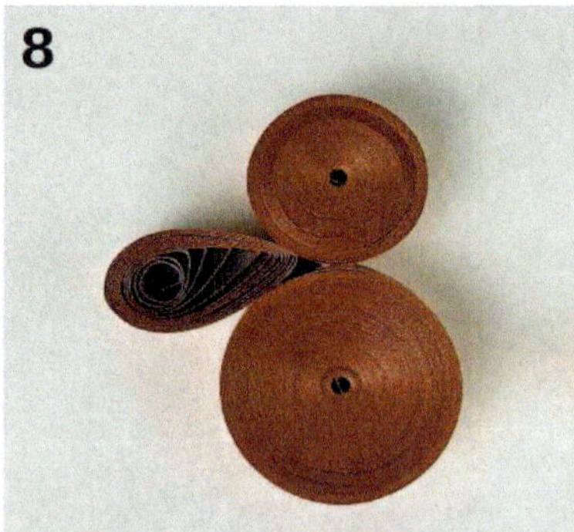

Glue the teardrop-shaped arm on the left side of the body coil

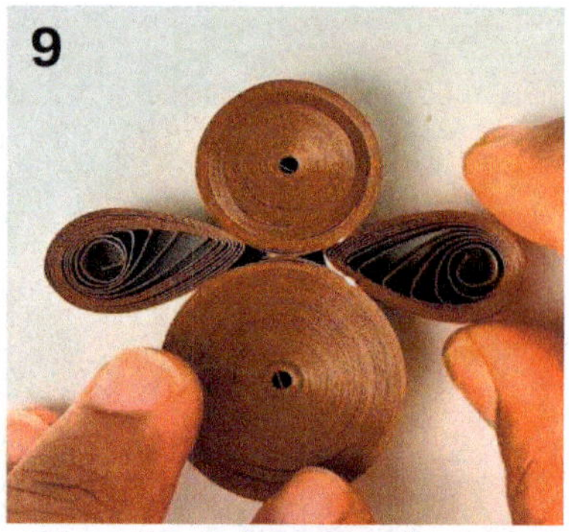

Glue the other teardrop-shaped arm on the right side of the body coil

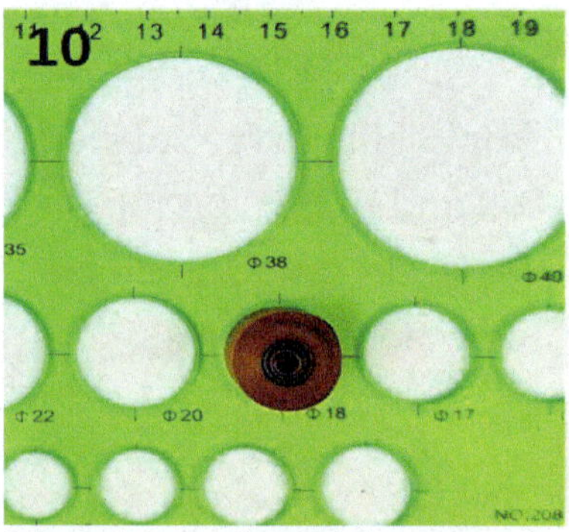

Glue the ends of 2 brown strips and roll into a coil and place it into a circular template (Size 18) to allow it to expand evenly. Secure the ends with the glue

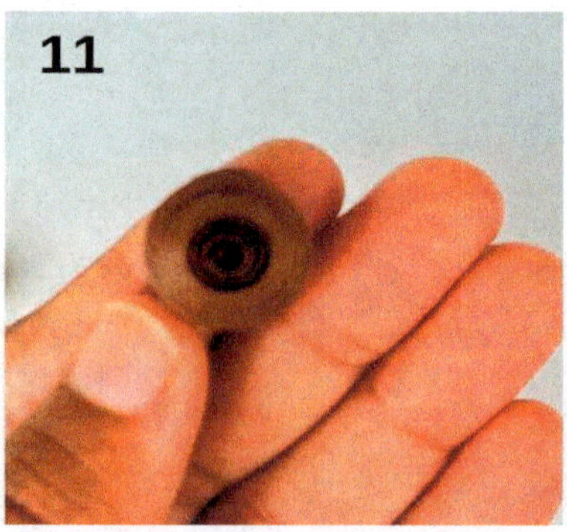

This coil will be shaped to legs

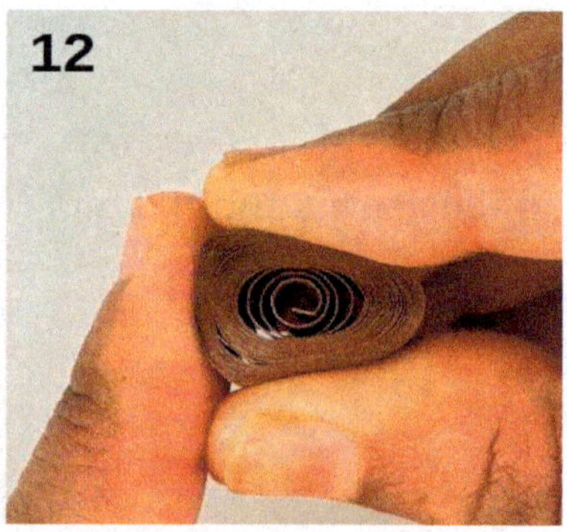

Press the small part of the coil against the finger and flatten it.

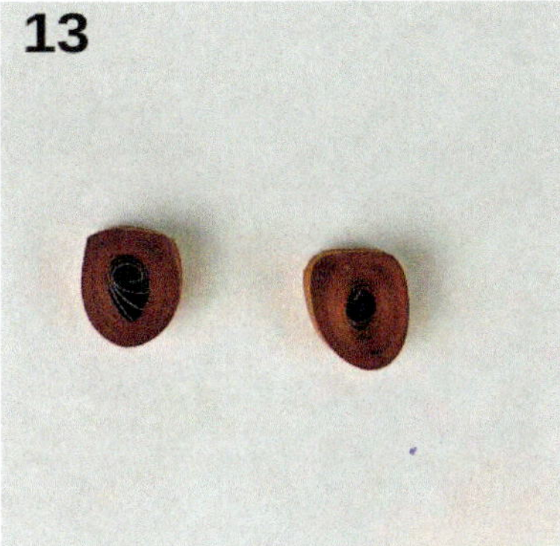

Make 2 legs of similar size

Glue the shaped leg at the bottom of the body coil

Glue the other leg at the bottom as shown

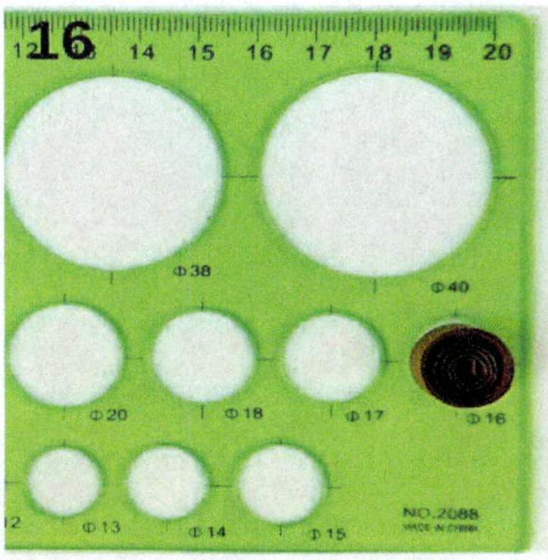

Roll ½ cut brown colour strip into a coil and place the coil into a circular template (Size 16) to allow it to expand evenly. Secure the ends with the glue

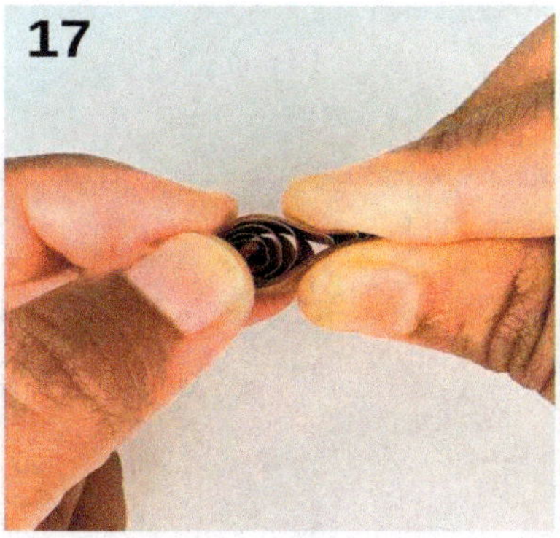

Shape them into teardrops by pinching at one end

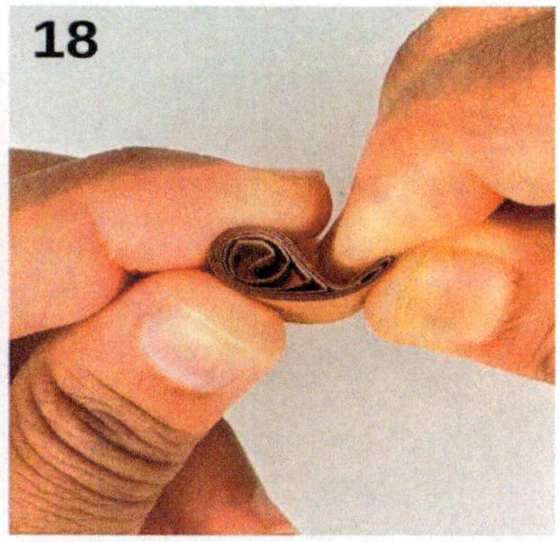

Gently curve the pointed end

Glue the curved teardrop to the bottom of the leg

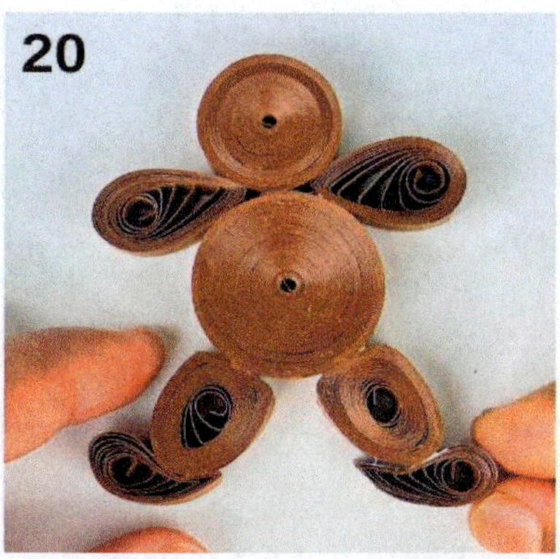

Repeat the same and glue another curved teardrop at the bottom of the other leg

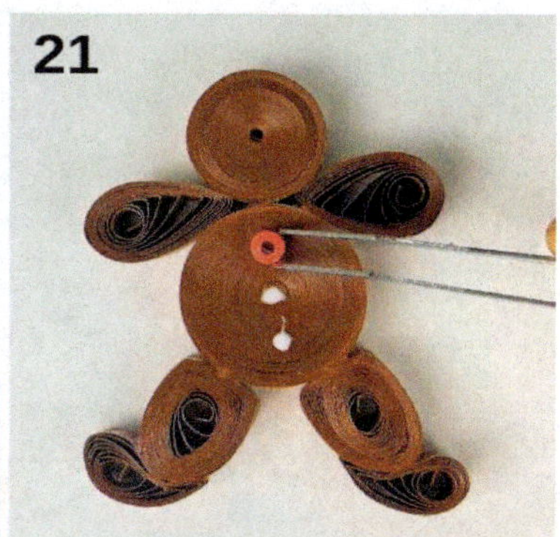

Roll ½ cut3mm red quilling strips into tight coils for the buttons. Attach it to the body as shown

Attach these buttons vertically on the body

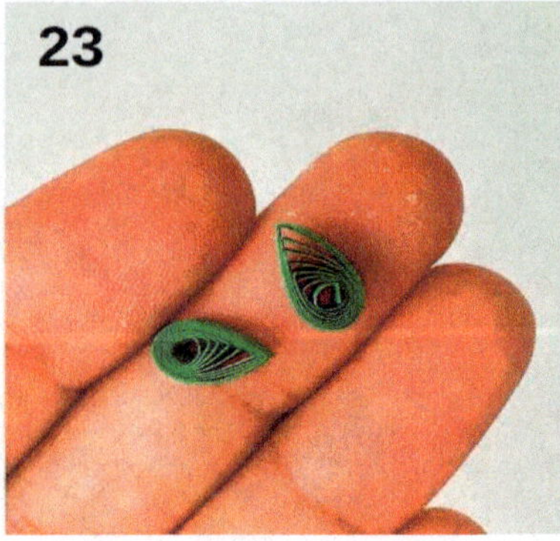

Make 2 tear drops from ½ cut 3mm green paper strips

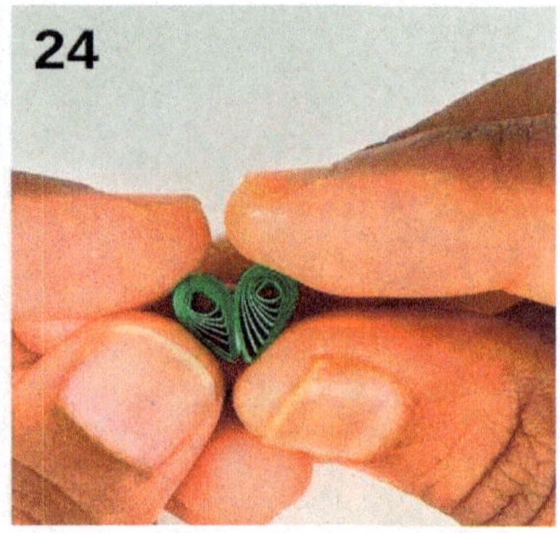

Glue the two tear drops together to make one half of the bowtie

Make 2 similar shapes

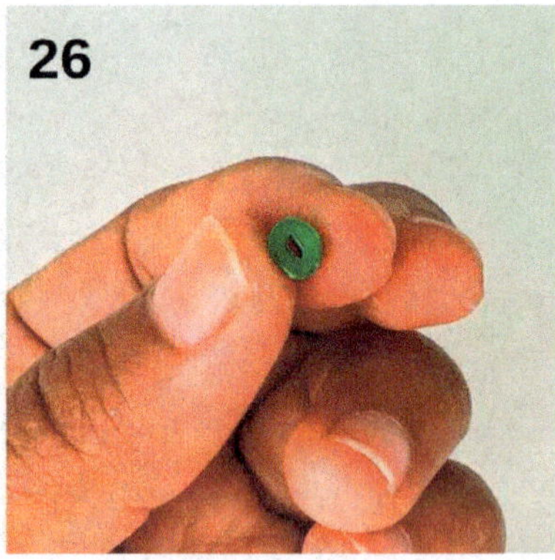

Create a tiny green coil from ½ cut strip for the centre of the bowtie

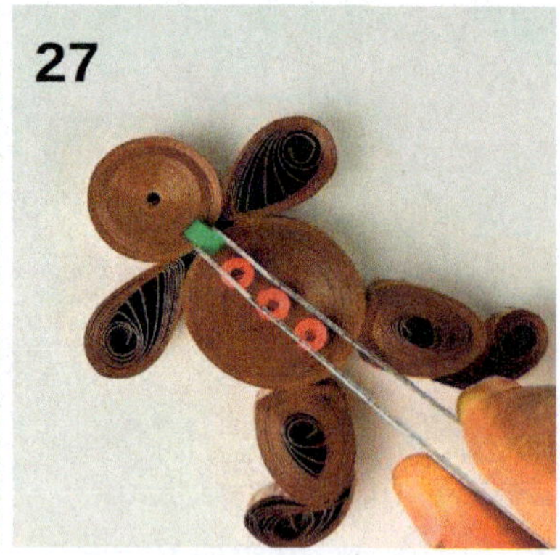

Attach the green coil under the gingerbread man's head at the centre

Attach one half of the bowtie to the tight coil

Attach the other half of the bowtie to the left of the tight coil

Roll ¼ cut 3mm black strip into a tight coil and this will be the eyes. Glue it on to the face

Glue the other eye onto the gingerbread man's face

Roll a ½ cut red strip into a small coil and glue it below the eyes at the centre

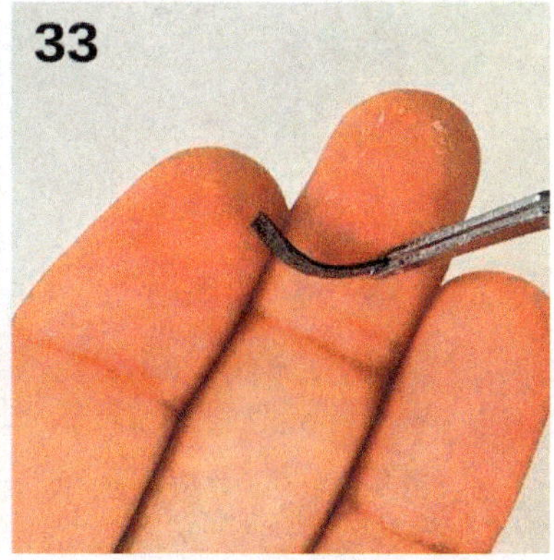

Shape a small black strip into a small crescent shape by slightly bending it.

Attach the mouth just below the nose.

If needed, apply a thin layer of varnish along the front and back of the gingerbread man to reinforce its shape

Allow the varnish to dry completely before handling your gingerbread man

SANTA CLAUS

Paper quilled Santa Claus is a festive and intricate craft that uses rolled and shaped paper strips to create a detailed Santa design. This handmade project is perfect for holiday cards, ornaments, or seasonal decor, adding a cheerful and creative touch to your Christmas celebrations. It's a fun way to capture the magic of Santa in a unique, artistic form.

Materials Needed:

- Quilling paper strips 10 mm wide in Skin Tone, Red, Black and Cream
- Quilling paper strips 3 mm wide in Cream, Black and Yellow
- Slotted Quilling tool
- White glue
- Small scissors
- Tweezers
- Quilling board / Circular ruler
- Fine brush
- Varnish (Optional)

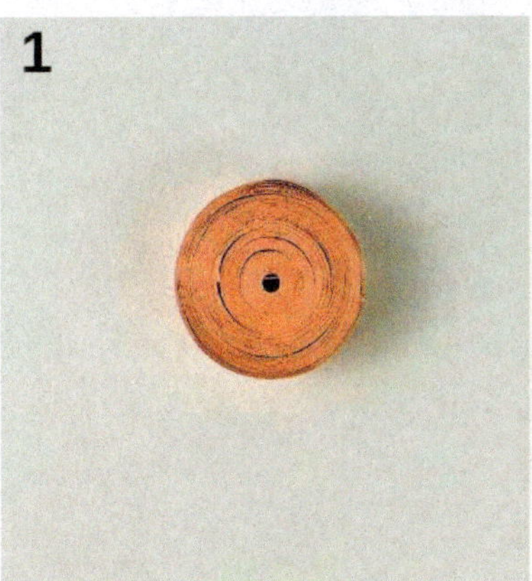

Glue the ends of 10 skin tone colour strips into a tight coil

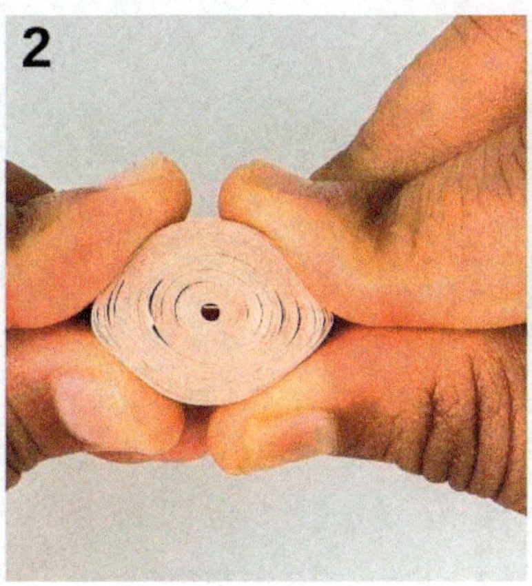

Gently press the coil to form an oval shape

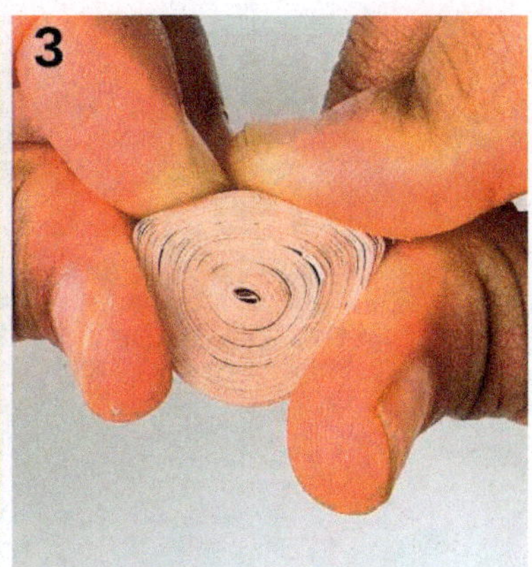

Flatten one of the sides. This will be the base of Santa's face

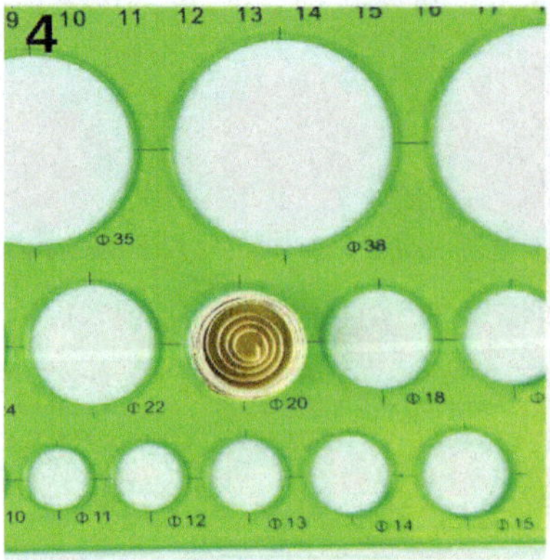

Glue the ends of 3 cream colour strip and roll into a coil and place the coil into a circular template (Size 16) to allow it to expand evenly. Secure the ends with the glue

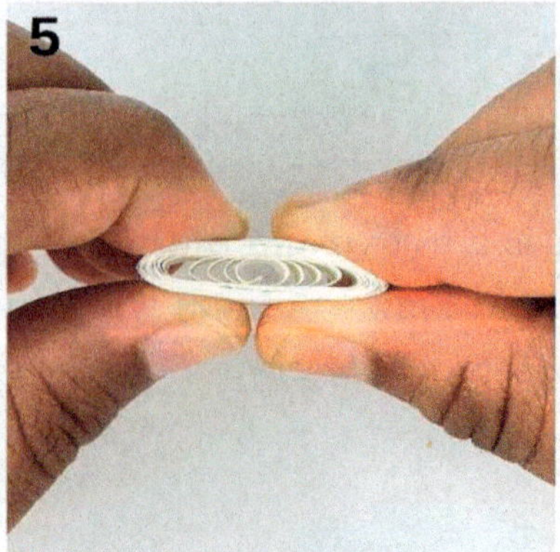

Pinch both ends to form a pointed oval shape for the top of Santa's hat

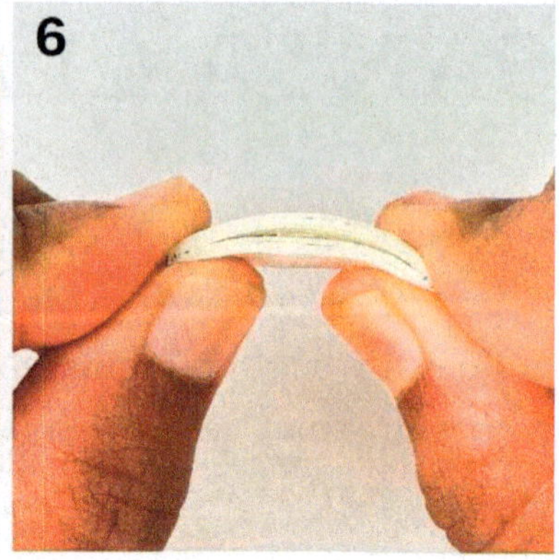

Bend it slightly

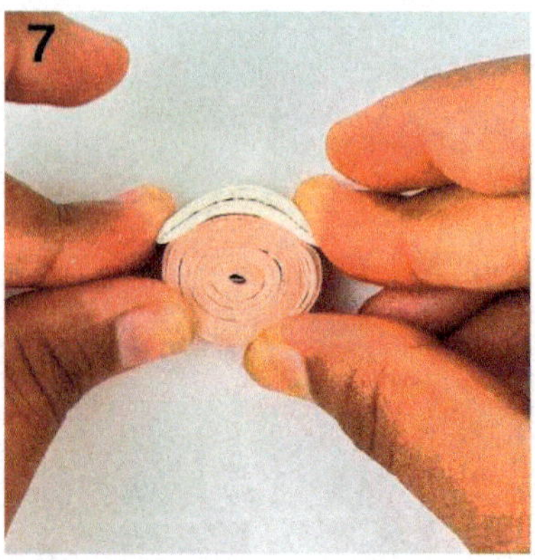

Glue it to the top of the Santa's face

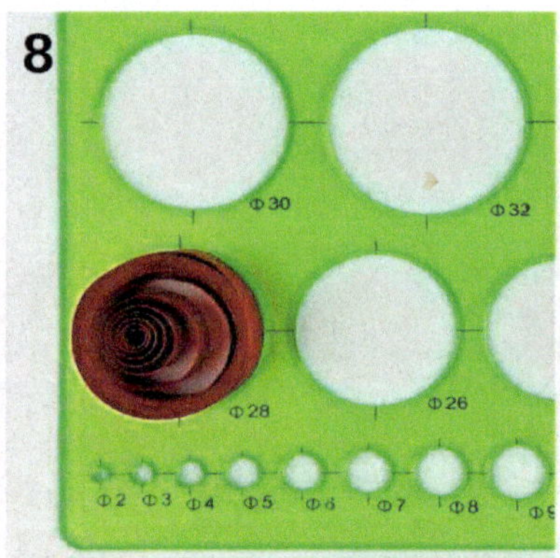

Glue the ends of 4 red colour strip and roll into a coil and place the coil into a circular template (Size 28) to allow it to expand evenly. Secure the ends with the glue

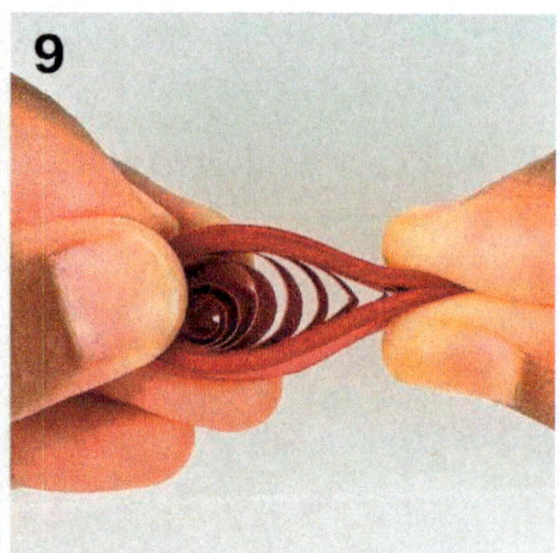

Pinch at one end to create a tear drop

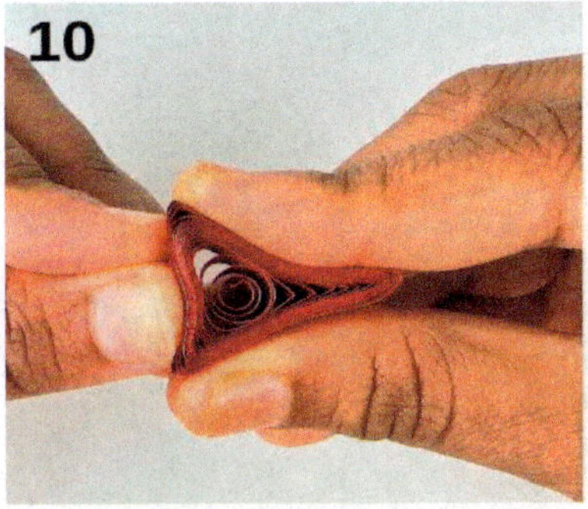

Press and flatten the rounded edge of the coil

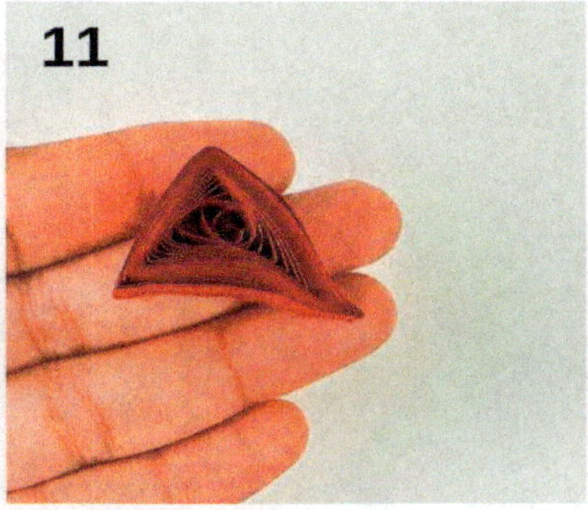

This will result in a triangle shape

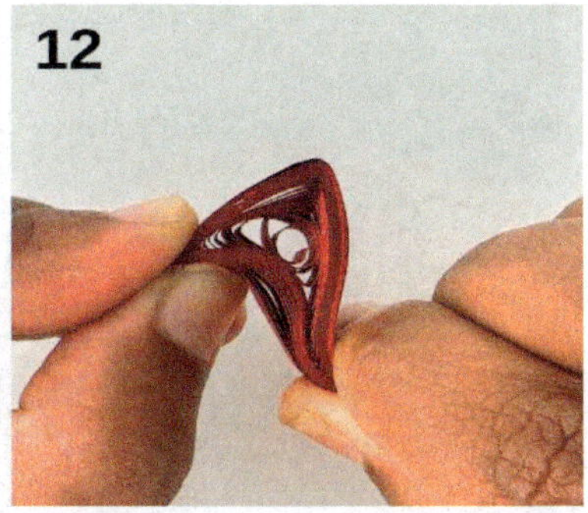

Curve the pointed edge of the triangle

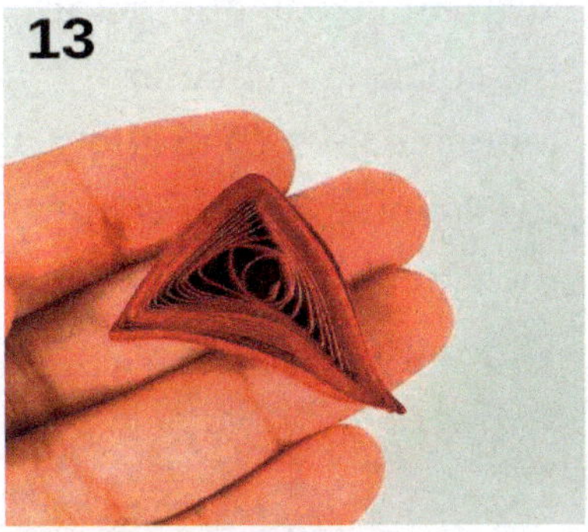

This will be the main part of Santa's hat.

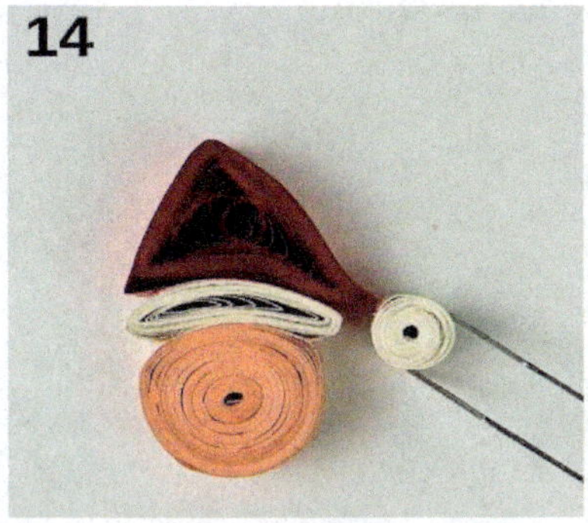

Place the triangular red hat above the face coil. Ensure the pointed end is facing up. Glue 2 cream strips and roll it a tight coil for the pom-pom of the hat and glue it to the end of the hat

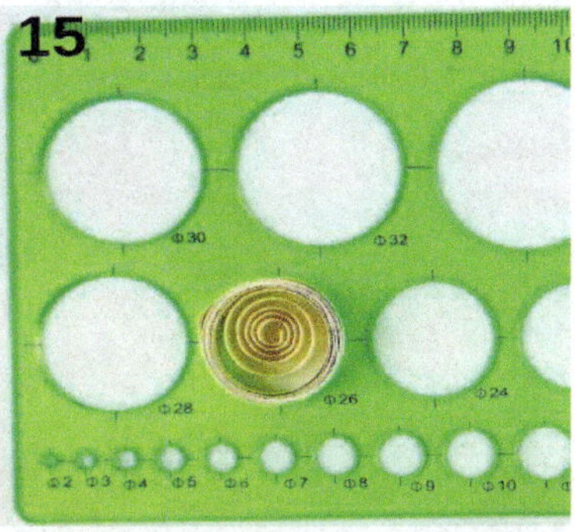

Glue the ends of 4 cream colour strip and roll into a coil and place the coil into a circular template (Size 26) to allow it to expand evenly. Secure the ends with the glue

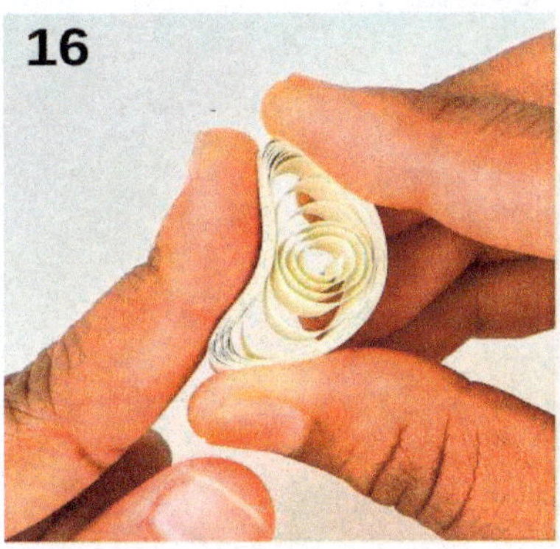

Shape it into a crescent

This will form Santa's beard

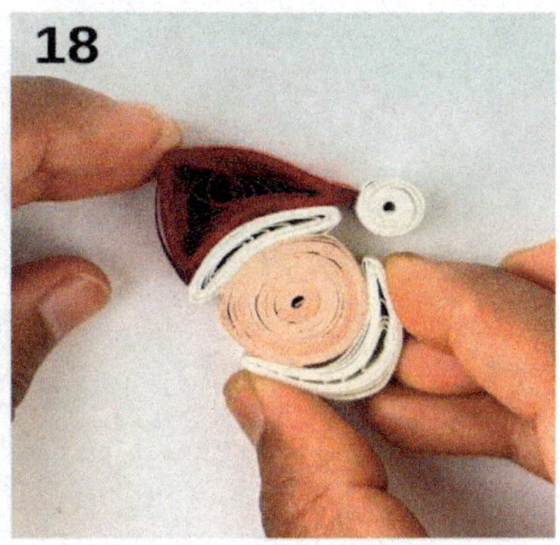

Glue the beard crescent below the face coil, ensuring it covers the bottom half of the face

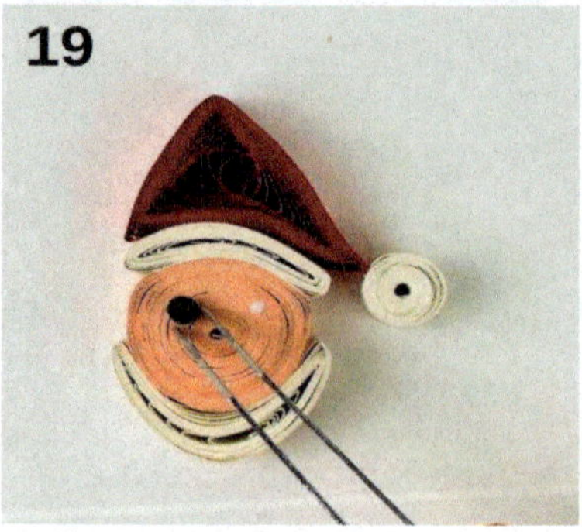

Roll ¼ cut 3mm black strip into tight coils for the eyes. Attach one eye on to the face

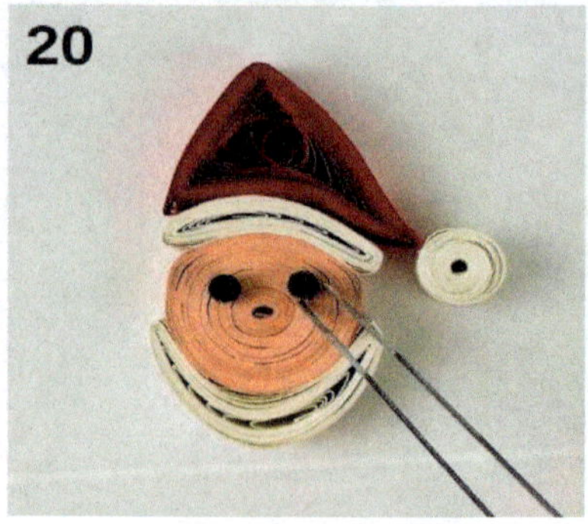

Glue the second eye on the face as shown

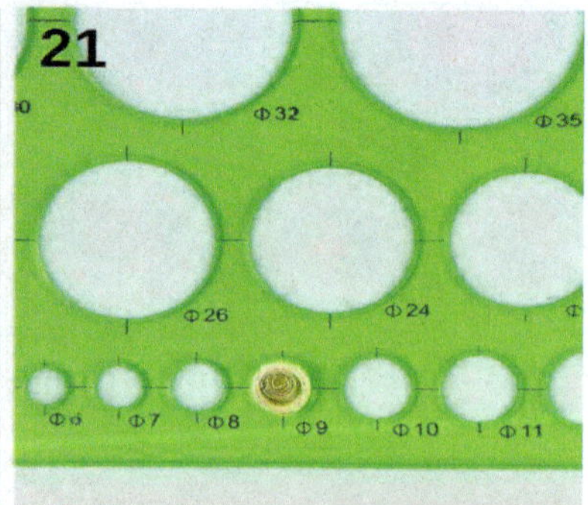

Roll 1 3mm cream colour strip into a coil and place the coil into a circular template (Size 9) to allow it to expand evenly. Secure the ends with the glue

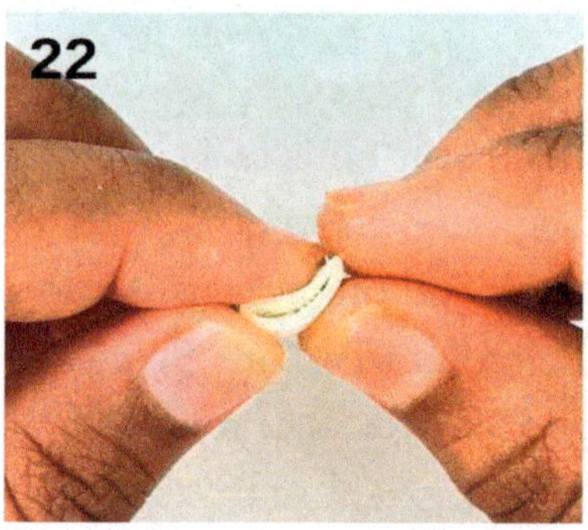

Shape them into smaller crescents

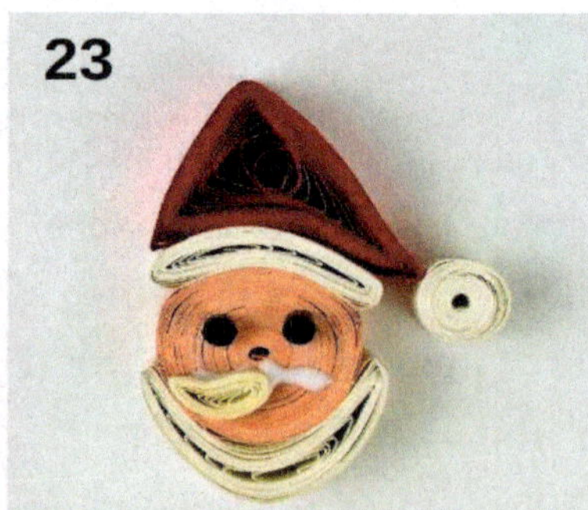

Attach these above the beard, on either side of the face, to form Santa's moustache

Santa's face is now complete

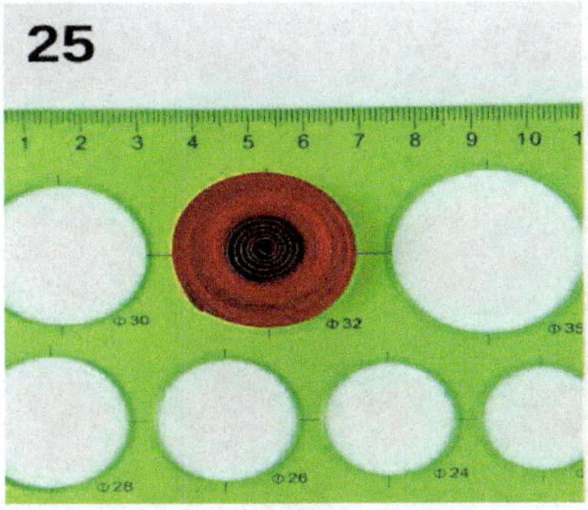

Glue 12 red quilling strips together and roll into a coil and place the coil into a circular template (Size 32) to allow it to expand evenly. Secure the ends with the glue

Hold the coil between the fingers slightly flatten the opposite ends to form the main part of Santa's body

Glue the shape beneath Santa's head, forming the upper part of his body

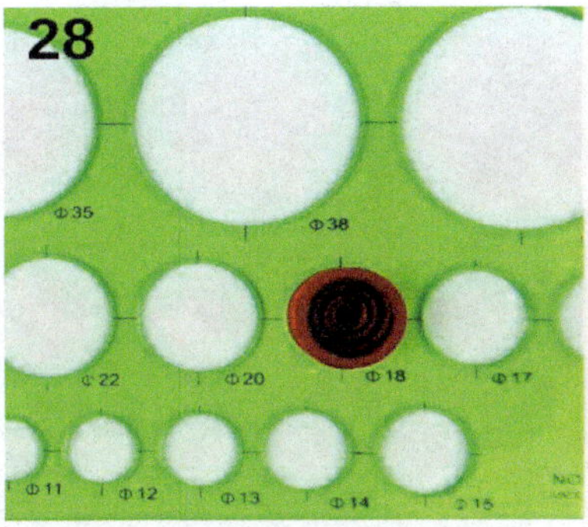

Glue 2 red quilling strips together and roll into a coil and place the coil into a circular template (Size 18) to allow it to expand evenly. Secure the ends with the glue

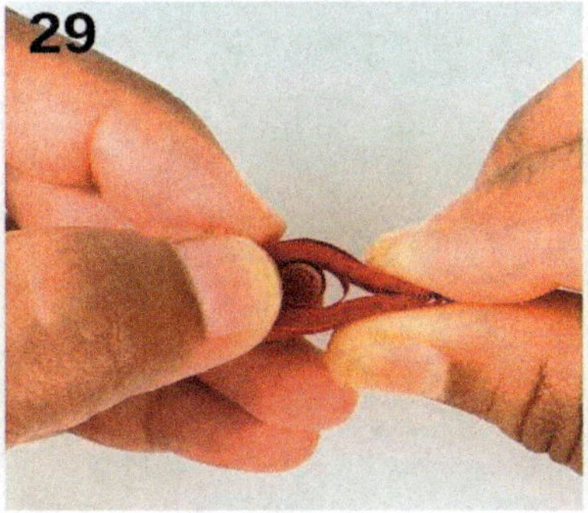

Shape these coils into teardrops

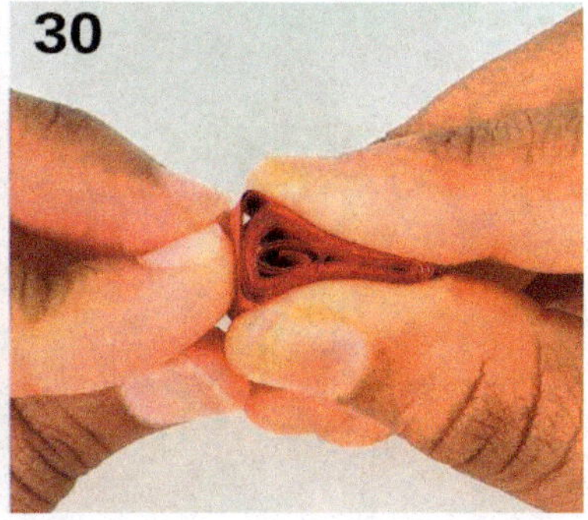

Further pinch the sides to form a more triangular shape

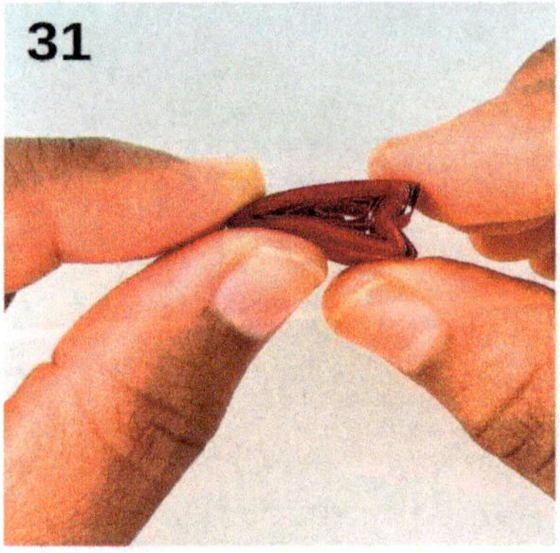

Slightly bend the pointed end of the triangle. Shape the wider part of the triangle by bringing in both the edges. This results a V shape

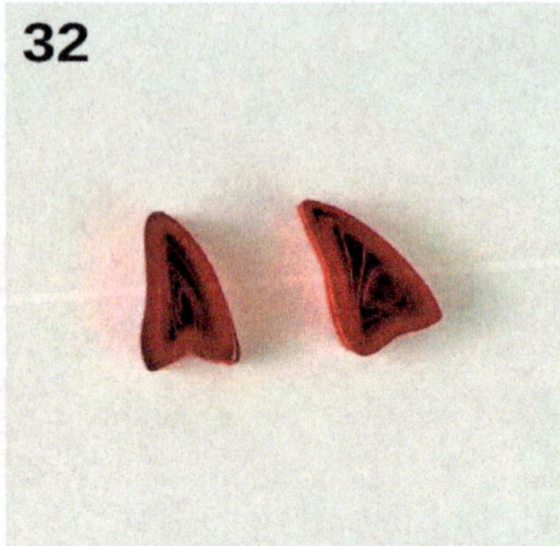

Make 2 similar sized shape. These will be Santa's arms

Glue the triangular-shaped arm coils on either side of Santa's body

Make sure they are evenly placed and aligned

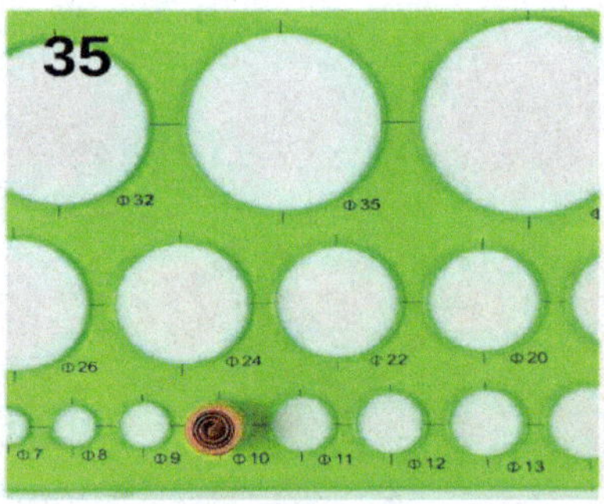

Roll 1 skin tone strip into a coil and place the coil into a circular template (Size 10) to allow it to expand evenly. Secure the ends with the glue

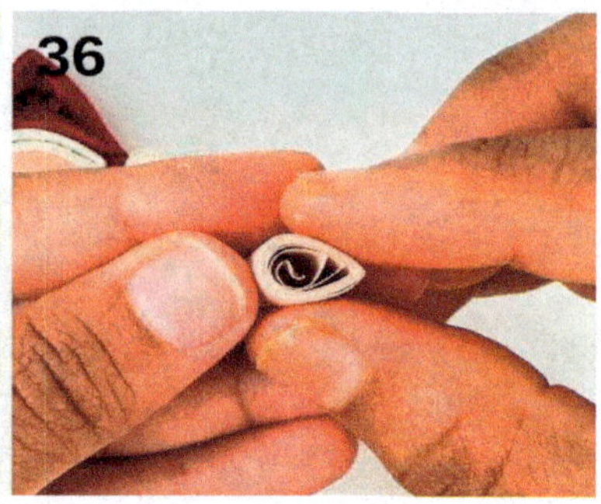

Pinch one end of the coil to convert into tear drop shape

Glue the hand coils to the ends of the arms

Make sure they are aligned and facing downwards

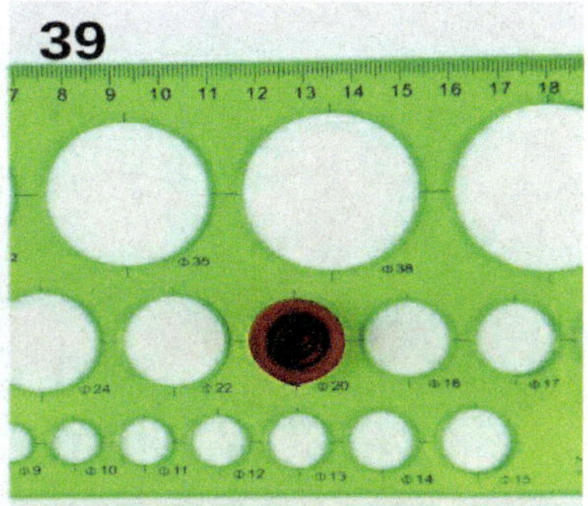

Glue 3 red quilling strips together and roll into a coil and place the coil into a circular template (Size 20) to allow it to expand evenly. Secure the ends with the glue

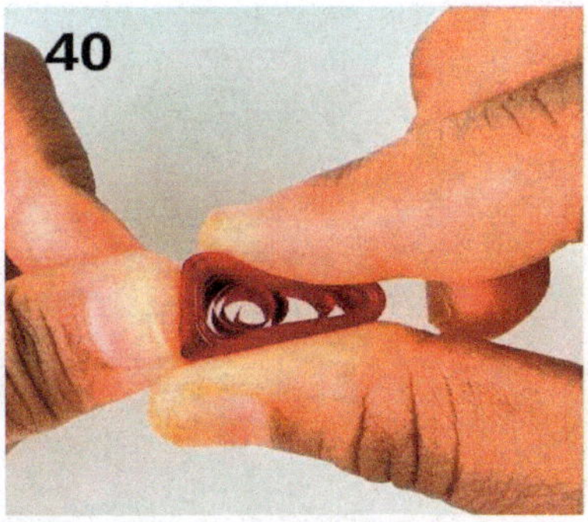

Shape these coils into a teardrop and slightly flatten the rounded edge of the teardrop

Flatten the opposite side and convert it to a small square-like shape with rounded corners

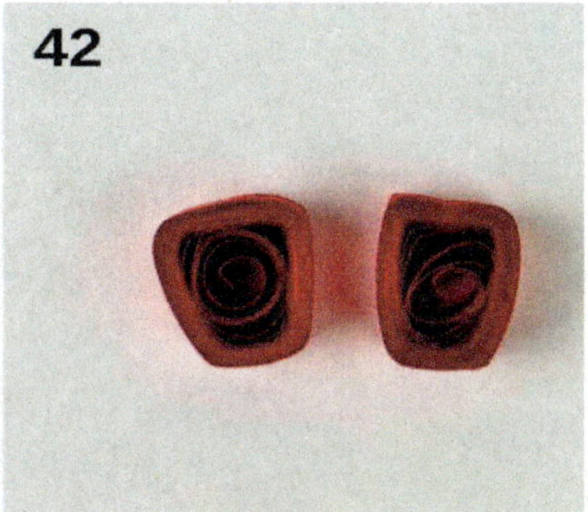

Make 2 similar sized shape. These will serve as Santa's legs

Glue the leg to the bottom of Santa's body

Ensure they are symmetrically placed and aligned

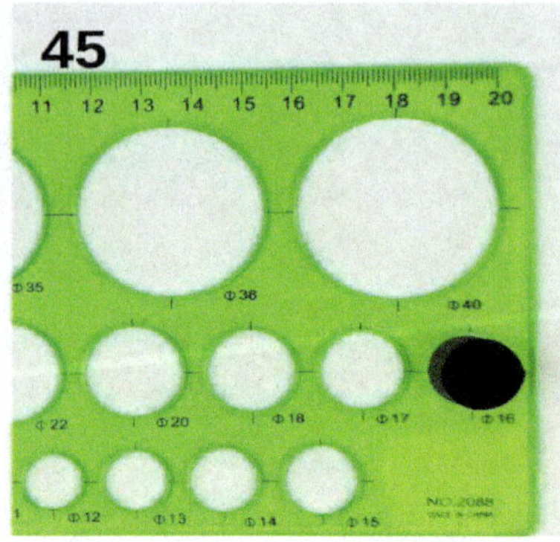

Glue 2 black quilling strips together and roll into a coil and place the coil into a circular template (Size 16) to allow it to expand evenly. Secure the ends with the glue

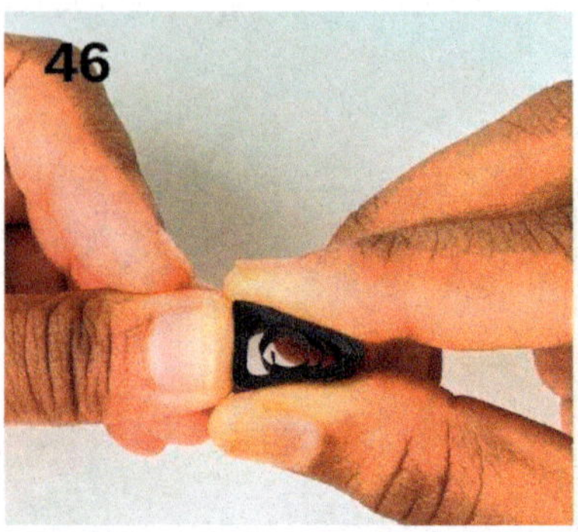

Shape each coil into a triangle by pinching three sides

Further shape into a rounded triangle-like form with one pointed end and one rounded end

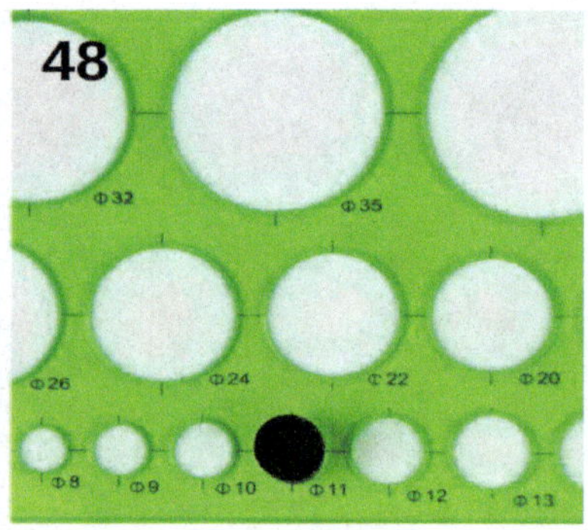

Roll 1 black paper strip into a coil and place the coil into a circular template (Size 11) to allow it to expand evenly. Secure the ends with the glue

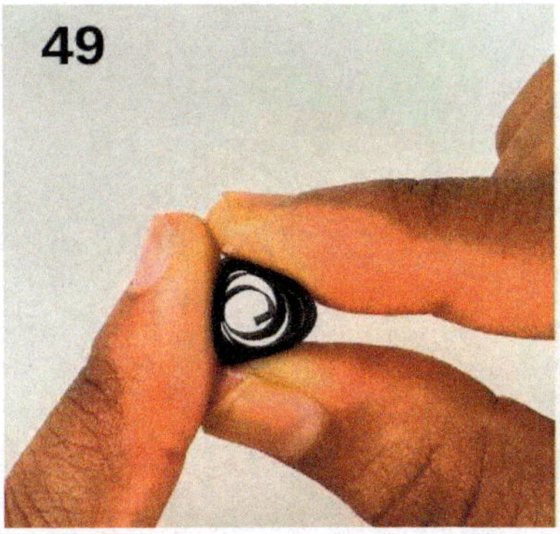

Flatten one side of the coil and convert it to a semicircle

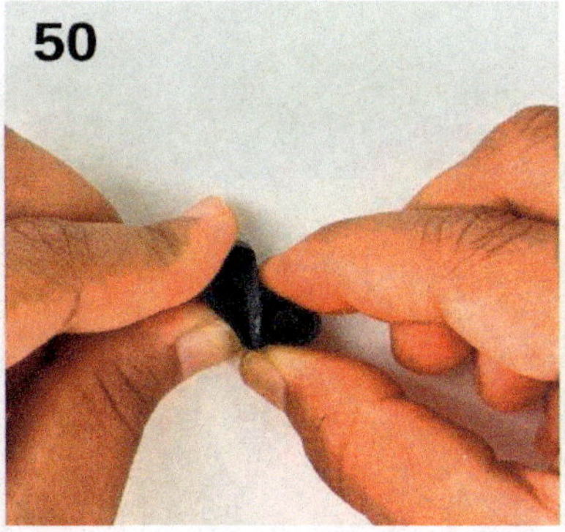

Attach the semicircle to the previously made shape

These will serve as Santa's boots

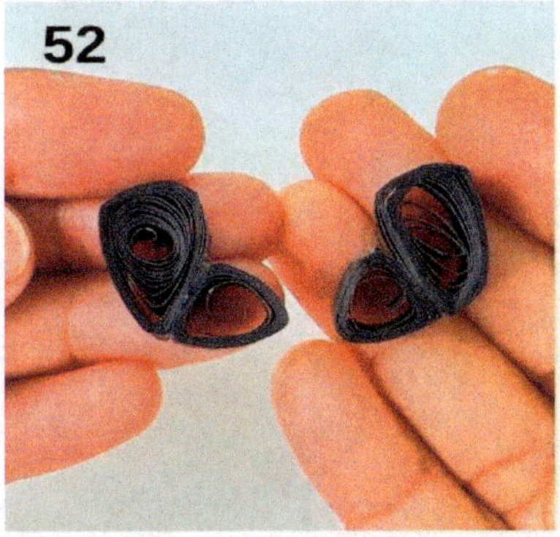

Make 2 similar size boots

Glue the black boot coils to the bottom of Santa’s legs

Ensure that they are symmetrical and aligned properly

Roll ½ cut 3mm black colour strip into a tight coil. Make 3 similar tight coils. This will be the buttons. Attach the first button below the beard at the centre

Attach the remaining 2 buttons in a vertical line

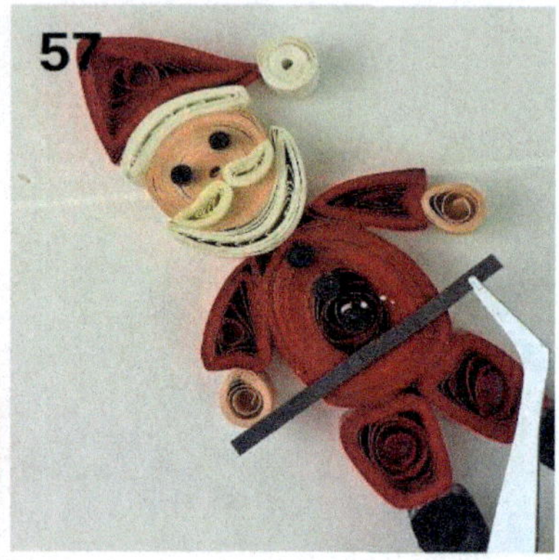

Wrap a 3mm black colour strip in the Santa's body just above where the legs are attached

This is to create the illusion of a belt

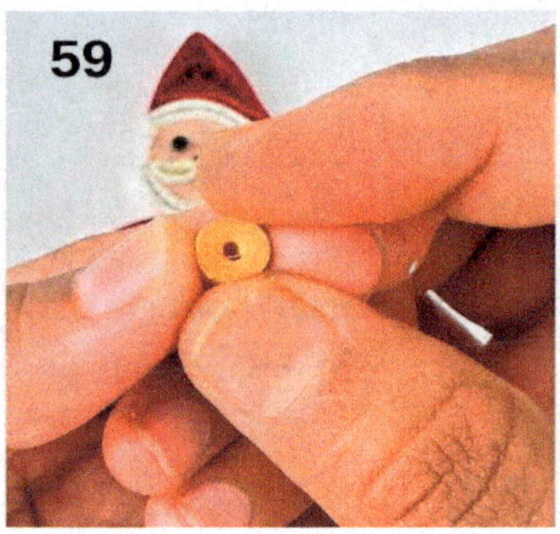

Roll 1 3mm yellow strip into a tight coil

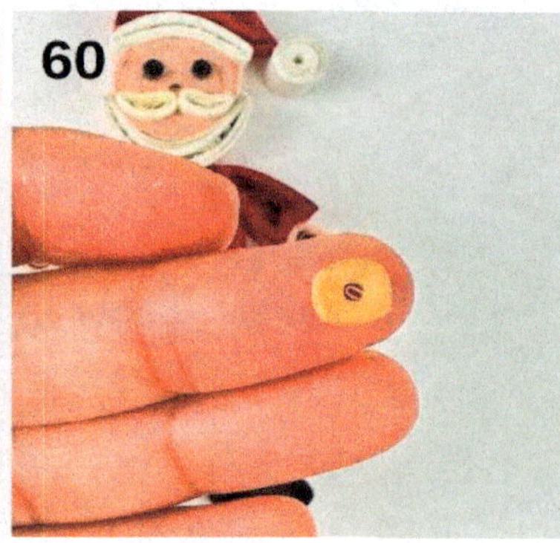

Convert this to a small square

Attach it at the centre of the belt

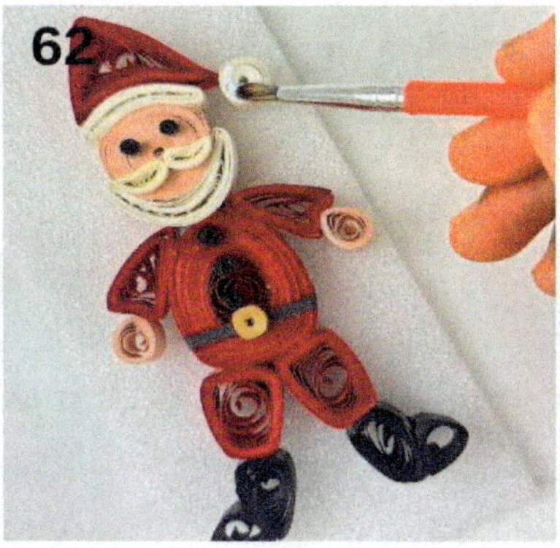

If needed, apply a thin layer of varnish along the front and back of the Santa Claus to reinforce its shape

Once dry, your paper quilled Santa Claus is now fully complete and ready to be used as a holiday decoration or gift

DISPLAYING AND PRESERVING THE ORNAMENTS

Attaching strings to paper quilled Christmas ornaments is a crucial step to ensure they are ready for display or gifting. This section will guide you through the process of adding strings or ribbon to your quilled ornaments, making them ready to adorn your Christmas tree or any festive setting.

Cut a piece of ribbon or string about 6-8 inches long. This length allows for easy hanging and adjustment. Fold the ribbon or string into a loop of your desired size. Secure the ends of the ribbon or string together with a small knot or glue.

Position the loop at the top of the quilled ornament. Use a small amount of glue to secure the loop to the ornament. Ensure the glue is placed where it will be covered by other elements or is not visible. Hold the loop in place until the glue dries to ensure it stays securely attached.

Ensure that the ribbon, string is securely attached and can hold the weight of the ornament. Trim any excess length to ensure a neat appearance.

Make sure the ornament hangs straight and is balanced. Adjust the loop if necessary to achieve the desired hanging position. Handle the ornaments gently during the attachment process to avoid damaging the delicate quilled designs.

This process adds both functionality and a professional touch to your beautiful quilled creations. Enjoy the final step of preparing your ornaments for a joyous holiday season!

Steps to Store Paper Quilled Christmas Ornaments

Storing paper quilled Christmas ornaments properly ensures that they remain in pristine condition year after year. Paper quilled ornaments are delicate and can be easily damaged if not handled and stored correctly. This section provides detailed steps for storing your quilled ornaments to maintain their beauty and longevity

Materials Needed:

- Acid-Free Tissue Paper or Parchment Paper: For wrapping ornaments
- Small Boxes or Plastic Containers: For individual storage
- Bubble Wrap: For added protection
- Zip-Lock Bags or Clear Plastic Wrap: For extra protection

- Labels or Tags: For identifying contents
- Cotton Balls or Foam Inserts: For cushioning and preventing movement

Step-by-Step Instructions

Step 1: Prepare the Ornaments for Storage

- Ensure each ornament is clean and free from dust. Gently brush off any dust using a soft, dry brush.
- Check each ornament for any loose parts or damage. Repair any minor issues before storing them.

Step 2: Wrap the Ornaments

- Lay out a piece of acid-free tissue paper or parchment paper.
- Place the ornament in the centre of the paper and gently fold the paper around it to wrap it securely.
- For extra protection, wrap the tissue-paper-covered ornament in a layer of bubble wrap. Secure the bubble wrap with a small piece of tape, ensuring it is snug but not overly tight.

Step 3: Pack the Ornaments

- Select small boxes or plastic containers that are appropriately sized for your ornaments. Ensure the containers are clean, dry, and free from any potential sources of damage.
- Place a layer of cotton balls or foam inserts at the bottom of the container to provide cushioning. Place the wrapped ornaments on top of this layer, ensuring they are not touching each other to prevent any potential damage.
- Add additional cotton balls or foam inserts around the ornaments to fill any gaps and prevent movement. Ensure the ornaments are snugly packed but not too tightly compressed.

Step 4: Seal and Label

- Close the box or container securely. If using plastic containers, ensure the lid is tightly sealed.
- Attach a label or tag to the container indicating the contents and any special handling instructions. This helps in quickly identifying the ornaments and handling them properly.

Step 5: Store in a Suitable Environment

- Store the containers in a dry, cool, and dark location to avoid exposure to moisture, heat, or direct sunlight. Avoid areas with fluctuating temperatures or high humidity.
- Ensure the containers are not stacked with heavy objects on top of them to avoid crushing or deformation of the ornaments.
- If possible, store the ornaments in a climate-controlled environment to maintain consistent temperature and humidity levels.

Tips

- Always handle quilled ornaments gently to avoid any damage.
- Periodically check the condition of the stored ornaments and ensure they are still well-protected.
- Consider adding silica gel packets to the storage containers to absorb any excess moisture.

By following these detailed steps, you can effectively store your paper quilled Christmas ornaments, preserving their beauty and ensuring they are ready for enjoyment in future holiday seasons. Proper storage is essential to maintaining the quality and longevity of your delicate quilled creations.

ACKNOWLEDGEMENTS

Creating this book has been a truly rewarding journey, and I am filled with gratitude for the opportunity to share my passion for paper quilling with you.
This book would not have been possible without the unwavering support and encouragement of my husband, Nagappan. His constant belief in my abilities, from the very beginning, has been my greatest source of strength. Thank you for always standing by my side and providing me with the motivation to pursue my creative dreams.

I would also like to express my heartfelt thanks to everyone who has supported and encouraged me throughout this creative process. Your belief in my work has been a constant source of inspiration.

I am incredibly proud to have designed, created, photographed, edited, and published this book on my own. Every page is a reflection of my love for crafting and my desire to help others discover the joy of creating beautiful paper quilled ornaments.

To my family and friends, thank you for your unwavering support and patience as I dedicated countless hours to bring this project to life. Your encouragement and enthusiasm have been invaluable.

Finally, to you, the reader, thank you for choosing this book. I hope that these 20 paper quilled Christmas ornaments bring as much joy to your holiday season as they did to mine in creating them. This book is dedicated to all of you who find joy in creating beautiful things with your hands. May this book inspire your creativity and fill your home with the warmth of handmade holiday decor.

Happy quilling!
Warm regards,
Anusha

ABOUT THE AUTHOR

Anusha has been immersed in the world of crafting since childhood, constantly exploring and experimenting with various materials and techniques. With a lifelong passion for creativity, Anusha has developed a deep expertise in a wide range of crafts, including paper quilling, yarn crafts, Jewellery making and dollhouse miniatures.

Over the years, Anusha has transformed this passion into a journey of artistic expression, creating beautiful, intricate designs that reflect a love for detail and a dedication to the craft. This journey has culminated in the creation of "*Festive Quilling: 20 Beautiful Christmas Ornaments,*" a book that showcases her talent for turning simple strips of paper into stunning holiday decorations.

As someone who has always found joy in the process of making and sharing, she took on every aspect of this book's creation-from designing and crafting each ornament to photographing, editing, and publishing the final product. This book is not just a collection of projects; it's a reflection of years of exploration, creativity, and a deep-seated love for the art of quilling.

Beyond the pages of this book, she continues to explore the vast world of crafting, always seeking new ways to inspire others and share the joy of handmade creations. Through a popular YouTube channel and various online platforms, she connects with a growing community of fellow craft enthusiasts, offering tutorials and insights that make crafting accessible to everyone.

Anusha lives in the UK, where she continues to create, teach, and inspire others with her endless curiosity and passion for crafting. With this book, she hopes to bring the magic of handmade ornaments into homes around the world, spreading joy through the simple act of creating.

Printed in Dunstable, United Kingdom

64038584R00092